Genre Worlds

A VOLUME IN THE SERIES
Page and Screen

EDITED BY
Kate Eichhorn

Genre Worlds

POPULAR FICTION AND TWENTY-FIRST-CENTURY BOOK CULTURE

Kim Wilkins · Beth Driscoll · Lisa Fletcher

University of Massachusetts Press

Amherst and Boston

Copyright © 2022 by University of Massachusetts Press
All rights reserved
Printed in the United States of America

ISBN 978-1-62534-661-2 (paper); 662-9 (hardcover)

Designed by Sally Nichols
Set in Dante MT Pro
Printed and bound by Books International, Inc.

Cover design by adam b. bohannon
Cover images: Moschiorini

Library of Congress Cataloging-in-Publication Data
Names: Wilkins, Kim, author. | Driscoll, Beth, author. | Fletcher, Lisa,
1972– author.
Title: Genre worlds : popular fiction and twenty-first-century book culture
/ Kim Wilkins, Beth Driscoll, and Lisa Fletcher.
Description: Amherst : University of Massachusetts Press, [2022] | Series:
Page and screen | Includes bibliographical references and index.
Identifiers: LCCN 2021054474 (print) | LCCN 2021054475 (ebook) | ISBN
9781625346612 (paperback) | ISBN 9781625346629 (hardcover) | ISBN
9781613769393 (ebook) | ISBN 9781613769409 (ebook)
Subjects: LCSH: Fiction genres. | Fiction—Publishing. |
Fiction—Authorship. | Fiction—Social aspects. | Books and
reading—History—21st century. | LCGFT: Literary criticism.
Classification: LCC PN3427 .W55 2022 (print) | LCC PN3427 (ebook) | DDC
808.3—dc23/eng/20211220
LC record available at https://lccn.loc.gov/2021054474
LC ebook record available at https://lccn.loc.gov/2021054475

British Library Cataloguing-in-Publication Data
A catalog record for this book is available from the British Library.

For our children:
Astrid, Ben, Julia, Lily, Luka, and Zhana

Contents

Prologue

....

Getting Hooked and Reading On

The afternoon is warm, and the breeze off the ocean rattles in the palms above your hammock. A cocktail is within arm's reach. In your hands is a small book printed on yellowing paper with slightly blurry text. You're reading the prologue. The book is a thriller, and the setup is dramatic: a detective is in the midst of an impossible hostage situation at an abandoned warehouse. Wait. The book is a romance. You're reading it on an e-reader. A surly duke paces through the prologue as heavy snow falls outside his palace windows. A carriage is approaching. The book changes again. Now it's set in a kingdom ruled by a cruel elven tribe. A young woman is burying her husband and child when she sees a mounted band of rebels on the horizon. She resolves to join them, and you will join this adventure with her. The maps and family trees that fill the front matter tell you there is a whole new world waiting.

Works of genre fiction are a source of enjoyment. They are read during cherished leisure time and in incidental moments of relaxation found between other activities or duties. Readers may avoid some kinds of books (too scary, too much kissing, more bloody wizards) or delightedly return to them over and over again (a murder in chapter 1, triumphant sex scenes, a whole coven of wizards!). Favorite books are pressed fervently into the hands of friends, parents, or children. In our case, we get to read them for work. The book you hold in your hands (or see on your screen) is the result of a multiyear research project. We wanted to know the stories behind the stories of contemporary genre fiction. How do people's personal tastes, social connections, craft expertise, and industry knowledge feed into popular genres and shape their imaginative realms?

In this prologue, we cannot provide a snowed-in palace or a hostage situation, but we can create a set of expectations and anticipations. We offer you a hint of our setting: What times and places does this book span, and what do they make possible? We gesture toward characters: Who wants what, and what are they prepared to do to get it? What allegiances will they pledge? What conflicts drive behavior in this world, and how do they make characters change? The idea is to pose enough enticing questions to make you turn the page. After all, genre fiction runs on forward motion.

The world of genre fiction is many worlds. The key genres—crime, fantasy, and romance—come with well-honed narrative conventions and textual modes. Think of noir thrillers, with wise-cracking detectives and femmes fatales. Think of epic fantasy battles and imagined cities brimming with magic. Think of laconic dukes, cowboys, or billionaires surprised to passion by quick-witted, unconventional women. There is more to genres than stock tropes of character, setting, and plot, of course, but they provide the shorthand cues that usher readers into their worlds.

Our setting is the twenty-first century. This is something of a dystopia, at least if you listen to some publishing industry pundits. E-books have killed publishers and brick-and-mortar bookstores. Amazon rules us all. The novel is in decline at the same time as video streaming and social media are on the ascent, suckling a hollow-eyed zombie culture whose sole interest in books is speculating which teen star will play the main character in the inevitable screen adaptation. For others, optimism persists, but it lives alongside the trepidation that comes with rapid and large-scale change. Transmedia energizes the successful storyworlds of popular series and expands their audiences—but screen entertainment consumes time audiences might otherwise spend reading. Self-publishing is a vault of opportunity that is kick-starting new careers and supplementing the incomes of established authors—but the prestige of traditional print publication lingers in conversations about books in traditional media and literature classrooms. Digital media technologies and platforms mean that genre fans across the world can meet each other and interact with their favorite authors like never before—but they might struggle to get copies of the books they love, thanks to stubborn territorial intellectual property regimes. Anyone can make it as an author, agent, social media influencer, or publisher—but it sure helps if you write in English and live in London or New York.

The three of us—Kim Wilkins, Beth Driscoll, and Lisa Fletcher—are set in academia. Beth hails from the realm of publishing studies and book history, working in a web of media technologies, industry networks, and the materiality of book objects. Lisa inhabits the realm of literary studies, buried in books and digging meaning from the stories they tell and the worlds they imagine. And Kim dwells in the realm of creative writing studies, writing her own fantasy novels and mentoring others to find their places in an industry that requires both creativity and commercial smarts. We are involved in the concerns of academia: the crisis of traditional humanities disciplines, the growth of creative writing programs, and the juggernaut of media studies (which sometimes includes publishing studies, when people remember that books are media products). In relation to genre fiction communities, we take up positions as both outsiders and insiders. To different extents, each of us attends book-culture events, reads and writes genre fiction, supervises genre writers in research higher degrees, and has friends who are writers or work in the publishing industry. Such involvement with our research object is not, to us, a problem but rather an opportunity to study a contemporary phenomenon at least partially from the inside.

Researchers are just some of the characters in this story. This book has a cast of thousands: Superstar authors like Nora Roberts, James Patterson, and Neil Gaiman. Workaday midlist authors who steadily produce long-running series. Shiny new debut authors who carry the hopes of publishing houses on their ill-prepared shoulders and entrepreneurial authors self-publishing on Amazon. Canny agents and community-spirited booksellers, creative marketers and long-suffering publicists, disenchanted CEOs and meticulous editors. Passionate book bloggers, vloggers, and podcasters as well as stalwart beta readers and convention volunteers. Together, they constitute the human infrastructure that makes genre fiction happen.

This infrastructure largely seeks to do good in the world by nurturing creative work. And yet there are conflicts. There is industry rivalry as established publishers scramble to adjust to new industrial conditions, and savvy new entrants exploit gaps. Who will survive? There is competition between authors as the gap between best sellers and the long tail grows ever wider. Interpersonal tension exists right alongside friendships for the ages. There are harassment, inequity, and structural disadvantage; activism and backlash; progress and conservatism. Imprints are born and die, subgenres and tropes brighten and then fade, writers flare into public consciousness and then burn out, series fill bookstore windows and then stuff thrift-store bins.

These are genre worlds. Are you hooked yet?

Genre
Worlds

CHAPTER 1

A Theory of Genre Worlds

Genre fiction books are not merely texts; they are also nodes of social and industrial activity. When you visit a bookshop—row after row of tempting covers enclosing crisp pages—you are standing among the results of extensive and intensive labor. When you scroll through a list of e-books, you witness the collaboration between writers, editors, typesetters, designers, digital production managers, and more that makes it possible for you to swipe through reflowable pages and immerse yourself in a world other than your own. Books are at the center of dynamic and invested networks, and genre fiction—with its active fan cultures, high-profile best sellers, and rapid pace of production—strikingly demonstrates this vibrancy.

This book offers a systematic study of the multiple, interdependent moving parts of genre fiction. Our central research question is this: How is contemporary genre fiction produced and circulated? Nested within this overarching inquiry are further specific questions: What is distinctive about the publishing processes of genre fiction? What role do genre communities play in the development and sharing of texts? And what aspects of writing craft are particular to the creation of genre fiction? The book answers these questions by proposing and developing a new conceptual model: genre worlds. The genre-worlds model recognizes that popular fiction's most compelling characteristics are its connected social, industrial, and textual practices, and the book uses this tripartite focus to work through nuanced facets of the production and circulation of genre fiction, including its relationship to digital technologies, its transnational and transmedia migrations, its involvement in global fan cultures and local communities, and its evolving textual features.

In this introductory chapter, we provide a definition of genre worlds and explain how the concept adapts and extends Howard S. Becker's "art worlds."[1] Becker argues that every work of art is located at the center of a network of cooperative activity and that this cooperation shapes—in large ways and in small—the final work of art. We apply this idea to the art worlds of genre fiction, or genre worlds, via the three key genres that are the focus of this book—crime, fantasy, and romance—and position our analysis and findings within an international context. With the concept of genre worlds and its associated methodologies, popular fiction studies can move away from the taxonomies and defenses that have dominated the field and see genre texts as the results of human creative collaboration, as the products of commercial negotiation and strategy, and as levers for social connection and engagement.

After introducing the genre-worlds model, this chapter traverses the scholarship that has inspired and informed us in building our conceptual framework. We explain how the genre-worlds model interacts with previous genre theories and establish the global scope of our model. We survey work done on genre fiction in the fields of popular fiction studies, literary studies, and publishing studies and elaborate how Becker's art worlds indicate a way forward for us. We then outline our sometimes unconventional methods and provide an overview of the structure of this book.

What Is a Genre World?

A genre world is a collection of people and practices that operates according to established and emerging patterns of collaborative activity, in order to produce the texts that make popular genres recognizable. A genre world enables the multifarious collective activities that go into the creation, circulation, and appreciation of genre texts and encompasses the formation and management of creative collaborations, industrial paradigms, and affective communities. Using a literary sociological approach, our research recognizes the multiple dimensionality of popular genres: as ever-expanding collections of texts; as social complexes that gather around, produce, and value those texts; and as distinctive sets of industrial practices with various national and transnational orientations. We have found it helpful to imagine a genre world as three stacked layers that cannot be easily prized apart: the industrial, the social, and the textual.

Figure 1 represents this conceptual model. This diagram (which we sometimes nickname the Genre Worlds Macaron or Genre Worlds Pancake Stack)

Figure 1. Model of a genre world

shows that the three domains of genre activity—industrial, social, and textual—overlap. Viewed from above our abstracted genre world appears to be a single entity, but viewed slantwise it reveals three connected domains. There are no genre-based social connections without textual patterns and expectations, and these patterns lose currency and power without the industrial machine to reproduce them.

There is a crime genre world, there is a fantasy genre world, and there is a romance genre world (as well as others). Within these worlds, subgenres such as Regency romance, high fantasy, or hard-boiled crime provide hubs—large and small—that contribute diversity while reproducing the logic of the genre world more broadly. Genre worlds have boundaries that create inside(r)s and outside(r)s. Centripetal forces, such as allegiance to and pleasure in core genre tropes, bind genre worlds together. Centrifugal forces, such as the way genre fiction texts are channeled into genre-specific publishing imprints, material formats, or cross-media adaptations, also define the edges of genre worlds by highlighting the differences between genres. Genre worlds are defined by badges of belonging as well as entry and exit points that regulate membership and cultural production. These boundaries can shift, or become fuzzy, when new forms of participation emerge or old forms fade into irrelevance.

Genre worlds are differentiated, and find their commonality, in how their social, textual, and industrial layers combine and interact. The genre-worlds model points to the coherence of individual genres and their capacity to hold together in shape, as well as highlighting structural features that apply across genres. The genre-worlds model can both account for the distinctiveness of specific genres and register the ways in which genres work in similar ways, and it is this that breaks new ground in the study of popular fiction.

Global Structures and Genre Worlds

Genre worlds are shaped by commercial and cultural power, and such power is not evenly distributed. Best-selling works of genre fiction are often the products of the companies with the biggest footprints in the global publishing industry, which have long been associated with the countries and cities where the money and might are concentrated. New York and London are the cities from which the biggest genre fiction names are published, and these authors often hail from the United States or the United Kingdom: Nora Roberts, Lee Child, George R. R. Martin, and Paula Hawkins, for example. Smaller and non-anglophone nations are typically better known globally for their literary novels than their commercial fiction. Japan's Haruki Murakami and Nigeria's Chimamanda Ngozi Adichie are high-profile literary successes, but historical romances and spy thrillers from Japan and Nigeria are less well known globally. Breakout exceptions sometimes happen, such as the Scandinoir crime trend that followed the success of Stieg Larsson's Millennium trilogy, but for the most part popular fiction from countries outside the United States and the United Kingdom finds it hard to travel.[2]

As Pascale Casanova argues in her influential 2004 monograph, *The World Republic of Letters,* international literary space functions according to a hierarchy of unequal power relations, with London and New York as the dominant anglophone centers (Casanova also highlights Paris as a literary center). Writers and books from peripheral or minor national literary cultures struggle for global visibility and legitimacy; the unequal hierarchy of the global publishing industry means authors from the periphery need to find a way to move to the center. Casanova traces examples of how this happens for writers of literary fiction, such as Samuel Beckett and Franz Kafka: routes include prestigious publishers and prizes. But apart from noting that the domestic U.S. market shapes global popular fiction trends, Casanova does not engage in detail with the hierarchies and obstacles that affect the production and circulation of popular fiction.[3]

We take up this challenge in our analysis because we are interested in this uneven distribution of power, and our vantage point in Australia gives us a sharpened view. Work on contemporary genre fiction and contemporary publishing alike is often derived from a focus on the United Kingdom and United States.[4] This book, by contrast, takes as one of its points of focus a peripheral (yet anglophone) national market, Australia, with a diverse range of players and practices. Our theoretical model shows that genre worlds manifest on local, regional, national, and global scales, forming both compact clusters and wide orbits.

Our position as researchers is inflected by our situation in Australia, a midsize culture and economy that is physically remote from the publishing and cultural centers of the United States and the United Kingdom but shares a language as part of broader anglophone networks and a history of (uneven, colonial) exchange of cultural products.[5] Many of our interviews are with Australian authors and industry professionals. This is partly for the pragmatic reason of access. But it is also an innovative way to appreciate an important dimension of genre worlds: the transnationalism of contemporary book cultures and industries. As David Carter writes, an Australian perspective "reveals both the mobility of books, genres and authors, and the barriers to that mobility."[6] The evolutions experienced by the publishing industry look very different when viewed from peripheral economic regions rather than from the centers of the United States and the United Kingdom.[7]

A key argument of this book is that genre worlds are both national and international. They are attuned to these different contexts, particularly the permeable boundaries between small and large publishing markets and the various challenges to that permeability. This attention to both the national and the international runs counter to a tendency in culture and academia to see popular fiction as part of a homogenized global market.[8] The very difficulty experienced by genre fiction books from peripheral markets in breaking into the global mainstream heightens the role of supportive national or regional genre worlds, even as participants keep an eye on global trends and larger markets.

The research in this book reveals the (sometimes difficult) transnational mobility of genre fiction participants and texts. For example, contemporary epic fantasy fiction is written by Australians, but the genre's conventional medieval settings and European concerns mean that it rarely depicts Australian people or places: as Kim Wilkins has argued, "Australian fantasy fiction therefore *is* Australian literature and yet somehow *is not* Australian literature at the same time."[9] The "is and is not" Australianness of popular fiction applies—with varying intensity—across contemporary Australian fantasy, crime, and romance. Consider the work of Perth-based author Anna Hackett, whose action romances include works set in space and works featuring U.S. Navy SEALs, or Michael Robotham, a former president of the Australian Crime Writers Association, whose work is often set in the United Kingdom or the United States, who has always been published by Penguin UK, and whose biggest market is in Germany. At the same time as we reaffirm these transnational interactions, we notice and record traces and influences of the national, so that our research contributes to the troubling of this binary and the cementing of popular fiction in the sphere of national literary studies. Any working definition of national or international cultural formations—and this is true not only for books but also for music or art—breaks down into a series of hard-to-reconcile incongruities. These incongruities are part of the texture of genre worlds. Our model allows the ambiguities of transnationality to stand: popular fiction is traversed by a range of textual, social, and industrial influences and practices that are sometimes but not always national.

Genre Worlds and Genre Theories

Multiple scholarly fields inform this book, and one of the most pertinent is genre theory. Genre theory evidences a solid history of understanding how genres are contingent on and responsive to their social milieus. Whereas Northrop Frye treats genres including lyric, epic, and drama as archetypal and ahistorical categories, Gerard Genette (while adopting the same genres) sees them as more socially and culturally dependent, with histories that are far from frictionless. The much-cited works of Tzvetan Todorov and Hans Robert Jauss dislodge a concern with taxonomy and categorization, where lyric, drama, and epic were held as natural and enduring forms, by emphasizing the historicity of genres and the agency of texts to change genres over time: while texts are in one sense a product of an existing "combinatorial system," they also necessarily act as "a transformation of that system." Jauss acknowledges that certain texts can evoke genre expectations while also changing the "rules of the game" over time and with historical specificity. John Frow calls this an "immanent poetics" that assigns certain texts to certain genres implicitly and in specific cultural contexts, a poetics that "can be glimpsed in such things as the principles by which anthologies are organised."[10]

Frow's work on genre, like Jauss's, is not about popular genres of fiction (strictly speaking neither is Todorov's, but as the research is about "the fantastic" it is regularly cited in studies of fantasy fiction). Frow admits he is interested mostly in a "high-level" concept of genre as a "universal dimension of textuality" rather than producing detailed studies of genres of fiction, film, and so on (notwithstanding his examples from the musical *Showboat*). Frow's ideas are useful, however, in understanding how popular genres of fiction operate. He writes about the tendency of theories of genre to circle back to taxonomy, particularly the many biological metaphors that are evoked in such an enterprise (genus, species, evolution, and so on), but suggests "none of this is particularly useful for thinking about the literary or other kinds, for the good reason that genres are facts of culture which can only with difficulty be mapped onto facts of nature." He uses the example of a row of shops (for example, butcher, baker, hardware store), suggesting what they sell is determined "by convention and [is] culturally specific," not inherent and unchanging. T. G. Pavel picks up the explicitly cultural aspect of genre, arguing that genres resemble social conventions "in the sense that the whole community recognises them as obligations." The idea of the social, or a "code of behaviour" between writer and reader, as Heather Dubrow calls it, is at the heart of more recent thinking about how genre may be negotiated between people. Ria Cheyne's research on genre and disability, for example, recognizes the shared work that writers and readers do "with a conscious or unconscious sense of the genre tradition," emphasizing the affective and reflexive nature of this work. Kim Wilkins calls this the "process of genre," writing that genres are organized around "loose rules of plausibility and probability which mean that certain generic elements are *expected* and therefore indispensible if a genre is to be recognisable (to authors, readers, institutions) *at specific times*."[11] Wilkins's interest in the institutions of genre—for example, publishing houses, university courses, literary review sites—points to the participants in genre outside the writer-reader dyad.

We argue that genres are formed not only textually (that is, by recognizable and categorizable textual features) but also socially and through industrial processes. Our ideas of genre have been shaped by film and television theorists, who have written about screen genres in this way. Steve Neale suggests that genre is formed partly in the social systems and institutions that bring audiences to texts, arguing these systems offer "a means of recognition and understanding." He does not, however, do away with texts, insisting that the study of genre institutions and audiences take place *"in addition to* texts not *instead of* texts." The perspective across text, audience, and industry enables analysis of what Jason Mittell calls "a circuit of cultural practice operative in multiple sites, instead of a singular realm of textual criticism or institutional analysis."[12] Such a perspective on genre unlocks rich evidence about the various interrelated sites of cultural agency that are activated by genre fiction.

Our genre-worlds model also bears similarities to Jeremy Rosen's recent work on genre fiction, particularly his three methodological axes of genre study: cultural, formal, and industrial. Rosen's interest in industry mirrors our own, and his attention to the formal properties of genre is mirrored by our focus on creative writing practice and what happens on the page of genre fiction. Rosen's attention to cultural factors is somewhat different from our approach, however. Rosen is interested in how "a genre's conventional form and thematic preoccupations make legible the social and political concerns of the historical moment at which that genre flourishes."[13] Rather than reading a text to apprehend society, we have chosen to look more directly at the social conditions through which genre texts are created and circulated, by interviewing multiple participants and analyzing genre-based associations, conventions, and interpersonal relationships.

Genre Worlds and Cultural and Literary Studies

In addition to high-level work on genre itself, popular or genre fiction has been studied by scholars working in a number of academic disciplines. As the coauthors of this book, we are based in diverse disciplines ourselves: creative writing, publishing studies and book history, and literary studies. This is a strength when approaching a topic located between or across established areas of scholarly inquiry. Internationally, popular fiction studies has been a well-attended field of research since at least John Cawelti's 1976 monograph, *Adventure, Mystery, and Romance: Formula Stories as Art and Popular Culture,* and John Sutherland's *Bestsellers: Popular Fiction of the 1970s.* The field has developed despite the fact that no discipline has wholly claimed popular fiction as its own. For example, literary studies usually positions genre fiction on the margins of its interests, while cultural studies has tended to focus on nonwritten texts: this is what Michael Butter calls popular fiction's "double otherness."[14]

The rise of cultural and media studies from the mid-twentieth century encouraged scholars to pay attention to popular media products as texts, while also supporting a turn to considering modes of production and consumption. Literary studies took up this interest in popular texts through a number of dedicated publications. This includes journals: while there is no academic association or journal dedicated to genre fiction in the broadest sense, there are specialist journals for every major genre with more appearing almost every year, from *Science Fiction Studies,* established in the 1970s; to *Clues: A Journal of Detection,* established in the 1980s; and to the *Journal of Popular Romance Studies,* established in 2010. The Finnish Society for Science Fiction and Fantasy Research has published *Fafnir* since 2014, and in 2019 Edinburgh University Press announced *Crime Fiction Studies,* dedicated to publishing research on the genre from its beginnings to today.[15] Even more tightly focused publications include the *International Journal of James Bond Studies* and *Pennywise Dreadful: The Journal of Stephen King Studies,* both launched in 2017.

Book-length studies of popular fiction have often tended to focus on single genres. Groundbreaking scholarship in the 1980s and 1990s included Janice Radway's *Reading the Romance,* about romance reading communities; Brian Attebery's *Strategies of Fantasy,* a writing-and-reception-focused study that centered on established authors such as Ursula K. Le Guin and J. R. R. Tolkien; and Rosemary Jackson's *Fantasy: The Literature of Subversion,* an analysis of the fantastic in literature. More recent monographs include those on romance fiction by Lisa Fletcher, Jayashree Kamblé, Lynne Pearce, Pamela Regis, Hsu-Ming Teo, and Jodi McAlister. In fantasy scholarship, the work of writers such as John Clute, Farah Mendlesohn, and Brian Stableford is influential, while scholarship on crime fiction points frequently to Stephen Knight and John Scaggs.[16] Recent edited cross-genre collections giving the field weight include *The Cambridge Companion to Popular Fiction, The Bloomsbury Introduction to Popular Fiction, Twenty-First-Century Popular Fiction,* and *New Directions in Popular Fiction: Genre, Distribution, Reproduction,* though the individual chapters tend to return to single-genre perspectives.[17]

Single-genre or single-author forums and projects add important depth to scholarship, but they cannot advance understanding of some of the common features of popular fiction, including its role in contemporary culture and the contemporary publishing industry. While these studies develop a range of conceptual frameworks with the potential for broader application, there has been an emphasis on defining specific generic classifications and tracing individual genre histories. For example, Regis argues that romance novels from throughout the genre's long history share eight essential narrative criteria, Clute defines fantasy as a metaphorical journey through various narrative checkpoints, and Knight and Scaggs have both written historical accounts of the development of crime fiction's key textual features. The method of textual analysis has been used to pay attention to the politics of genre fiction books. The argument that studying popular genres enhances understanding of the prevalence and power of dominant ideologies is exemplified by the rise of feminist criticism centered on popular genres in the 1990s. Sally Munt, for example, asks questions about the feminist transgressive potential (or otherwise) of crime fiction, while Anne Cranny-Francis calls genre texts "conservative" and argues they are in need of "radical revision." These critics use textual analysis to explicate the relationship between reading pleasure and ideology, with a view to explaining the appeal of seemingly conservative genres to writers and readers. Many of these studies share a preoccupation with the politics of popular writing and reading. For example, Jackson takes issue with epic high fantasy's "nostalgic humanistic vision" as a barrier to progressive political change, while arguing for the subversive potential of the fantastic in the highbrow literature of Franz Kafka and Henry James, and Janice Radway—whose monograph straddles both ethnographic study of readers and analysis of romance fiction texts—is concerned with how romance reading may or may not make women's conventional roles tolerable in a patriarchal society.[18]

This important work on the textual conventions of specific genres can be built on by expanding our purview to include the practices and processes of contemporary genre fiction's creation and publication. While we value deep literary studies scholarship, we trace our genealogy more directly from broader cross-genre and interdisciplinary studies of genre fiction. In one of the first scholarly accounts of popular fiction, Cawelti argues that it should be evaluated on its own terms as a literary art, gestures to relationships to genre for both creators and audiences, and views adventure, mystery, and romance alongside each other. An increasing number of broad studies of popular fiction by literary studies scholars appeared in the 1990s. Thomas J. Roberts's work argues for a distinct aesthetics of popular fiction across westerns, crime, and romance, with a focus on their appeal to readers. Jerry Palmer's work examines genre conventions across media and argues against elitism in scholarship of popular narrative, while also analyzing the role of commercial operations in genre. Scott McCracken argues in his research for the important work performed by popular fiction, across genres, in mitigating late-twentieth-century disaffection with modernity.[19] The titles of these three works all use disparaging names for popular fiction in their titles: "junk fiction," "potboilers," "pulp." This is partly about reclaiming such labels from high-culture elitism; however, it also reinforces a hierarchy of low culture/high culture that can keep analyses of popular fiction trapped within a framework that centralizes literary value (or otherwise) as a defining characteristic.

A key text of the 2000s is Ken Gelder's *Popular Fiction* (2004). Gelder, a literary studies scholar, develops sociologist Pierre Bourdieu's influential model of the field of cultural production to account for the features of popular fiction. In contrast to Bourdieu, who places different forms of fiction (such as avant-garde and mainstream) together in a field, Gelder argues that popular fiction constitutes a field of its own, distinguished through its "logics and practices" and operating in relation to the field of Literature (with a capital *L*). Whereas Literature is indifferent to commercial success and the demands of the buying public, values originality over convention, and celebrates the intellectual work of slow, solitary reading, popular fiction—as Literature's "opposite"—actively engages with its audience and values market success. For Gelder, "Literature and popular fiction will necessarily not be read or 'processed' in the same way." Gelder identifies three terms that are fundamental to popular fiction and encapsulate its distinctiveness from Literature: "industry," "entertainment," and "genre."[20]

"Popular fiction" is an academic term, usually used as Gelder does to distinguish those works of fiction that are not "literary." The term "popular fiction" is rarely used in the industry. Publishers, agents, and others are more likely to talk about "commercial fiction" or "mass-market fiction." In both academic and industrial settings, though, these books are often classified (and evaluated) in terms of their genre. Though other, earlier, theorists may be more likely to use the term "popular fiction," saving genre for discussing specific cases, we follow Gelder's lead that the terms "popular fiction" and "genre fiction" are largely interchangeable: as Gelder writes, "popular fiction is genre fiction."[21] We use both "genre fiction" and "popular fiction" throughout this book.

Literary studies remains an important touchstone for our research, particularly work with a broad focus; however, we also draw on sociologically inflected, book history–informed scholarship on genre fiction. We are interested in investigating the ways people work together in publishing houses and other sites across genre worlds to produce the novels that fascinate us and so many others. We are therefore influenced by researchers who have addressed popular fiction's creation and publication, as well as (often) its reception. For example, as noted above, Janice Radway's *Reading the Romance* is partly an ethnographic study of a romance readers community in the pseudonymous town of "Smithton," while Frank Felsenstein and James J. Connolly's *What Middletown Read* situates a cache of data about library borrowing in Muncie, Indiana—including the borrowing of best-selling popular fiction titles—in a history of the town's cultural and civic development around the turn of the twentieth century. Nicola Humble's work on historical readers of popular fiction and Danielle Fuller's research into writing and reading communities in Newfoundland, Canada, are other examples of the broader sociological approach that inspires us. We follow, too, in the tradition of research that discusses popular fiction as a cultural and commercial sector of print culture, including David Carter's research on the historical middlebrow, Beth Driscoll's work on the contemporary middlebrow, and the work on the production and distribution of pulp fiction by Paula Rabinowitz, Erin Smith, and Michael Denning.[22]

Genre Worlds and Publishing Studies

Our broadly conceived study of genre fiction, then, needs to understand the operations and relationships characteristic of the publishing industry in order to fill out the comprehensive picture of a genre world. This is a multidirectional process: publishers do not force genre on passive readers.[23] The sense of mutually influencing nodes in the cycle of books and book culture recalls Robert Darnton's influential communications circuit, reworked and updated for the twenty-first century by Padmini Ray Murray and Claire Squires.[24]

The growing field of publishing studies—that is, research about the publishing industry—pursues a variety of approaches.[25] Sometimes scholarship focuses on the history of publishing houses or on the industry's business models.[26] Broader studies often adopt Bourdieu's model of the field of cultural production in order to represent the dynamics of the publishing field and the interactions between cultural and economic capital that determine its operations.[27] Casanova offers an explicitly global extension of this approach in her work on international power relations in the "world republic of letters," in which publishing personnel function as gatekeepers of culture.[28] International field dynamics have also been explored in relation to translation, international rights sales, and the media reception of transnational best sellers.[29]

Field theory has enabled high-level observation and scrutiny of the ways in which the publishing industry carries out its commercial and artistic aims. This research has charted the shift of the publishing industry from a "gentleman's profession," through an era of mergers and acquisitions that produced an industry dominated by publishing conglomerates, and now to an industry reshaped by technological companies such as Amazon.[30] Sociological research that approaches the world of books as a field usefully highlights the uneven structure of the industry: some players are giants, and some are minuscule. It shows also that the publishing industry is globally dispersed according to colonial patterns, with power concentrated in London and New York, especially for anglophone publishing. It is connected to, and is a subset of, larger media and entertainment (and retail and educational) industries. These valuable larger-scale claims, however, need to be enriched and complicated with research on a granular level.

Such detailed research is sometimes hindered by the paucity of reliable data on book sales, which can occlude the importance of genre fiction. It is notoriously difficult to find and verify accurate data about the publishing industry, a difficulty that has been compounded by the rapid emergence of new routes from author to reader. For example, while Nielsen BookScan is one of the leading sources of sales data in many countries, at the time of writing it does not include all e-book sales on Amazon, including sales of self-published titles.

Publishing studies also often works closely with industry accounts; as Simone Murray writes, "In the absence of a substantial, self-defined body of academic publishing research, scholars may profitably mine vocational and industry-oriented discussions for quantitative data capable of supporting qualitative analyses." Industry insights and reports are indispensable, despite their tendency toward partiality and reliance on "descriptive rather than critical modes of analysis";[31] textbooks sometimes summarize this kind of research.[32] Paying close attention to industry also informs primary research in publishing. David Throsby, Jan Zwar, and Thomas Longden, for example, use interviews and surveys of industry personnel for insight into the changing circumstances of authors and publishers.[33] We have also drawn inspiration from industry-oriented approaches to data from broader research into creative industries, which frequently considers publishing.[34] In addition to providing data about broad trends in the numbers and types of books published and sold, such gray literature can reveal areas of upheaval within the industry. Digitization has been—and remains—one such locus of heightened industry attention.[35] The industry response to the "digital revolution" (a key phrase in countless media articles about publishing) is especially relevant for understanding the production of genre fiction and appreciating the perspectives of the people writing and publishing it today.

Between literary studies, genre theory, and publishing studies, the picture of how popular fiction operates is becoming more and more detailed. However, there are large gaps in extant scholarship of the late twentieth and early twenty-first centuries. This is, in part, because conceptual frameworks developed with reference to book industries and cultures of past centuries can become weak explanatory models when applied to the contemporary literary sphere. For example, much work on fiction publishing draws on Bourdieu's model, which is based on an analysis of nineteenth-century French literary culture.[36] While Bourdieu does not fade entirely from view in this book, he is not central to our understanding of twenty-first-century popular fiction. Our experience of popular fiction, as readers, researchers, and writers, led us to seek new ways of understanding this cultural sector. Our aim has been to produce a major new study of genre fiction that is panoramic in outlook, innovative in methodology, and deeply engaged with conversations beyond academia. We therefore sought a theory that would help us understand the interconnectedness of the people and processes that make and circulate genre novels. The theorist who helped us address these aspects of genre fiction was Howard S. Becker.

From Art Worlds to Genre Worlds

Becker, born in Chicago, was playing piano in strip joints by the time he was a teen. While he always considered himself more a musician, he is best known as a sociologist. Becker's enduring attachment to music, however, has given him an insider status from which to conceptualize the sociology of art. His 1982 book, *Art Worlds* (frequently reprinted and updated and revised for a twenty-fifth anniversary edition in 2008), offers a sociological study of how art (taken broadly to include visual art, music, drama, literature, and so on) is produced, circulated, and appreciated. For Becker, art is the result of collective activity. He acknowledges the centrality of the artist, but locates the artist within a radiating network whose "cooperative activity, organized via their joint knowledge of conventional means of doing things, produces the kind of art works that art world is noted for." Everything that the artist does not do "must be done by someone else," and wherever the artist relies on someone from this "cast of characters," Becker asserts that "a cooperative link exists." The artist, as well as the others in the radiating network, embodies knowledge about how things are done within the art world via "conventions" that are "known to all or almost all well-socialized members."[37]

Becker accounts only obliquely for the world of books and publishing, but his conceptualization is particularly apposite for the study of genre fiction, which is organized by highly networked communities with a strong orientation toward conventional behavior (social, amateur, professional, industrial) focused on conventional texts that reproduce and reconfigure well-known tropes. To date, Becker's conceptual tools have not regularly been used to investigate the publishing industry, but they are clearly amenable to such use. Like Bourdieu, Becker focuses on the many people who contribute to the production and circulation of an artwork or cultural product. In relation to novels, this includes publishers, agents, book designers, and editors. For Becker, the difference between his concept of a "world" and Bourdieu's "field" is that people in a field are not "flesh-and-blood" but "caricatures." Becker's account may give Bourdieu's model unnecessarily short shrift, but it usefully points to Becker's emphasis on people's real-world practices. For Becker, the metaphor of the world is not spatial but centers on collective activity between people. A world is not a "closed unit," not an "analytic convenience"; it is "more empirically grounded" and encompasses "things that we can observe—people doing things, rather than 'forces,' 'trajectories,' 'inertia,' which are not observable in social life, if you understand these terms in the technical sense given to them in physics." That is, a world "consists of real people who are trying to get things done, largely by getting other people to do things that will assist them in their project."[38] Differentiating his work from Bourdieu's less open approach, Becker writes, "The basic question of an analysis centered on 'world' is who is doing what with who that affects the resulting work of art? The basic question of an analysis centered on field seems to me to be, who dominates who, using what strategies and resources, with what results?" The real people who are the focus of Becker's account do not operate alone but interact to produce artworks. Analyzing an art world starts with identifying "its characteristic kinds of workers and the bundle of tasks each one does." This, we argue, is an apt description of the publishing industry and the creative practices that underpin genre fiction. We recognize artists as principal players in the production of new creative work; in genre worlds, writers are usually at the center of the radiating networks of cooperation that give those worlds their purpose and identity. Placing the artist at the center of a network, methodologically, is consonant with the understandings at work in genre worlds themselves: as one publisher told us, "At the end of the day the heart of the team is always the author because there is absolutely no way we'd be able to do what we do without them."[39] Becker's work, then, suggested to us a concept that could underpin an innovative approach to popular fiction. We call this concept genre worlds.

As outlined above, a genre world is a textual, social, and industrial complex in which people work together to create and circulate specific types of books. An analysis of the component parts of a genre world and their interrelation involves identifying the "cast of characters" and examining the "cooperative links" between them, in whatever material, digital, or even imaginary place those links occur. It includes, therefore, a focus on industrial and social dimensions of the production of genre texts. Further, Becker holds that artworks "always shows signs of that cooperation." A genre-worlds analysis therefore also involves tracing the influence that the cast of characters and their dynamic links exert on works of art, that is, genre novels. Importantly, in Becker's conceptualization, the work of art (a painting, a sculpture, a published novel) is not an object in stasis, even abstractly. Instead, the people who receive, respond to, or critique works of art are included in the collective whose cooperative activities define art worlds. While close and comparative reading of genre texts and their paratexts—book covers, blurbs, titles—is an important part of mapping the operations of genre worlds, so too is attending to the collaborative social and industrial networks in which genre texts arise. Robert Cluley provides a pithy summation of Becker's key insight for the study of text-based cultures and industries: "Cultural texts allow people to interact and are produced by people interacting."[40]

This book examines genre texts as products of distinctive interactional worlds (crime, fantasy, or romance) while remaining sensitive to industry-wide structures that produce similarities between genre worlds. Genre worlds are distinctive, but they are not unique. This is evident in the more or less fluid movement of people between genres, such as an agent who represents both fantasy and romance authors, an author who writes romance but is an avid reader of crime, or an omnivorous reader of best sellers who publishes reviews on Amazon across multiple genres.

Our genre-worlds theory not only newly applies Becker's "art worlds" concepts to the cultural sector of genre fiction but also updates Becker's theory in a number of key ways. For example, the art-worlds model does not account for the dramatic effects of digital technological changes on genre worlds over the past two decades. These changes cannot be conceptualized in a blunt, monolithic way. Attention must be paid to the varied changes mediated by platforms and their affordances, which include a shifting value placed on physical and live practices. This is what it means to be postdigital, that is, in an environment where ongoing digital change is the new norm and digital and nondigital practices coexist and interact.[41] Each of the chapters of this book is engaged with the postdigital and the influence of digital technologies on the production of genre texts.

Moreover, while Becker accounts for networks and the activities that create and sustain them, he does not account for the pleasurable investments in community that motivate contributors. As each of the chapters in this book reveals, our interviewees frequently traced their love of a specific genre to reading books, but then explained the myriad ways in which books helped them find their way to a professional and affective community, including enduring friendships and supportive relationships. Thus, while Becker's theory gave us a starting point, our model develops a fuller picture of the functioning of the multiple and dynamic aspects of genre worlds, including their transnationality and transmediality. Our approach to genre fiction in this book takes aspects of Becker's art-worlds theory—particularly his emphasis on cooperative activity and conventional behaviors—and develops and updates them to account for the creation and circulation of contemporary genre fiction.

Scoping the Research: Crime, Fantasy, and Romance

We are particularly interested in the genre worlds of crime, fantasy, and romance. These three genres provide the focal points for this book, as specific genre worlds. We use the terms "crime," "fantasy," and "romance" in a broad and flexible sense, recognizing that the worlds they describe are constituted through continual discussion and evolving practice. Genres are often understood by their textual features: we all know where to sort fire-breathing dragons, rakish earls, and spinster sleuths (which is not to say they can never appear in the same—thrilling!—novel). It is in the joint recognition of genres that genre is formed, however, not in the textual features alone. There are plenty of fantasy novels without dragons, and readers recognize them easily enough. Similarly, books with dragons may not be fantasy. Kazuo Ishiguro's novel *The Buried Giant,* which included dragons and several other recognized fantasy conventions, inspired a vigorous debate in literary pages and online, which caught up Neil Gaiman and Ursula K. Le Guin, about whether it was a fantasy novel: in the words of *Guardian* journalist David Barnett, "Another day, another argument about whether a book about dragons is fantasy or not." Ishiguro himself refused the fantasy category, commenting, "I don't know what's going to happen. Will readers follow me into this? Will they understand what I'm trying to do, or will they be prejudiced against the surface elements? Are they going to say this is fantasy?"[42] Ishiguro's questions signal that genres are decided communally. That is, the presence of genre conventions may raise the possibility that a text belongs to a specific genre, but it is ultimately in the public realm of social and industrial discourse that genres are haggled over and assigned. Academic debates over how a genre such as crime or fantasy or romance should be defined, as described in our literature review above, can be lengthy and are themselves part of the process of genre formation.

In our research, we use the practical and capacious industry terms "crime," "fantasy," and "romance." The industry usage of "fantasy," for example, captures science fiction, horror, and any other books where the "not real" is a chief selling point. While the term "speculative fiction" is sometimes used for this category, it is not as meaningful a term in an industry sense. In the United States, the Book Industry Studies Group's BISAC Subject Codes do not include "speculative fiction," offering instead fifteen subcategories of fantasy; Nielsen BookScan also has no speculative fiction category.

"Romance fiction," too, has a clear industry meaning, informed by the long history of Mills & Boon and Harlequin publishing. There exists a distinction in romance between category romance and single-title romance. The former are associated with shorter lengths, cheaper price points, and distribution through mail and newsagents; the latter are lengthier stand-alone stories distributed via bookstores and with a longer shelf life. At the same time, romance fiction is involved in debates about the edges of its genre world, particularly when texts shade into categories such as commercial women's fiction and chick lit. "Crime" encompasses mysteries, detective novels, and, increasingly in the twenty-first century, the psychological thrillers that regularly top best-seller charts. "Fantasy," "romance," and "crime" are broad terms that denote a certain kind of book in the marketplace, and the terms allow us to talk about these books without becoming beholden to taxonomies that seek to impose rigidity, given elasticity is valued by many stakeholders in genre worlds. At the same time, we are interested in critiquing industry practices around genre—including attempts to shift authors between genres and creation of new genres and subgenres that capitalize on sales trends—and bring our academic expertise to bear on this task.

Researching Contemporary Genre Fiction: Our Methods

We introduced ourselves in the prologue to this book as, to varying degrees, partial insiders in relation to genre fiction communities, and our research has sought to leverage the opportunities that arise from traffic between the professional world of academia and genre worlds. We are, variously, a writer of genre fiction, enthusiastic readers and attendees at genre events, and academics. Even in our academic roles, we occupy an intriguing insider-outsider position; Becker writes of criticism as one of the activities that sustains art worlds, and we too see academic critique (or its absence) as a fundamental component of how genre worlds are situated.

Among the advantages of an insider-outsider approach, especially when it is undertaken in collaborative research, is an understanding of different ways of being involved in genre worlds. Gelder talks about different ways in which scholars, writers, and others may be "in the game" of popular fiction, noting this as a Bourdieusian concept to do with the personal and professional investments that are made in a field. Bernard Lahire also responds to Bourdieu, though more critically, when he describes "the divided habitus," where members of one field may also have investments in another.[43] We too see different levels of interest and involvement in genre worlds, including from academics. Insider-outsider movements between academia and genre fiction writers are increasingly common: there is burgeoning growth in university creative writing programs that may employ genre fiction writers,[44] and there are professional jobs in genre fiction that build on university qualifications (for example, publishing degrees, creative writing degrees, and generalist undergraduate degrees with majors in English or work-experience components). Among our interviewees were faculty staff, PhD students, and publishing personnel who deliver guest lectures, consult on internships or course design, and partner in research projects. Different institutional attachments, roles, and practices are at play for genre-world participants, and these affect how the edges of genre worlds are traced.

And so we operate from the standpoints of those who are active in the genre, seeking and reporting the perspectives of genre-world participants and acknowledging our own positions as academics who find pleasure in romance, crime, and fantasy fiction.

Aca-Fans and Autoethnography

Having accepted that we are to some extent "in the game," in the Bourdieusian sense of having professional and personal interests in the genre fiction worlds we study, we now think through how this shapes our research. The first concept we consider is that of the "aca-fan," a term defined by Henry Jenkins as "a hybrid creature which is part fan and part academic." As Cécile Cristofari and Matthieu J. Guitton note, this challenges the idea of the academic as detached: fans embody emotion, subjectivity, passionate investment, amateurism, and "unorthodox or marginal forms of knowledge," whereas academics have often been imagined in terms of "critical distance, professional language, rationality, intellectual orthodoxy." However, these binaries around academic and fan are "partly artificial" and may foreclose certain important functions the aca-fan can perform. Jenkins holds that his role is "to bridge the gap between these two worlds," while Cristofari and Guitton agree on the important role an aca-fan may play as "a crucial node where knowledge from the community is passed on into the academic world." Jenkins sees the aca-fan breaking cultural theory "out of the academic bookstore ghetto" to "open up a larger space to talk about the media that matters to us from a consumer's point of view." Jenkins's focus on pleasure and meaning bears similarities to a movement within literary studies—including work by Rita Felski, Heather Love, and others—that identifies with a "postcritical" position, attuned more to enjoyment and pleasure and less to what Paul de Ricoeur calls a "hermeneutics of suspicion," although those scholars are primarily interested in shifting styles of reading within the university rather than opening the university up to more engagement with the public and industry.[45]

Catherine M. Roach explored the aca-fan approach in her research around the romance genre, with her stated purpose being to "swing discussion about popular romance in a different direction" by not taking an outsider position. To enact this, she began writing romance novels under a pseudonym and conducted participant-observation fieldwork at a "con" (explained in chapter 5), the Romance Writers of America convention. She combined these activities into a "performative ethnography," which even manifests in the language of her academic text: "Academic-scholarly intellectuals aren't supposed to wear velvet, especially without underwear." She describes how one romance-convention participant became defensive about her approach: "It helped me to see how a 'real' insider could read my participatory research as disrespect, infiltration, inauthenticity—even blasphemy."[46] Roach's account alerts us to the possibility that adopting the aca-fan position from the "aca" entrance point may create tension.

Our challenge, then, was to balance critical distance and personal investment and model a kind of critical proximity. Like Cristofari and Guitton, we believe that the academic impulse deriving from cultural studies to sort fan behavior into progressive or reactionary brings a "risk of bias when applied to a community, especially one as diverse and complex as fandom."[47] Conversely, there is always a danger that an aca-fan might take a defensive stance when they see their object of affection under threat (from highbrow academics, for example), where a more neutral stance would be appropriate. The mixed nature of our team, with one of us more embedded in a genre world than the others, helped us to maintain a productive balance, affording us an insider position with outsider objectivity.

Another approach that aligns with our methods is that of autoethnography. Cristofari and Guitton see this as a potentially productive adjunct approach for aca-fans. In genre worlds, aca-fans could autoethnographically study their own performance in genre-world contexts or consider the narration of observations by themselves and others. Cristofari and Guitton recognize that previous work on the aca-fan has eschewed this approach, seeking to observe only the community and not themselves, offering the examples of Matt Hills and Henry Jenkins.[48] This eschewal is not for us, as at least one of us is genuinely from the community under observation.

Autoethnography is rooted in a researcher's personal experience, values their relationships with other participants in a group, is self-reflective, adopts a social justice ethos, and balances intellectual rigor and emotional investment.[49] The theory of autoethnography, like that around aca-fans, also questions the idealized view of the rational and distant academic. In fact, it is highly critical of goals such as distilling universal truths from social relations, making stable claims about human experiences, the bias against emotion, and the refusal of different ways of knowing (for example, storytelling, amateur interpretation). The reflexivity embodied in autoethnography mitigates against several "ethically questionable ethnographic stances" such as "custodian's rip-off," "enthusiast's infatuation," and "curator's exhibitionism."[50] In such a view, a team makeup such as ours can be genuinely emotionally invested in genre worlds while also remaining reflexively ethical and providing room for critical distance.

Becker writes, "You can only learn current conventions by participating in what is going on," that is, by being situated inside the art world.[51] We agree and leverage our insider status to enhance our knowledge of current practices. A genre-worlds research project examines routine activities; including researchers engaged in routine participation in the world is a distinct advantage.[52] Our critically proximate approach blends the enthusiastic but analytical research orientation of the aca-fan, the reflexive ethics of autoethnography, and a collaborative approach in which the researchers have different levels of investment and experience in genre communities.

Our Mixed-Methods, Medium-Data Approach

Popular fiction can seem resistant to some scholarly research habits. The time lines typical of academic research are incompatible with the rapid pace of contemporary popular fiction production, to say nothing of the sheer number and often length of the texts themselves. We address this challenge through an innovative methodology that attends both to the texts and to the processes and practices by which they are brought into being.

We used mixed methods to conduct the research for this book. Methodologically, our approach was to select ten case-study titles from each of our focus genres: romance, fantasy, and crime.[53] The case-study approach ensured we weren't overreliant on generalizations. Headlines for media articles about genre fiction often focus on data about the volume of production, sales, and circulation: "Four Writers That Have Sold More than 125 Million Books and the Creator of HBO'S *True Detective* Praise a New Novel Causing It to Sell Out at Bookstores Nationwide Overnight," "Oxfam Charity Shop Given So Many Copies of *Fifty Shades of Grey* It Turned Them into a Fort," and "Science Fiction and Fantasy Book Sales Have Doubled since 2010."[54] The data that inspires these articles and the associated online discussion is valuable, and some of it informs the arguments of this book. But genre fiction is more than a commercial phenomenon. We offer case studies of selected novels and series to provide in-depth, fine-grained knowledge of genre fiction texts and the people involved in their production and circulation. Case-study texts (a full list is provided in the appendix) were selected to provide a meaningful cross-section of the textual, social, and industrial dimensions of contemporary genre fiction. We chose case studies that would help us to understand the specificity of popular fiction across genres, from different points in author careers, and at different places on the spectrum of commercial success. This selection enables investigation of the breadth and diversity of genre fiction without claiming comprehensiveness. Our case studies range from a high-profile thriller coauthored by James Patterson and early career writer Candice Fox to a series of Regency romances authored by seasoned writer Anne Gracie and a *Star Wars* novelization by Sean Williams.

Having selected our case-study titles, we conducted interviews with authors, editors, agents, and others associated with the books. We also conducted a number of more general interviews with bloggers, managing editors, literary agents, and highly prolific authors that gave insights into genre worlds. For this project, we interviewed seventy-eight writers and industry professionals and transcribed panel discussions with a further twelve participants from a symposium on popular fiction that we held in 2016. Interviewing is an established method for producing rich data concerning the contemporary production, circulation, and appreciation of texts and is particularly suitable for a study of popular fiction.[55] We agree with Danielle Fuller, who argues that interviews enable researchers to discover new knowledge by "learning to listen carefully and critically to the analyses, definitions and interpretations provided by those people who are most intimately involved with creating, publishing and evaluating" relevant texts.[56] Semistructured interviews enabled us to explore a framework of themes but left open the possibility of our interviewees revealing unexpected insights into practices, processes, and contexts.

We conducted our interviews with an awareness of the limitations of this method. For example, we recognized that interviews necessarily produce partial accounts, and these are shaped by the context in which they occur. In our case, respondents gave their answers to us, as academics, knowing that they would be used for a research project. This inevitably created particular power relations and framing for the discussion, so that some knowledge was not shared. For example, some interviewees chose not to discuss material or financial constraints that affect their participation in genre worlds. Some people turned out to have reputations for being unpleasant to work with or for exaggerating their fame or fortune, none of which was discussed on the record with us. We recognize the transcripts of our interviews as invested and incomplete. Interviews also capture moments in time, following which situations may change; we have learned since conducting the interviews, for example, that some of the relationships depicted positively by participants have subsequently broken down, while new relationships have formed.

We also recognize distinctions and overlaps between articulations of lived experience, general commentary, and marketing spin. In our analysis, we elected to prioritize interview quotations about the interviewee's direct, personal experience rather than those that articulate their perceptions or assessment of the industry, culture, or genre world as a whole—often received ideas or wisdom—or that expressly seek to sell or promote the book or author under discussion. However, we also recognize the heuristic value of general statements made by our interviewees. The frequent repetition of often unattributed pearls of wisdom is one way in which knowledge circulates and has effects. In *Race and the Cultural Industries,* Anamik Saha develops Timothy Haven's concept of "industry lore" to describe the often implicit knowledge of creative managers, which is gleaned from a range of sources, including "market research, experience and gut feeling." This lore informs decisions about which cultural commodities are produced and can lead to narrow representations of racial and ethnic groups and perpetuate unconscious bias: often "racialist logic is disguised as common business sense."[57] In genre worlds, some general, clichéd comments become self-fulfilling prophecies because of how often and to whom they are articulated (for example, "Short stories don't sell," "Most readers are white women")—at least until they are interrupted by new data ("The print book is dead" alternates with "The e-book is dead"). We made a commitment to reflect carefully on the different kinds of knowledge that might be gleaned from each interview.

While being aware of potential gaps, blind spots, omissions, or partiality, throughout our research we have recognized the expertise of the individuals we have interviewed. This is one of the ways in which we share Becker's antielitist approach to cultural sociology: our aim has not been to show that "when actors think they are doing one thing, they are really doing something else."[58] We believe in interviews as a method for producing grounded, nuanced, detailed information about contemporary practice. We complemented our interviews with industry data drawn from both scholarly and commercial sources (including the bibliographic database AustLit, the sales-tracking service Nielsen BookScan, German library deposit records, and industry "gray literature," such as magazine reports). We also read extensively across the three genres of fantasy, romance, and crime published internationally over the past twenty years.

This produced what we call medium data: a data set that is not massive to the point of being unable to be read but is also larger than a study of a single book or author. Our medium-data approach builds knowledge on a scale that should be useful and readily adaptable, especially for scholars of publishing seeking to understand some of the finer-grained elements of the contemporary industry and for scholars in literary studies seeking to contextualize the text- or author-based studies that remain their methodological norm.

The Structure of This Book

The chapters that follow grow organically out of findings from our interviews, alongside our interpretation of relevant industry data and our broader reading and thinking on contemporary genre fiction. We have divided the book into three sections that correspond to the three dimensions of our genre-worlds model: industrial, social, and textual.

Chapters 2 and 3 are concerned with the industrial aspects of genre worlds. Chapter 2 details the contemporary publishing industry's investment in genre fiction, considering participants' lived experience of cooperative and competitive networks as they bring crime, romance, and fantasy books into being. The chapter closely examines four evolving arenas of activity that are shaping the twenty-first-century production and circulation of genre fiction: editing, distribution, self-publishing, and algorithms. Chapter 3 is interested in industrial borders and how genre worlds are constituted in movement between markets and media. Using Casanova's ideas about unequal power relations in the "world of letters," we trace the access points and blockages experienced by genre-world participants from a medium-size anglophone market as they attempt to move the texts they are invested in toward the international center. We then turn to the ways that an increasingly converged media landscape leads to another type of border crossing: between one medium and another. The international inflections of genre worlds are highly visible when books become content vying for large-scale, global audience share.

Chapters 4 and 5 center around the social aspects of genre worlds. While the social in terms of audiences and reading is regularly accounted for in other scholarship on genre fiction, our emphasis pushes well beyond these topics. Genre-worlds theory insists that we consider the many other ways people interact with books, including writing them, talking about them, studying them, reviewing them, attending conventions, interacting with fandoms, and so on. These kinds of interactions underpin both formal associations and informal relationships. Chapter 4 takes as its lead the affective nature of genre worlds as expressed in the interviewees' accounts of genre community and uses Gee's affinity space theory to examine what outcomes community achieves in genre worlds, especially with regards to the creative relationships that facilitate the writing of books. Chapter 5 looks more closely at the public formations of genre worlds, locating them both within digital space across social media and in physical spaces with a sustained analysis of the role of professional conventions, or "cons."

Genre-worlds theory, while explicitly interested in the industrial and the social, cannot ignore participants' accounts of the centrality of the *textual* dimensions of their worlds: genre worlds exist because of genre books. Chapter 6 asks how we might read genre books while remaining mindful of the many participants in genre worlds. This chapter closely reads genre texts to demonstrate how the social and the industrial aspects of genre worlds are visible on the page. It focuses on examples of genre fiction titles in depth, including Indigenous Australian author Claire G. Coleman's fantasy novel

Terra Nullius. This chapter thinks through the kind of social and industrial work that writers can use genre conventions to do—including progressive or conservative ideological work.

Finally, chapter 7 sums up our argument that genre worlds are composed of layers of textual, social, and industrial collaborative activity but emphasizes that these are subject to change over time and as different practices and tastes take hold among the structures and individuals that form them. The chapter discusses genre-world futures and the question of how a genre world might change, tracing as an example the turns toward (and against) increased diversity and inclusivity in genre worlds.

. . .

And so, the story has begun. The opening chapter draws to a close. Just as it does, a shadow falls. What strange beast casts that shadow? A benevolent god? A crushing oppressor? Ah, 'tis the publishing industry, and the great storytellers say it is sliding into chaos . . .

CHAPTER 2

Genre Worlds and the Publishing Industry

In the first chapter, we argued that studying genre worlds requires a tripartite focus: on the industrial, social, and textual aspects of genre fiction. These aspects influence each other in myriad mundane and profound ways, so much so that they are impossible to prize apart fully, yet it is helpful for analytical purposes to consider each in turn. This chapter and the next directly address the industrial conditions of twenty-first-century genre fiction. We agree with Ann Steiner that the "contemporary book business is globalized and digitalized," and this chapter locates popular fiction and the specific genre worlds of crime, fantasy, and romance within the overall structure of this global, digitized industry.[1] Chapter 3 follows this discussion by considering the boundaries of industrial formations through an investigation of the transnational and transmedia movements of genre fiction texts.

Genre has long been a central mechanism of fiction publishing, providing both practical arrangements for the organization of books and marketing tools to assist reader choices.[2] Industry practices to do with genre have been affected by rapidly changing conditions in the early decades of the twenty-first century. The emergence of new economic structures of publishing and bookselling, particularly those driven by Amazon, has strikingly affected the production and circulation of genre fiction, which, with its relatively fast production cycle and responsiveness to market, is often first impacted and most deeply implicated in changes to the publishing industry.

Genre worlds are made up of people. Rather than being a monolith, the publishing industry is a collection of people, often performing routine tasks in conventional ways. As times change, those people, tasks, and conventions must also change. This chapter takes the view from the now, a time in the early twenty-first century, when a long history of publishing personnel, tasks, and conventions lies behind us and a new future of publishing personnel, tasks, and conventions lies ahead. That is not to say that the now in which we are writing is a single pivot point in the story of publishing; rather, we wish to contextualize the environment we write about in this chapter with the recent and the near, to understand some of its subtle shifts and sudden movements, through the perspective of the real people who materially do the work of bringing genre fiction to market. We ask, what place does genre fiction now occupy in small, medium, and large publishing houses and in the growing sphere of self-publishing? Are there typical or distinctive publishing protocols for genre fiction that persist throughout the industry or that vary according to the scale of the publishing house: publication schedules, acquisitions, or rights sales? How has genre fiction contributed to the digital shift in publishing, and where has the contribution been greatest? And how have those digital shifts affected the material work of the publishing industry, how it is viewed, and how it is valued?

The Contemporary Publishing Industry and Genre Fiction: Setting the Scene

Throughout the contemporary fiction industry, and for every kind of organization from multinationals to small presses to technology companies and self-publishers, genre is an organizing principle. This is apparent in myriad ways. Categorization schemes such as BISAC, Thema, and Amazon's own categories operate behind the scenes, assigning genre labels to books as part of their metadata. Genre-branded imprints and established iconographies of cover design and format make genre texts easy to identify, as do the organization of the fiction shelves in brick-and-mortar bookstores and the direct-marketing strategies used by e-retailers, publishers, and authors.[3] Genre in this industrial sense influences creative and commercial decisions and workflows throughout the publishing industry. To put it more abstractly, genre is one of the categories of perception through which the distribution of economic and cultural power occurs and through which the interactions of print and digital technologies are materially experienced.

Two decades into the twenty-first century, publishing remains an industry largely made up of organizations recognizable from the twentieth century. Piecing together the available data on the number of books produced and sold across territories and formats, we can make the following observations about the contemporary industry. First, the market is dominated by a small group of very large multinational publishers (themselves owned by media conglomerates). At the time of writing they are Penguin Random House, HarperCollins, Simon & Schuster, Macmillan, and Hachette. One estimate suggests that these companies account for 80 percent of the U.S. trade fiction market.[4] Industry conversations often referred to the "Big Six," then the "Big Five"; the recent announcement that Bertelsmann, owner of Penguin Random House, intends to purchase Simon & Schuster indicates we may soon be down to a "Big Four." In this book, we use the term "Big Few" to point to the concentration of multinational publishing companies (and to future-proof our book somewhat against further consolidations). These companies control much of the most visible genre fiction, whether visibility is measured through book sales or through the cultural and commercial expansion achieved through adaptations for film and television. For these companies, genre fiction provides each year's most reliable moneymaking books. Multinational companies publish the most brand-name genre fiction authors, such as Nora Roberts, Lee Child, Danielle Steel, George R. R. Martin, and Stephen King. As noted in chapter 1, these authors are usually based in the United States and the United Kingdom, and it is the London and New York offices of these multinational companies that exert the most power. The Big Few tend to publish their genre fiction through specific imprints, such as HarperCollins's Avon imprint for romance, Hachette's Orbit imprint for fantasy, or Penguin Random House's Arrow imprint for commercial fiction, including such best-selling writers as Diana Gabaldon and James Patterson.

In addition to the few large players, there are a multitude of small presses. Independently owned publishing companies may range from tiny kitchen-table operations to quite large businesses. These companies often specialize in a single type of fiction, so that crime, fantasy, or romance fiction may be their core business as well as an expression of their own taste and enthusiasm. Small presses continue to play a vital role in genre worlds as research and development spaces that discover and support new voices and sometimes break out new authors or trends that are subsequently capitalized on by Big Few publishers.[5] They can also be important sites for the nurturing of genre communities.

Alongside these traditional kinds of publishing organizations, new players have emerged in the twenty-first century: technological companies taking an interest in publishing. These include powerhouses such as Amazon (and, to a lesser extent, Facebook, Google, and Apple) and a host of small, medium, and large digital service providers, including print-on-demand companies. Technology-focused companies are particularly linked to the growing phenomenon of self-publishing, which has generated and continues to generate a vast array of texts circulating primarily online. These forms of publishing produce a range of products and enable a range of career paths: they constitute and alter the who, what, and how of the publishing industry.

The People of Publishing: Activity, Practices, Conventions

The theory of genre worlds, like Becker's art worlds, is "a way of talking about people who routinely participate" in the making of a work of genre fiction.[6] The genre-worlds model therefore fosters an appreciation of the many and various publishing personnel who interact with genre fiction texts, at any point in the workflow from first idea to reaching readers. These people may include agents, scouts, editors (acquiring editors, commissioning editors, structural editors, copy editors, proofreaders), publishers, sales and marketing staff, publicists, designers, production managers, printers, distributors, warehousers, and booksellers. They may work for large or small companies or as freelancers.

The demographics of publishing industry personnel are concentrated in a fairly narrow set of categories. Publishing has a recognized diversity problem: those who participate are predominantly white, middle class, and, in the lower professional ranks only, female.[7] Moreover, anglophone book culture's centralization in London and New York (and in the metropolitan centers of other countries, such as Sydney or Toronto) has exclusionary effects on who has the capacity and opportunity to fulfill the professional roles in publishing. This affects genre worlds; some viewpoints and experiences are not included, and industry professionals who do not fit the template may experience friction or difficulty as participants in genre worlds. There are signs these demographics may be shifting slowly: the feminization of the industry, for example, has helped it shake off its reputation as an "old-fashioned gentleman's industry," but in this regard change is slow.[8] We pay attention throughout this book to the ways that publishing's diversity problems affect people, practices, and texts.

Less slow to shift are the roles people perform in twenty-first-century publishing, as a changing digital environment creates role confusion or overlap. Our interviewees who have changed roles tended to link their need or decision to reprofile to the opportunities or limitations of digital change, and several of the people we interviewed performed multiple roles in the production of genre texts. Romance author Kelly Hunter, for example, both writes and edits for publisher Tule. Becker's phrases "kinds of workers" and "each kind of person" are anachronistic to describe the labor force for the production of genre texts, in an age of increased self-publishing and proliferating small presses.[9] The self-publishing of genre fiction has changed the professional profile of the publishing industry, complicating and blurring the lines between author, agent, editor, cover designer, typesetter, publisher, and bookseller. There are new opportunities for readers, too, to become involved in the professional activities of publishing genre fiction. Amazon's Kindle Direct Publishing, Wattpad, and fan-fiction sites such as Archive of Our Own and Fanfiction enable the paraprofessional and professional work of fans and readers, some of whom also play other roles in the wider publishing ecosystem.[10] Self-publishing and related enterprises show the need for fluidity in descriptive and interpretive models for studying publishing. Roles are not inert in this dynamic industrial space. And it is not only roles that are in flux; so too are practices.

The publishing activities undertaken in a genre world are myriad. They include managing submissions, editing, designing, printing, distributing, rights trading, and promoting. Accomplishing these tasks requires collaboration, which often happens in conventional ways, from shared publication schedules to cooperative distribution arrangements. In her interview with us, commercial fiction publisher at HarperCollins Australia Anna Valdinger cited variously the work of book designers, typesetters, translators, rights managers, and agents but confirmed these roles are not siloed. In her account, she described a particular instance when personnel stepped outside their roles to join in the promotion of Daniel O'Malley's fantasy novel *The Rook:* "You could see people, all in different departments around the office, started reading it and getting excited." It was the collective activity of these people that kicked off the publisher's marketing campaign for the book:

> One of the things we did end up doing to support it was a kind of guerrilla marketing thing that was quite fun. We printed off a bunch of "Dear You" letters [a plot point from the book] and put them all

in all-black envelopes with "Dear You" written on the front, I think. Then we just, the squad of staff members just went and dropped them around the place in Sydney, all over the place, people were tucking them into freezers in supermarkets and leaving them on pub tables and leaving them on trains and stuff. It had the logo of *The Rook*. . . . People really felt passionate, and they're all coming to my desk to pick up their clutch of "Dear You" letters and then scurrying out to drop them off in the world. Because people felt really attached to the book, and still do.[11]

This quotation reveals people from many different departments in a publishing office cooperating to get word of the book out "in the world," speaking to both the conventional activities of genre worlds and the moments when the divisions between these roles are put aside in response to new circumstances.

Publishing industry conventions are accepted as a means to minimize risk and more reliably make money. To take an industry-wide example, it is conventional to make international rights deals at the Frankfurt Book Fair, where much of the industry gathers in person for a specific period, enhancing the efficiency of communications while also fueling the word-of-mouth buzz of certain properties. Literary agent Jenny Darling told us that rights sales at fairs were particularly suitable for new properties: "If you had a new author, like [debut author Jane Harper's best-selling crime novel] *The Dry*, you'd really want to play that up and maybe do that at the fairs."[12]

Genre publishing conventions also include choices about material formats. The size of Tolkien's epic fantasy *The Lord of the Rings* required his publisher to break it into three separate volumes to contain costs (a common practice in publishing before the twenty-first century), yet in a different technological age the trilogy form remains a staple publishing convention in the fantasy genre. Genre fiction texts are made discoverable and appealing by conventions that dictate physical book aspects. Paper size and quality, cover design and font choice, and format and binding are highly relevant to genre fiction, marketing texts to readers. These material aspects may differ across different markets. Australia is very attached to the trade paperback C-format for its commercial fiction, as both literary agent Jenny Darling and publisher Anna Valdinger pointed out, though it has not always been the case.[13] Romance blogger Kat Mayo attributes the attachment to the C-format in Australia to the demands of the large discount chain stores such as Big W and K-Mart. Cover design is often highly conventional, both in general terms (the bold colors and typography of thrillers, the cinch or topless torso of a romance cover) and in specific ones (look-alike covers that mimic a best-selling genre work, such as *Fifty Shades of Grey*).

Decisions about materiality tend to be risk averse, which can result in unintended consequences. An extended example illustrates this. One of the authors we interviewed for this book was Sulari Gentill, an Australian crime writer of Sri Lankan background. Gentill is the author of numerous crime novels, including a series set in regional Australia during the 1930s featuring the charismatic Rowland Sinclair. The first book in this series, and Gentill's first published novel, is *A Few Right Thinking Men*. Two conventions affected Gentill's entry into the crime genre world: an expectation about the length of author names and an expectation about the perceived ethnicity of authors of historical Australian crime. "Gentill" is a pseudonym; the author's real name is Sulari Goonetilleke. As Gentill relates, the decision to publish under a pseudonym was related to the material conventions of the size of a book spine and the font size of text on the spine. She says, "It's about spine space. I either had to shorten my name or shorten the title, and for me the title was more important than my name, and so I just took a few letters out of 'Goonetilleke' and I ended up with 'Gentill.'" It was important for Gentill that the name was still connected to her surname—"It did feel very related to my name"—and she also emphasized that she didn't feel pressured by her publisher. Gentill acknowledged that the shortened version of her name does not as clearly flag as nonwhite to readers: "It's kind of an awkward thing to talk about, but I'm also very aware that I am writing Australian white history and I'm not white. And I did not want to make that particularly obvious. It's not that I wanted to hide who I was, but I didn't want to hit people in the face with it at the time when I was trying to establish a readership because at the time any, any reason for people not to pick up your book is a problem." Here, Gentill links her Sri Lankan surname to a potential loss of market share. Gentill shows a pragmatic understanding of the book market and reader expectations. She expands on how her surname may be linked to genre expectations, too: "I was also aware of the prejudice working in the other way in that when people see a name like Goonetilleke, they assume it's going to be an immigrant or a refugee story. And I wanted people to go to my books. I didn't want them to be looking for an immigrant refugee story and suddenly have [her detective character]

Rowland Sinclair and be disappointed. So, part of a writer's name, I suppose, is to point people . . ."[14] This was a practical decision for Gentill, one that highlights the impact of industry conventions and reader expectations on authors of color.

Another material aspect of genre publishing is timing of publication. Publishers schedule books to have the biggest impact in the market, basing their decisions on a range of factors. As Penguin Random House publisher Beverley Cousins told us:

> I mean, it is very strategic. If you take an author on, you're thinking, what's the best month for them? Are there any promotions? Is this going to be a Mother's Day, so we'll publish in March, April, May, maybe? Is this Father's Day? Okay, so it's going to be that. And [discount department store] Big W has Big Book Bonanza promotions twice a year. Will we publish it for that? Or it's a debut writer. There's no way we want to publish them in the last six months of the year. They've got to be in the first six months of the year. January's notoriously quiet. Maybe we'll publish the debut in January because not many people are publishing then, so they'll get more—there's more chance of getting space in stores and things like that. So it is very strategic on who the market is and when we can sell the most copies, obviously, and not clashing with other books that we've got on the list.[15]

The number of timing considerations in this interview is remarkable and firmly linked to conventions of the industry. Debut authors are vulnerable and get lost in the last half of the year; the post-Christmas retail slump makes January a bad month to publish. Certain genres may be better suited to seasonal occasions (romance and women's fiction for Mother's Day, crime and thrillers for Father's Day), and the discount department stores have a striking influence on publisher schedules through their in-store promotions. Again, genre is implicated here, as retail promotions like the Big Book Bonanza favor popular titles rather than experimental or avant-garde literary texts (which discount department stores rarely stock). Considering the logic of publication schedules brings home very clearly the interconnectedness and mutual influence of players in a genre world.

The strength of genre as an organizing principle within the publishing industry has consequences for every practice related to publishing. In our

interview with him, U.K. agent Mark Lucas suggested that genre categories create "channels down which writers and their reputations can travel
and gather momentum." The metaphor he used was a "six-lane highway
or a series of trunk roads" that may reduce options to explore but help
you "get from A to B very effectively."[16] Lucas outlined a vision of genre
fiction as a route of convention-driven activities—encompassing editorial,
cover design, marketing methods, prize submissions, and bookstore place-
ments—that reduce options but smooth progress.

Conventions may produce stability and reliability, but they are not static.[17]
Sometimes, genre-world conventions are broken in ways that innovate. For
example, U.S. author James Patterson's Book Shots series was designed to
publish shorter than usual crime fiction titles, for sale in airports (now also
as e-books and audiobooks). Published by Penguin, this series is described
on its website with the tagline "Stories at the speed of life"; they are "short,
high impact stories by James Patterson and other writers" that "can be read
in one sitting" and provide "a shot of pure and satisfying entertainment."[18]
This series breaks with some conventions while enacting others, negotiating
a path through the expected and the unexpected. The publishing industry
values both points of difference and points of conformity. In this case, the
risk of breaking with conventions to do with format and price is mitigated
by the highly recognizable author name on the covers and the bookseller
location, which is associated with safe sales. For a debut author seeking to
bend or break genre expectations, the conventionalized activity of acquisition is perhaps more resistant to change, though change is still possible.
Anna Valdinger told of acquiring *The Rook*:

> I took it to acquisitions, and I was like, "This is, I don't even know
> what box we would put it in, but it's fantastic." And people just loved
> it. But it wasn't a straightforward buy because how do you pitch it?
> It doesn't slot very neatly into a genre. It's clearly a genre book, but
> what genre? Because it crosses over so, you can't easily say this is just
> another George R. R. Martin–esque. You start, and you can see in
> the reviews for *The Rook:* it's like the *X-Men* meets *Harry Potter,* meets
> this, meets that, meets Douglas Adams, meets Ben Aaronovitch,
> meets . . . And the way that the publishing proposals work: anything
> I take to acquisitions, you do your spiel and what is the book about
> and all of this, and then you have to bring your comparison numbers.

And I was trying to find, but what are the obvious and immediate comparisons for this? Ben Aaronovitch, I think, is a good one. And you can say Jasper Fforde and you can say Douglas Adams and stuff, but, and then just find the appropriate level that you would pitch it at, so what money you could offer depending on what we really think we can sell. And because it's a bit out of the box, we ended up making a fairly modest offer.[19]

Because the novel was not clearly salable as high fantasy, the subgenre most associated with fantasy ("George R. R. Martin–esque"), it presented a challenge to the conventionalized channels of marketing and distribution. The enthusiasm for the project carried the book through acquisition, but with only "a fairly modest" advance, although it went on to be highly successful.

Publishing industry conventions can seem arbitrary, but this does not mean they are easy to change. As Becker notes, for example, the customary allocation of tasks within a network can be considered "quasi-sacred"; attempts to change conventions are a form of "work politics." Such politics, we note, are a form of struggle and refute the simplified understanding of Becker as preoccupied with cooperation (in opposition to Bourdieu, who is similarly simplistically thought of as preoccupied with conflict).[20] In genre worlds, an example of such conflict can be found in the conventions that divide the profits from the recommended retail price (RRP) on a book between author, publisher, and bookseller and the tensions that result when people attempt to change this: for example, when booksellers seek deeper than usual discounts from publishers, when agents seek higher royalty rates for e-books, or when publishers try to pay authors a royalty based on net receipts instead of RRP. *New York Times* best-selling romance author Stephanie Laurens explained her transition to hybrid authorship to us in terms of what she saw as the major publishers' unfair treatment following the advent of e-books in the early twenty-first century:

All the major publishers came to all the authors and said we need you to sign these forms, and, you know, this is, it will be 25 percent net on e-books, whereas our actual contract said 50 percent. But they said we can't do it at 50, we need the 25, until the market gets going, and then you know, so it's only for a few years, until we get the markets. Well, so a lot of us accepted that. We thought, I mean our agents thought, they were being correct and that was all fine. So we signed those amendments. And subsequently, the publishers have never, have never, changed, and they've refused to go back and redo those, you know, change the amendments back again, which was naive on the part of a lot of people to accept that. But up to that point there wasn't anything odd about it, until e-books took off and they refused to revert those contracts. And they also continued to keep, to hang on to, that 25 percent net, which is, once the whole thing took off, which is just inexcusable. But what they didn't see was the self-publishing coming.[21]

In this quotation, we can see the major publishers' desire to control risk by maximizing their revenue from the new format of e-books and their paradoxical loss of control due to unforeseen consequences (self-publishing). Laurens's account is, of course, partial: she describes the publishers' behavior as "inexcusable," where we might imagine a publisher would be able to justify the decision to reduce author royalties by citing the value of the publishers' editorial input and handling of digital production processes and the small profit margins on e-books that mean less funds available to support that work.

There are clearly many types of publishing activities, and while the activities may seem to belong to the industry as though it is a monolith, they are carried out by people, all of whom have their own skills and biases and all of whom are trying to work in cooperation to bring genre books into the world. In a postdigital paradigm, the various value propositions of publishing are being recalibrated. Below we look closely at two of the offerings that have traditionally been viewed as handled best by established publishing conventions: editing and distribution.

Editing: The Guidelines and Expectations of Genre

The term "editing" can be used in a narrow or broad sense. In its broad sense, Becker uses it as a master term for the work of support personnel "who make (or help the artist to make) the choices which give the work its final shape." But he also uses it in the narrow sense of the editor in a publishing house as a "nonartist participant" who edits a text.[22] Genre worlds have established systems and mechanisms to enable and expedite editing in its narrowest and broadest senses. Editorial moments occur in the context of established patterns of making, justifying, and implementing decisions about the kind of book in development. Industry personnel have clear expectations of genre texts, including their structure, characterization, and language, and often have strong views about the willingness of readers to engage with books that challenge these expectations.

Many of our interviewees discussed the direct influence on their works of editors in the narrow professional sense. For example, Harlequin romance author Carol Marinelli told us, "I've never chosen my titles; the editors do that."[23] The book buyer for major Australian discount department store Big W has exerted direct influence on the design of romance fiction covers, as reported by publishers and authors. The broader sense of editing—as in the exercise of indirect influence to make or direct choices—was also evident in our interviews. In genre worlds, one of the prime responsibilities of agents and editors who recognize a new manuscript's potential in a specific genre or subgenre is to reshape it to fit comfortably within that category. Michael Robotham tells us:

> I didn't realize I was becoming a crime writer, because I saw that first novel very much in that sort of Hitchcockian man-in-the-wrong-place-at-the-wrong-time sort of mystery, but I didn't think I was becoming a crime writer. . . . When they turned around and said, "What are you going to write next?" and I had this idea, completely left-field idea, and I was told, "You can't do that," and I said, "Why?" and they said, "Well, you've got to write something similar to what you've written," and I said, "Where does it say that?" "In your contract."[24]

It was not until Robotham proposed something that was not crime that he realized his position in the genre world. In many cases, engaging with industry personnel marks the moment when an author first enters a genre world, a kind of professionalizing moment when they slot (willingly or otherwise) inside the genre more tidily and must take on a host of behaviors and practices appropriate to the production of that genre's texts.

As an extended example of how editing shapes a genre text, consider the processes of Harlequin, a publisher of romance fiction that now owns its former rival, Mills & Boon, and is in turn owned by multinational company HarperCollins. The production of category romance—short titles in a defined series—is a distinctive feature of the romance genre world. Harlequin provides a strong example of scaffolded and streamlined industry decision making in relation to its category romances, in which publisher-set specifications influence the text.

The reputation of Harlequin is largely anchored in the promise that its publications will comply with strict textual conventions, not least of all the "happily ever after" ending. The influence of the publisher on texts is visible in the website that sets out expectations for submitted texts. While the Harlequin submission-manager site avoids the word "formula," it does link certain textual "elements" to imprints and editorial lines (these correspond to a range of subgenres, such as medical romance, and heat levels, such as sweet or sexy romances). For example, the Harlequin Desire imprint seeks stories of fifty thousand words with the elements of an "independent heroine," an "alpha hero" who can still be "vulnerable," the fantasy of wealth, and secondary characters in the background. The Harlequin Heartwarming imprint seeks stories of seventy thousand words that are "wholesome" and based in a strong community, with no premarital sex represented (though "secret babies" are welcome).[25]

Further editorial moments emerge in interactions between romance publishers and authors. From the perspectives of our interviewees, the editing strictures of category romance are not a cynical or solely commercial strategy to sell books (although higher sales is always a goal) but a means to achieve a level of emotional intensity that attracts and satisfies readers in a format that they recognize and trust. At the level of the individual text, the highly conventionalized and strictly controlled editing regime of category romance provides a series of checks and balances to guarantee that each book will be written, packaged, sold, and experienced in expected, satisfying ways.

Carol Marinelli describes accessing the Harlequin guidelines at the beginning of her romance writing career, in her early twenties. During this period, before the ubiquity of the Internet, Harlequin was known to have a cassette tape with a recording of its editorial guidelines. Marinelli told us that she "sent off . . . to get a tape . . . the guidelines tape. . . . It was wonderful; I probably have it in my garage somewhere."[26] Her first novel, *The Outback Nurse,* a medical romance, was published in 2001, and, at the time of writing, she was working on her 105th book for Harlequin.

The publisher's famous guidelines are a form of genre training as well as early or preemptive editorial intervention. A consequence of these tradi-tions—and the various methods by which the publisher communicates, sus-tains, and reviews them—is that they streamline and expedite the standard processes of editing a finished manuscript to bring it to print and distribu-tion. Former Harlequin editor Haylee Nash commented on the publisher's "rigorous efficiency," which includes its editing process. This sense that cat-egory romance novels are edited quickly was corroborated by Sue Brock-hoff, who acknowledged the publisher's reputation for speed and efficiency when she talked about Harlequin's efforts to show bookshops that their new imprint, HQ, will be distinguished by "quality editing."[27]

Sometimes working outside editorial conventions highlights the fact that they exist so strongly. Harlequin's strict interventions are thrown into relief by the lighter editorial touch applied to noncategory romance fic-tion published by other imprints or publishers. Bec Sampson, reflecting on her writing buddy Rachael Johns's breakout book, *Jilted,* a romance in which a successful soap-opera star returns to her hometown in Western Australia, linked its success to Johns's desire to escape Mills & Boon con-straints: "Rachael wanted to write in Rachael's voice. The guidelines and the lines make it very difficult with Mills & Boon to . . . write naturally." Johns echoed this reading of her relationship with the two kinds of genre fiction writing: "I've got freedom with my Australian books, you know, and I don't necessarily follow the rules all the time. I think, you know, that's okay, but with sort of the category romance, you have more rules to fol-low."[28] Johns emphasizes here the editorial "rules" that shape the content of category romance. Harlequin is a striking example of the constraints that can characterize a publisher's editorial process and of how romance writers work within these constraints to shape their stories and voices.

Harlequin's model of consistency applies not only to editorial shaping of texts but also to the standardized paratexts of the novels; as Lisa Fletcher et al. write, "The promise of a Mills & Boon novel . . . , with its template cover and prioritisation of publisher and line over author and title, is typi-cality."[29] Standardization also, famously, extends to the distribution of Har-lequin titles. For many decades, Harlequin provided mail-order subscrip-tion services for readers of romance, where readers subscribed to specific lines, such as medical romance or historical romance. This regularization of the distribution of romances, with lines released in monthly catalogs, enabled predictable print runs and minimized waste and returns.[30] These days, Harlequin's digital distribution systems are just as savvy, with links to the next title in a series embedded within e-books, online promotion of imprints, and targeted marketing. Distribution, in fact, is another key site of conventional industry practice in genre fiction publishing that has traditionally been seen as best handled by publishers, for their corporate heft and established pathways.

Distribution: Established and Emerging Pathways to Readers

A written genre work does not have an in-built mechanism to market. Genre worlds, like Becker's art worlds, "provide distribution systems which integrate artists into their society's economy, bringing art works to publics which appreciate them and will pay enough so that the work can proceed." Distribution materially affects the creation of the work; as Becker puts it, "Art works always bear the marks of the system which distributes them."[31] Distribution processes shape genre worlds and mark their texts. This includes the way that distribution processes enable and block opportunities for texts to travel; a focus on distribution highlights the territories of the global publishing industry.

The publishing industry is historically shaped so that it reflects and reinforces particular power dynamics, including those of colonialism and late capitalism. Contemporary publishing distribution systems for genre worlds are transnational, with a center in the United States. Multinational publishers have local offices that operate as subsidiaries. Distribution has long been a particular challenge for small presses, who may not have the resources to move their books to diverse and geographically disparate locations, and for particular markets, such as Canada and Australia, where a medium-size industry must grapple with large geographical areas and poor connective infrastructure. Small presses may face particular obstacles to transnational distribution, if they cannot afford to conduct rights trading at venues such as the Frankfurt Book Fair or lack access to book retailers overseas. On the other hand, if a writer publishes with an international small press, they may not have their work available for sale in their home country. Fantasy author Angela Slatter, who has published with both Australian small presses (Ticonderoga, Twelfth Planet Press) and international small presses (Tartarus, PS Publishing), told us:

If your publisher is overseas, then you can't guarantee when you're going to get stocked; you can't guarantee they'll be willing to send a heap of stock. You have to deal with the money yourself, and I'm not a merchant. You know, I have no intention of setting up my shingle as a book merchant. So . . . unless there's a convention at which you can have a launch, you don't have a guarantee of the kind of captive audience, which is a really important consideration—you know, "Who is going to buy your book? . . . [W]here are they going to be?"[32]

The questions of who and where are conflated here, because even in a digital global publishing environment, geography matters. Power relations affect the ease of travel between periphery and center, and the industry is convergent, not wholly digitized.

A focus on distribution reveals much about different kinds of publishing organizations and how they operate. Multinational publishers would, in Becker's terminology, be called "culture industries." They "deal with very large audiences that are almost totally unknown to them."[33] Small or boutique presses operate in the style of "dealers" in the art worlds Becker describes. Consider as an example anthologies of fantasy fiction published by small genre-dedicated presses, a staple publication in the genre world of fantasy. These volumes are often distributed among fan communities and sympathetic independent bookstores, as well as online. FableCroft Press's *Cranky Ladies of History* anthology crowdsourced funding online through Pozible to pay its writers and publication costs and then leveraged that same community for sales and word-of-mouth recommendation. FableCroft defines itself as a "boutique" publisher, and *Cranky Ladies* supports this definition, through, for example, making available limited-edition hardcovers for audiences who collect unique books.[34] Small-press distribution channels highlight the social core of genre worlds, which can be masked by the commercial imperatives that drive larger publishers. The size of publishers leaves a strong mark on genre texts.

A big shift in the twenty-first century has been the digital disruption of distribution. Digitization has enabled print-on-demand fulfillment centers to augment traditional distribution, reducing the unit cost of small print runs, and e-book platforms to provide readers instant access to some titles. Digital publishers and self-publishing platforms and e-readers are creating new route-to-market conventions for genre fiction texts, including new forms of marketing, new contractual arrangements, and cultures of licensing rather than owning texts. For self-publishers, a growing and increasingly influential group within genre worlds, distribution entails new systems and raises new challenges that require agile business approaches. Self-publishing is a more laborious and therefore, arguably, less prized career option than traditional publishing, yet the situation may be changing, as new intermediaries such as Ingram and Amazon make distribution easier and more regularized.

If there is revolutionary change happening in genre worlds, it is happening at least partly through the rapid developments in digital technology, at which the examples above hint. We turn, now, to an in-depth examination of self-publishing to see some of the dynamics of change in the publishing systems of genre worlds. What happens when the who, what, and how of publishing are changed or cut out all together?

Self-Publishing: Shifting Roles and the Expansion of Genre Worlds

A feature of the publishing industry since around 2010 has been high-profile self-publishing successes, with sales levels that rival those of best-selling authors with large commercial presses. U.K. author Mark Dawson's crime series, self-published on Amazon, has accrued more than 2 million downloads since 2013, while U.S. romance author Anna Todd's 2014 novel, *After*, originally fan fiction based on the band One Direction, drew more than 1.5 billion reads on Wattpad, an Internet reading and writing community, before eventually being acquired by Simon & Schuster and then adapted for film.[35] Hugh Howey started his climb up the best-seller list on the lowest rung, without the boost provided by the support of a trade publisher and without the customer base of an established author.[36] The news discourse about the large commercial successes of some self-published writers—as one article introduces Dawson, "the literary sensation you've never heard of"—suggests that the long-established vertical logics of book cultures and markets are under strain in what journalist Alexandra Alter terms "the new digital publishing landscape."[37] But self-publishing is more than an addition to the pipeline of traditional publishing. A great deal of self-publishing consists of non-best-selling works that appeal to micro-niche audiences and cater to specific tastes (elfpunk fantasy, prison-planet romance, LGBT [lesbian, gay, bisexual, and transgender] military romance, futuristic crime noir). Self-publishing sometimes occurs in close interaction with traditional publishing and sometimes proceeds entirely within its own infrastructure.

Digital self-publishing is a relatively advanced practice in the world of genre fiction, where it is linked with agile, hybrid new business models; this is a twenty-first-century publishing practice in which genre fiction is leading the way. Romance fiction, for example, has proliferated into niche subgenres almost entirely enabled by digital self-publishing, while fantasy fiction's traditional fan creativity has spurred the growth of user-writer sites such as Wattpad and Inkitt. As noted above in relation to personnel, self-publishing fragments and confuses roles across the literary field and thus offers a serious challenge to how scholars typically theorize the power relations of literary culture. This challenge suggests a Bourdieusian view of self-publishing as a field-changing event, but it also complements an "art worlds" approach. While artists may aim to work with existing systems, the corollary of this, we argue, is that artists are attuned to changes in this system—the onslaught of e-books or the meteoric rise of audiobooks, for example. Change is sometimes resisted due to the weight of tradition, but members of genre worlds are also entrepreneurs who seize new opportunities and take risks. At the moment that constraints are released, genre writers rush in. This is exactly what has happened with self-publishing, made easy and financially appealing by Amazon. Between the e-book platform Kindle Direct Publishing, launched in 2007, and Amazon's print-on-demand service, Create Space, acquired in the same year, hundreds of thousands of texts have been self-published.

Amazon does not release data about its Kindle Direct Publishing. However, we have prepared some data on Australian self-publishing activity, in conjunction with AustLit, the Australian literary database maintained by a consortium of researchers. Our research with AustLit shows the number of self-published books in crime, fantasy, and romance, across three time slices. We defined self-published as published by a person or an organization that we manually checked and found to have published fewer than ten books by fewer than three authors.

This graph shows a tremendous rate of growth in self-published Australian popular fiction since 2000. Romance, with its highly active readership, has grown the fastest; romance authors and readers are not only digitally savvy and participatory but also often entrepreneurial, alive to the financial

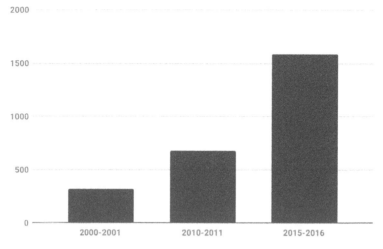

Figure 2. Number of Australian crime, fantasy, and romance titles self-published, as recorded in the AustLit database.

benefits of self-publishing. Fantasy authors have also embraced self-publishing enthusiastically, while crime remains more closely locked to the more sedate growth patterns of mainstream publishing, with only moderate (but still striking) growth in self-publishing.

Numbers tell part of the story, but our data is also qualitative and tries to unpack what self-publishing is and means. Self-publishing is not a monolith, and there is no single answer to the question of why an author might self-publish a book. The ready stereotype, perhaps, is that debut authors do it in order to bypass publishers, the traditional gatekeepers, and certainly this happens. However, our research shows that for romance and fantasy writers particularly, self-publishing is often one strategy in a complex, hybrid career, which includes both traditionally published and self-published works. Some of our case studies illustrate this.

Stephanie Laurens is one of the world's most successful romance novelists. She is a resident of regional Victoria, Australia, whose sales are mostly in the United States, and at the time of writing she is the author of sixty-nine novels, thirty-eight of which have been *New York Times* best sellers. Her career began with writing Mills & Boon/Harlequin Regencies, and she then moved to HarperCollins. In 2012 Laurens gave a keynote address to the Romance Writers of America convention. She used the opportunity to reflect on industry change and soon afterward began reconfiguring her own publishing arrangements. In 2014, with her agent, she negotiated a new deal with Harlequin, so that they publish her print novels while she self-publishes the e-book versions. She also self-publishes novellas that are prequels to, or that sit in between, the novels in her traditionally published series. Laurens produces her e-books through her own company, Savdek Management, Ltd., and distributes them through Kindle Direct Publishing as well as Kobo and other outlets. Her agent tried to negotiate this split deal with HarperCollins, but they declined; Harlequin (since 2015, in a twist, owned by HarperCollins) was prepared to give it a go.

Laurens's story is one of power—of a prolific, already established author with significant brand recognition and loyal fans, an author who can afford to take risks, who realizes that self-publishing potentially offers her a better deal and has been able to pursue that while still retaining ties to a traditional publisher. Her career complicates any view of self-publishing as second best. Laurens's self-publishing is an experiment for her and for Harlequin, a significant challenge to established economic models in the industry, with ramifications for how we understand the role of the publisher and indeed the agent and author. In line with this reading, and following Laurens's experiment, several of the other romance authors we interviewed were on the threshold of moving to hybrid careers and were experimenting with self-publishing some of their works.

Romance author Kylie Scott, for example, has published her "rock-star romances"—such as *Lick,* which begins with heroine Evelyn waking up in a Las Vegas hotel room unexpectedly married to tattooed famous guitarist David—with multinational company Macmillan. When we interviewed Scott, she was just about to self-publish her first young adult (YA) romance, *Trust,* saying that her primary reason for doing so was that "I wanted to get it out quickly . . . so that I could have two books out this year."[38] Self-publishing can be much faster and more nimble than traditional publishing, as well as allowing more experimentation with genres and subgenres.

The same tension between the relative speeds of publishing modes can also arise in relation to start-up small presses, which sometimes blur the lines between traditional and self-publishing in the new publishing economy. This was evident in our interview with Sulari Gentill. For her debut novel, *A Few Right Thinking Men,* Gentill had interest from three publishers: Pan Macmillan, Penguin, and brand-new-at-the-time small press Pantera.

Gentill chose to publish with Pantera, and one of her reasons, in addition to their evident passion for her novel, was the speed they offered. She said, "Once you've been in publishing for a while, you sort of learn to accept the eighteen-month time lines, but at the time, it seemed to me, 'Oh, I've got a book finished. I want it out next week.'" Gentill has gone on to become thoroughly networked in the Australian crime-writing community and now brings considerable industry knowledge to bear on her publishing choices. Scott, too, recognizes the value of her traditional publishing experience, saying, "I'm grateful that I started the way I did and went the way I did because I know my patience levels, and I would have just gone, with my first book, 'I'm publishing it. This is genius.' And it wasn't. I needed to do the work."[39] Traditional publishing, for Scott, operated as a kind of training ground that then enabled self-publishing, a complement to the arguments we develop in chapter 4 about how people learn genre competence.

Paranormal romance author Keri Arthur, another well-established figure, was also about to release her "first fully self-published book" when we interviewed her.[40] Self-publishing is not only a financially attractive route for Arthur's primary output, giving her a greater percentage of royalties, but also opens up different options for her to experiment creatively. She noted that a recent novel she had written in a different genre for her—high fantasy—was receiving little interest from publishers and suggested she might self-publish that one, too. Her plan was not to transition fully to being a self-published author but to become a "hybrid" author, exploiting different routes to market and the different economic arrangements they offer.

However, self-publishing is not a preferred route for everyone. Crime author Iain Ryan self-published three novels before signing with Bonnier imprint Echo, who published his crime novel *The Student* in 2017, touting it as a "high-paced, hardboiled regional noir." Ryan was pleased to have switched to a traditional publisher. When we asked him what the editing process was like with Echo, he replied, "It was glorious. It was like having a patron come along and give you $10,000–$15,000 worth of commercializing, and after . . . two, three years of self-publishing, I knew the commercial value of it."[41] This quotation indicates clearly that editing is one of the enduring value propositions of traditional publishing.

U.S. author Barbara Dunlop told us about a book that "I had originally self-published, but I really didn't enjoy self-publishing, so I just pushed that over to Tule, and they've been working with that one as well."[42] She has gone on to publish several other books with Tule, an author co-op model of a publisher run by Jane Porter, whom Dunlop met and became friends with at a Romance Writers of America convention. Tule Publishing is a small, largely digital publisher with a limited print-on-demand service that has exploited the possibilities of a digitized book business but is firmly anchored in the genre's textual heartland. Rather than publishing in new subgenres, Tule remains energized by the genre tropes that dedicated readers still care about (central to genre competency and its very real commercial imperatives), and the author profiles on its website speak to their strong attachment to particular localities and regions. Tule benefits from networks among writers developed at the Romance Writers of America conventions and the experiences of many of its authors with publishers such as Harlequin, profiting from the professional sociality enabled by multinational romance publishing. While it is an author-led model, it is highly connected to the professionalized world of genre fiction publishing.

A similarly complicated story of traditional and self-publishing is that of Mitchell Hogan, a Sydney-based author of fantasy and science fiction. In 2013 his debut novel, *A Crucible of Souls,* became the first self-published work to win an Aurealis Award for Best Australian Fantasy Novel. In an interview with us, Hogan explained his reasons for self-publishing. After writing the manuscript, he revised it with mentoring through the New South Wales Writers Centre; paid for a structural edit and assessment from an agent and editor in the United Kingdom, John Gerald; and pitched it to agents. While waiting for feedback, he became interested in digital publishing. Then, as he told us, "when I got the edit back from John Gerald, he said, 'Look, it's a good book, but publishers aren't looking for good; they're looking for special. So whether or not you'll be able to get it published . . . is another story.' So then I decided to self-publish it. . . . And I hired another editor to do a copyedit and a proofread, and then I self-published it in July 2013." *A Crucible of Souls* did extremely well as a self-published book, selling more than seven thousand copies in two months and then going on to win the Aurealis Award. What is particularly interesting in terms of the development of the field is what happened next. Hogan signed a deal for the series with HarperCollins. This meant pulling both *A Crucible of Souls* and its sequel, which he had already written and self-published, from Kindle Direct Publishing, so that they could be rereleased under the HarperCollins imprint. So far, so expected; the self-published author picked up by a major multinational publisher is a story that has become familiar. But there is a twist. Hogan's deal was for that series only, and when it came time for him to release his second series of novels, he went back to self-publishing. His reasoning hinged on audio rights, noting a "surge in audiobooks" sales since the mid-2010s. He told us, "I was lucky enough to sign with Audible first for my first series. And they've sold really, really well. They've sold over seventy-two thousand audiobooks." Hogan prizes his "great relationship with Audible." When it came time to publish Hogan's second series, Harper Voyager "said they're going to insist on audio rights, and if audio isn't part of any deal, don't bother submitting to them. And that's now, I guess from what I've heard, a blanket policy on all of the big publishers and some of the major smaller publishers, like Kensington, as well." Hogan reflected on his direct relationship with Audible, the "great narrator" they already had, and their capacity to promote his audiobook sales—for example, through two-for-one sales—and so really the question was "How valuable were my audio rights to me? Are they worth signing to a, signing them over to a big publisher? . . . The reality was I thought, 'Well, I'm going to self-publish this series then.'"[43]

Audible is an Amazon company—a disruptive operator, opening up new pathways to publication. Hogan's decision to self-publish was made because HarperCollins, a Big Few multinational trade publisher, insisted on licensing all rights, including audio rights. The implication of this story is that some multinational publishers are resisting the fragmentation of the industry; publishers have usually sought as many rights as possible, but whether they successfully negotiate this point depends on power relations in the market. Audible's growing power enables it to make financially lucrative offers to authors for their audio rights. These offers are especially appealing to authors with the confidence and connections to self-publish their print and e-books. For now, fragmentation creates opportunities for small, nimble players, including genre fiction authors, but there is also a pattern here, a drift toward more power for Amazon, the new dominant institution of contemporary fiction. Amazon owns more and more of the fragments: not just Audible but also data services, the Kindle Direct Publishing platform, online retail, and the reader-review platform Goodreads. Amazon has harnessed and fostered self-publishing activity so that self-publishing has become a key driver within this fragmented yet monopolistic ecosystem and one of the most significant forces reshaping the publishing industry—and genre worlds.

Algorithms: The New Digital Processes of Contemporary Genre Worlds

Amazon's power is linked to another development in the publishing economy: the increasing role of digital algorithms. Algorithms—processes designed to solve problems—can be understood in a broad sense as what Tarleton Gillespie terms "sociotechnical assemblages" that include both computational steps and human decision making.[44] Algorithms are omnipresent in digital publishing as processes that make books visible and link them with potential readers. Algorithms, especially as activated across digital sites, are forms of marketing (both formally and informally activated) that disrupt conventional practices in the publishing industry. The algorithms of the new publishing economy fundamentally affect the visibility of books in an age of abundant content—their capacity to be discovered and read. Algorithms are designed by people, but the personnel profile here is significantly different from that of traditional publishing, and the norms surrounding their use are still emerging. As such, digital algorithms drive a change of conventions, influencing in some unexpected ways the cooperative activity of people in genre worlds.

The world of publishing is often seen as unpredictable. No one knows what the next megaseller will be or why some books succeed and others fail. Algorithms have long been part of the publishing industry's attempts to regularize practices and thus minimize risk, especially when algorithms are understood at the level of processes that sort information according to categories. Genre, itself, aligns with algorithmic processes. Genre fiction has some qualities that mitigate against the unpredictability of book publishing, including an overarching commitment to familiarity alongside newness. All genre fiction offers familiar tropes that reduce uncertainty for publishers and readers alike. Furthermore, much genre fiction—especially crime—is invested in seriality, allowing for reader attachments as well as relatively predictable sales patterns across several books. Genre fiction is amenable to algorithms because, at the most fundamental level, genre fiction is also organized by categories: genres, subgenres, and microgenres that align with taste preferences, regularizing the process of book production and consumption. In the digital realm, genres, subgenres, and microgenres can be identified and sorted so that they find their readers.

There are several different algorithms at work on Amazon, and these are kept secret so that it is unclear to what extent publishers can influence their results. Publishers have been asked by Amazon for "promotional fees" that directly affect the visibility of their titles; in addition, publishers must continually optimize their marketing activities in order to work strategically with algorithms that they may not fully understand or that may suddenly change without notice.[45] Romance publishers explain their involvement most clearly. Kate Cuthbert, then managing editor of Harlequin's Australian digital imprint, Escape, told us that the bulk of her marketing budget went to point-of-sale advertising on book retail websites. She said, "We do next-to-no traditional advertising, and the vast majority of our advertising budget goes to point of sale, so all of the promotions—for example, through Apple or Amazon—the publisher has to pay for those promotions; they don't just get picked up, necessarily. So, we put a lot of our marketing budget into making sure that when somebody's going to that website, and they are actively looking for books to buy, that they're going to see our books." These are ways in which the publisher's marketing spend can interact with a site's algorithms: as Cuthbert told us, the site is "algorithm based, but the more money that a publisher puts into sales, the higher your algorithm." Cuthbert's second-largest marketing spend was targeted at increasing online reader reviews. As she put it:

> I said just earlier that we put most of our money into point-of-sale marketing, which is true. The big chunk of the leftover goes into trying to get readers to leave reviews on Goodreads and [at] the point of sale. We spend a lot of time, and a lot of money, doing that, because it's about the only thing that we've ever found that actually works. Reviews left on Amazon, reviews left on Apple and Kobo, the star ratings—not only do they play into the algorithms of whether or not that book is going to get visible; they're also the only thing that leads directly to sales. Everything else is more about brand building and general awareness.[46]

Goodreads reviews, and reader reviews across other sites, are crucial to the new commerce of publishing. This is perhaps why they are treated with suspicion by some academics, even as the text of reviews themselves can reveal sincere engagements with reading experiences.[47] Algorithms that draw on the content of reviews may serve the needs of readers, while also creating market effects that entrench a disparity in power between technology companies such as Amazon (which also owns Goodreads) and publishers. Publishers, and certainly romance publishers, are keenly aware of algorithms and try to harness their power—without necessarily being fully privy to how they work.

Algorithms are not simple or monolithic, and their effects vary across national markets and time. One Amazon algorithm that has received a lot of attention is its recommendation algorithm, which it describes as item-to-item collaborative filtering. It uses person-based behavior to create links between products: people who bought A often also buy B; therefore, A and B are connected. This core algorithm is supplemented by a range of other recommendation algorithms, all of which become personalized if a customer logs in to Amazon. At that point, according to algorithm designers Brent Smith and Greg Linden, the whole online store changes; they use the metaphor of bookshop shelves shuffling forward and back.[48] Amazon's recommendation algorithms are sophisticated, allowing for diverse consumption patterns and effects. Compare, for example, the recommendations for a single title: Melbourne author Emma Viskic's debut crime novel, *Resurrection Bay*. On Amazon.com.au, where the Australian edition is for sale, most recommendations lead to other Australian titles, apart from those in the "Products related to this product" section, which is flagged as "sponsored." On Amazon.com, where the U.K. edition is for sale, the recommendations are titled "More items to explore" and include a great deal of romantic suspense. Earlier versions of these websites linked *Resurrection Bay*, respectively, to Australian literary fiction and to British and American crime. Genre intersects with nationality in these shifting algorithmic recommendations.

These algorithms are highly visible to ordinary consumers. In fact, part of the appeal of Amazon's recommendation tool is its apparent transparency. Consumers can see how Amazon comes up with recommendations, because the process is often in the heading (for example, "Customers who bought this also bought"), which makes the recommendations reassuringly comprehensible. Other aspects of algorithms, however, are buried deeper. As discussed above, publishers can influence algorithms through some of their marketing activities, and so can authors. Miriam Kriss, who is Keri Arthur's literary agent, has noted that when hybrid authors self-publish books, this can have a positive effect on the algorithms that recommend their traditionally published work. Kriss says, "Frankly, the activity that authors generate with their self-published or indie-published . . . it feeds the algorithms, and it does drive more readers to their older titles as well."[49] There's a symbiosis here between self-publishing and traditional publishing that shows they are not always opposed in the new publishing economy but interact.

Author Iain Ryan's experience with self-publishing means he also has a high awareness of the effort that self-published authors put in to understand and work with algorithms. Ryan describes his observations of self-publishing authors who put out three or four books a year, "pumping out these pulp novels":

> I learnt a lot about what happens in the interior of those books that sell, which is that they['ve] got to hit the tropes down the middle. Essentially. So you can have a likable protagonist, you can have a setting that doesn't need a lot of setting up—they don't want to know about what the islands of Australia are like, or what the setting or the climate is; they want to get into the thing. . . . You have to list your books with six keywords. They're used to categorize the book. . . . Over a period of about a week to a fortnight, algorithmically Amazon will come along and say, "This book's working," and they have the biggest mailing list of readers in the world, so they can literally put you into this grinder and the books just sell. If it's priced correctly and the blurb is good and everything like that. So it's all about trying to get onto those lists, the right lists, getting on there in a timely fashion, trying to generate sales that either are organic or look organic.[50]

He also notes, "A lot of [self-publishers] are ex-coders . . . , so they come from that 'Get it to market while it's barely working and then fix it when the first round of beta feedback comes.' When you're getting smashed with one-star reviews on Amazon, you actually take that as data and go back and correct there." Ryan also acknowledges the leading role played by romance fiction in this area, saying, "That's one thing you also learn when you start looking at self-publishing exclusively is that all the other genres you're dealing with what romance has discovered three or four months ago. Or a year ago. That's where the entrepreneurial feel is." As well as being an insight into how entrepreneurial skills more associated with the innovation field have made their way into the creative arts, Ryan reminds us here that both users and designers of algorithms are people. As users, they may try to game the system. As designers, they may reproduce biases and assumptions that are then difficult to challenge once up and running.

Despite his embrace of traditional publishing for his own creative work, Ryan is engaged and interested in the use of algorithms by self-publishers. In an academic article published under his own name, Ian Rogers, he writes:

> The entrepreneurialism of self-published fiction trades off this sense of the tactical. Within the scene, Amazon best-seller charts aren't as much markers of prestige as systems to be hacked. . . . Over time, the self-publishing scene has become expert at decoding Amazon's monolithic Terms of Service, ever eager to find both advantage and risk as they attempt to lever the affordances of digital publishing against their own desire for profit and expression. This sense of mischief and slippage forms a big part of what self-publishing is.[51]

Rogers paints a somewhat romanticized view of self-publishers as mischief makers operating against the establishment. His narrativization infuses the digital technologies that are transforming the publishing industry with meaning. The urge to find storytelling structures that make sense of computational processes is a feature of the current moment. Artificial intelligence is itself moving in this direction, with chatbots that mimic humans in their interactions with customers. Similarly, storytelling and humanizing are ways of coming to understand the new digital economic environment of book publishing.

Another response to digital algorithms is to emphatically reject them. In his article "Algorithmic Culture," Ted Striphas argues that Amazon is an exemplar of humans delegating the work of culture to data-intensive computational processes. He develops this argument by analyzing how computerized algorithms influence power relations, writing that "what is at stake in algorithmic culture is the gradual abandonment of culture's publicness and thus the emergence of a new breed of elite culture purporting to be its opposite."[52] Here, he is pointing to the results of reliance on algorithms, which include a concentration of power with Amazon.

While Amazon is unusually powerful, its behavior is not entirely new—and romanticizing the old publishing economy should be avoided. A piece on the blog *Lithub* criticized Amazon's brick-and-mortar store, where stock is chosen algorithmically (on the basis of sales rank), and reminisced about an older model of the independent bookshop, the kind of bookstore owned and run by a mean old walrus with ketchup stains on his shirt and strata of nicotine marbled into his whiskers, and who turns out to be very knowledgeable and cool and non-creepy once you get to know him. And even though his shop is a musty mess, books piled up like little temples and triple-layered on the shelves and hoarded into far-fetched crannies, he always knows exactly where everything is (and you could always find something surprising and secret and wonderful in there). And then you sort of got to know him a little, and he gave you a dog-eared Pynchon novel when you went away to college, and it changed your taste in prose forever.[53]

This dramatic reconstruction misses some of the complications of book-selling. Independent bookstores can sometimes be very appealing spaces, but they also filter their content; in fact, that is their value proposition. Independent booksellers are trusted filters, a kind of mediator that is particularly significant for readers engaged in middlebrow practices.[54] The filtering process of Amazon is more crowdsourced, although still mediated, and it raises the visibility of different books—including, especially, genre fiction. This may be challenging for those with investments in particular ideals about literary value, but the problem is not necessarily algorithms as such. Algorithms are a first-level sort in a world of abundance. As the personalized and nationally distinctive elements of the Amazon algorithms show, there is still room for the human, the social, and even the serendipitous in digital algorithms. The most current industry discussion of algorithms suggests they must include serendipity; otherwise, recommendations feel too stale to consumers and lose their effectiveness.[55]

Self-publishing and algorithms, especially as facilitated by Amazon, are exerting powerful effects on the publishing economy and are being used intensively and creatively by publishers and authors of genre fiction. McGurl's claim about the genrefication of the publishing industry in the Age of Amazon has merit but not in a simple way: not all literary fiction will become trilogies or have a murder on the first page. Rather, the genrefication of contemporary fiction is evident in shifting relations and practices across the industry. The people, the practices, and the conventions of genre worlds will respond to change and shape the change; they are not separate from it but materially caught up in its currents.

Conclusion

Genre fiction affects the publishing industry and the publishing industry affects genre fiction, but the industry is not a monolith. The first part of this chapter investigated the personnel and activities of the publishing industry, which are integrally involved in the conventions of genre worlds. These personnel and their activities shape the structure of genre worlds but are also responsive to genre worlds' other participants, including authors and readers. The publishing industry also reveals the unevenness of power and agency in genre worlds. Multinational publishers have long had enormous heft, and some writers clearly have more power than others.

However, as the second part of the chapter has shown, the emergence of digital publishing technologies and the dominance of Amazon in the book industry have reshaped some of these dynamics. Self-publishing confuses roles and alters the hierarchy of credibility that pervades book culture, as well as diversifying the channels by which authors make money. Proliferating, ever more precise subgenres and algorithms change the way books are discovered and circulate, as authors, publishers, and readers work out ways to interact with the computational algorithms designed by technology companies, such as Amazon. The new publishing economy, led by genre fiction, is both fragmented and magnetically pulled toward new technological centers; it is shaped by both the digital and human creativity.

Digital technology has also propelled two kinds of movements that challenge the borders of genre worlds: the borders around local or national instantiations of genre worlds are challenged by transnational pulls, and the borders around books as the center of genre worlds are challenged by pulls toward transmedia adaptation. These are considered in the next chapter.

. . .

The tarot reader flips over a card: a knight on a rearing horse, a torch aloft.
"Travel," she predicts in a gravelly voice.
    "Overseas?" you ask, hopeful.
    She glances up, her pupils dilated. "Further," she says. "Other worlds."

CHAPTER 3

Transnational and Transmedia Genre Worlds

The previous chapter offered a genre-worlds analysis of the contemporary publishing industry, describing the personnel and activities that shape the production of twenty-first-century genre fiction and looking in particular detail at the changes wrought in this dynamic area by digital technology. This chapter zeroes in on questions of mobilities (between markets, between media forms) that have become more pressing and more complicated in that publishing economy. Digital transformation has made it easier for the people and products of genre worlds to cross boundaries, but there are also persistent obstacles to flow and exchange, as well as the emergence of new hurdles. This chapter explores transnational genre worlds and transmedia genre worlds through a close examination of the roles of key personnel, such as authors, publishers, agents, and bloggers, and through scrutiny of selected conventionalized activities, especially intellectual property distribution and adaptation of genre novels for the screen. This chapter also shows that transnational and transmedia movements of genre fiction books are related, affecting one another in a global and converged media landscape.

When we consider the global in relation to genre fiction, it reminds us of potential complications in using the metaphor of "world," as it is a word that operates in a number of contexts and at a number of conceptual levels, especially with regards to popular fiction. A "storyworld," for example, is a fictional enclosure of setting, lore, and logic in which stories (both official and participatory) take place, often across platforms (transmedia). At the same time, we are interested in keeping alive the spatial metaphorics of the term "world" to talk about places where genre books are written, published, and read, especially given the way that technology has enhanced the international aspects of cultural production. Referring to, for example, the "Australian crime genre world" or the "Filipino romance genre world" involves conceptualizing an object with both national borders and global qualities. It is perhaps apposite that both usages of the word "world" come together in this chapter.

The people who work within genre worlds are attuned to these different scales and modes. Our interviewees spoke readily of their national context and understood how that was linked to a global genre but not fully contained by it.[1] They also spoke of storyworlds as fictional spaces created by authors, with the potential for sharing with others for creativity and enjoyment, as well as leveraging market share.[2] Storyworlds and national context are ordinary complexions of genre worlds but also connect to the significant theoretical considerations around mobility across media and across the globe.

Transnational Genre Fiction

In this section, we look closely at how genre worlds allow and resist movements of texts and people transnationally, a word we use to mean between nations. This can mean "going global," or it can be a smaller-scale movement from one national setting to another. Such movements are quite concrete and specific. Examples include an author or agent physically touring a region or being interviewed by a blogger from a different country. Other movements happen through securing translations or rights sales for texts into another national market, signing a contract with a publisher or agent from another country, or collaborating with an author from another country. Movements may be configured as highly localized, regional, national, or international for particular purposes, but they may also operate on all of these scales simultaneously.

Our deliberately loose conceptualization of worlds—and particularly our insistence on the ongoing relevance of the national—runs in opposition to some narratives of globalization. For example, media rhetoric around Amazon's global hegemony might make it seem that national borders are increasingly irrelevant to popular fiction; similar ideas are emerging about the impact of Netflix or Disney+ on television.[3] There is a tendency to see mass culture, such as genre fiction, as aligned with global forces (including the global forces of capitalism) and more prestigious cultural forms, such as literary fiction, as aligned with national or regional structures.[4] However, the alignment of genre fiction with the global is both true and not true.

As we foregrounded in chapter 2, the contemporary publishing industry does have global dimensions fueled by digital technology. There is abundant evidence of the pull to the global in genre worlds. Genres create transnational communities, and these are often mediated online.[5] To take an example from our interviews, Australian romance author Kylie Scott credits American bloggers Maryse (www.maryse.net/) and Aestas (https://aestas-bookblog.com/) with driving the popularity of her books (and thanks book bloggers in the acknowledgments of her books, such as *Lick*).[6] Cultural mediators, such as bloggers, assist the transnational movement of books in genre worlds. The development of digital-first genre fiction publishers and imprints also supports such movement, not least through promoting global release dates and world rights, so that genre books can be simultaneously accessible to readers worldwide. There are, however, rubs and obstacles that defy the assumption of a single global market for genre fiction and show that genre worlds exist in smaller configurations.

National frameworks for the making and distribution of books are resilient, and we see no evidence of their imminent dissolution. A range of factors tie genre fiction production to national markets. Intellectual property (IP) regimes support the carving up of the publishing industry into a series of national or regional territories. The persistent importance of live and in-person author events in book marketing acts as a constraint on author careers. Niche subgenres may thrive in one market and not another.

One example of the national affiliations of genre worlds occurs when a subgenre becomes closely associated with a particular place of production, even if it is consumed globally. Think, for example, of "Tartan Noir," an informal term for the works of Scottish crime authors such as Denise Mina, Val McDermid, Ann Cleeves, and Peter May.[7] This is effectively a nationalized subgenre of hard-boiled crime thrillers. The authors of Tartan Noir are Scottish, and so are the settings; these elements combine to produce a package with exotic appeal for a global market (as well as a locus of national pride). The label "Tartan Noir" recalls the much more commercially successful "Scandinoir," which originated with the global megaseller by Stieg Larsson, *The Girl with a Dragon Tattoo* (published in Sweden in 2005 and in English translation in 2008). Not every nation has been able to produce its own "noir" suffix, though. We are yet to see Mexinoir or Russonoir, although the overseas success of Jane Harper's 2017 novel, *The Dry,* with its small-town Australian setting, created hopes of an Aussie Noir wave.[8]

Rather than making use of distinctive settings, crime (and other genre) novelists may deny or obscure local markers in their work. Australian crime writer Michael Robotham told us, "I identify myself as an Australian crime writer, but I'm not writing Australian crime."[9] Not only has he never set a crime novel in Australia, but he also has a U.K.-based agent and primary publisher. In our interviews, authors, publishers, editors, and agents described with detailed examples the distinctive histories and features of the different markets they operate within and traverse. There is constant, dynamic interplay between the global and the national when it comes to genre fiction. The movement of anglophone small-nation-authored crime, fantasy, and romance through international markets, and thus the extent to which national genre worlds embrace the globe, is usefully theorized with the work of Pascale Casanova.

Theorizing Transnational Genre Worlds

Our understanding of the power relations that affect transnational movements in genre worlds largely accords with Pascale Casanova's modeling of the global publishing ecosystem in *The World Republic of Letters*. Although consonant with Bourdieu's work, Casanova's model also aligns with Becker's account of inner circles, core participants, and fringes of art worlds and is useful for extending it into a geopolitical argument. Casanova argues that international literary space functions according to a hierarchy of unequal power relations, organized in a center-and-periphery structure. Centers are determined by language groups, and there can be more than one center for each, which is why London "continues to be central for Australians" and why both London and New York are centers within the anglophone area.[10] Centers have prestige and resources, including the institutions of large capital cities (such as public libraries and writers organizations), concentrations of publishing houses, and ease of access to leading trade events, such as the international rights sales behemoth the Frankfurt Book Fair.

In contrast, writers, publishers, and books from peripheral national book cultures struggle for visibility and legitimacy. These struggles can be all but invisible to those in power. As Casanova puts it, "The irremediable and violent discontinuity between the metropolitan literary world and its suburban outskirts is perceptible only to writers on the periphery, who, having to struggle in very tangible ways in order simply to find 'the gateway to the present' (as Octavio Paz put it), and then to gain admission to its central precincts, are more clearsighted than others about the nature and the form of the literary balance of power." The forms of domination exercised by the center against the periphery include linguistic domination (especially against countries where English is not the official language) and economic domination, "notably in the form of foreign control over publishing." Casanova insists, therefore, that "literary relations of power are forms of political relations of power."[11] Recent scholarship has been particularly attentive to how these power relations work for translations, affecting which books are translated and into what languages.[12] Literary power relations are also evident in the different status of literary prizes and in the settings and characters within books that are published.[13] We have noted elsewhere that "the sheer cultural force of London and New York as Anglophone publishing centers . . . mitigates against the inclusion of Australian content in popular fiction."[14]

The center-and-periphery structure is not a simple binary but a continuum, Casanova argues, as "the many forms of antagonism to which domination gives rise prevent a linear hierarchy from establishing itself." For Casanova, the old and established literary centers of Paris and London are affected by the growing influence of New York as part of "an increasingly powerful commercial pole [that] has profoundly altered publishing strategies, affecting not only patterns of distribution but also the selection of books and even their content." These effects are particularly powerful in the sphere of commercial fiction, where the emphasis on "immediate profitability" favors transnational circulation. "Bestsellers," she notes "have always sold across borders."[15]

According to Casanova, and from her Bourdieusian perspective, commercial fiction is attuned to consumer demand. This means that it often respects the "commercial customs" of national markets but also, increasingly, that commercial novelists write for the United States: "In the case of the United States, this market has now come to assume global proportions, giving rise to a new breed of novel whose international success is the combined result of the triumph of the commercial model in the publishing industry and of the universal adoption of popular American tastes in fiction." The most popular books in each nation, including their genre fiction, are affected by the tastes and conventions of the American domestic market. Casanova points to Hollywood and the rise of publishing conglomerates as factors in this.[16]

Other research on contemporary publishing offers support for this view of a concentrated, nondiverse global industry for popular fiction. Ann Steiner writes, for example, that "the bestseller industry is constantly driven towards international markets, spurred on both by large media conglomerates with publishing interests and by national publishing houses looking for the next success abroad and trying [to] capitalize on national bestsellers through international sales." Steiner finds that of the most significant megasellers of the twenty-first century, "at some point the major international publishers picked up all these authors," suggesting that real power tends to be centralized with the multinational conglomerates, in line with Casanova's claim.[17]

At the same time, different nations maintain distinctive book cultures.[18] This can be true for regions, too.[19] Indeed, it may be the particular pattern of oppression that has shaped the books of a nation. In Australia scholars have noted the ongoing legacy of British colonialism and the unequal relationship with America as fundamental to the self-understanding of historical and contemporary Australian writers and publishers, as both dependent on and independent from other markets.[20] We, too, see the aftermath and persistence of this inequality as evident in some ingrained attitudes to writing and reading genre fiction from the periphery.

As academics from Australia, we experience the perspective that comes from being located distantly from the powerful centers of the United States and the United Kingdom. This is a perspective attuned to the difficulties and barriers that travel imposes and the (symbolic and economic) effects of the conferral or withholding of legitimation from the center. For writers and publishers, this distance can also have positive effects, including the possibility of innovation. We are struck by Ronald Burt's argument, cited by Katherine Giuffre, that "people who stand near the holes in a social structure are at higher risk of having good ideas."[21] Those outside dominant cliques are more likely to have diverse networks and be exposed to divergent ideas. Burt notes, "This is not creativity born of genius; it is creativity as an import-export business. An idea mundane in one group can be a valuable insight in another."[22] This may be overly optimistic, and ignore the costs for fringe participants, but it does also point to some opportunities.

We argue that it is moments of transition between national markets, between small-scale communities and larger arenas, between peripheries and centers that produce some of the dynamism and excitement of book culture. Our focus on industry illuminates this, showing real-world obstacles and enablers and the extent to which the logistics of the (globalized, digitized) contemporary book business impact the composition and reach of genres. Practical examples below, drawn from our interviews, showcase these operations in more detail. How does a writer's or publisher's location affect their involvement in genre fiction publishing processes? And how does the national or regional flavor of some texts and subgenres—epic fantasy's European settings or romance's American epicenter—fuel or impede transnational movements?

Books across Markets: Peripheral Authors, Central Aspirations

The most common direction of transnational movement in genre worlds is from periphery to center. The publishing industry has a centripetal force, where objects move toward the center, in order to receive validation and increase commercial success. This means that many genre fiction authors develop a double mind-set: physically located—and in some ways attached to—one national market (engaged with local conventions and festivals, interacting with local readerships, teaching writing at local arts organizations) but mentally oriented, and connected in other ways, to another more powerful national market (negotiating contracts with international centers, performing remote marketing such as blog tours and phone interviews, timing social media posts for different time zones). Periodically, for example, the Australian media reports with surprise that an author living quietly and unknown in Australia is hugely popular in America. The *Sydney Morning Herald* writes of multiple *New York Times*–bestselling author Stephanie Laurens, "The reason Laurens isn't a household name in this country is that she doesn't sell many books in Australia."[23]

To take a more extended example, romance writer Anna Campbell is a writer from the peripheral market of Australia whose career has been oriented toward the United States and the United Kingdom. Campbell considers Australian romance fiction to have an Australianness on the page that comes from its strongly drawn and mature female characters—"I think there's an innate strength that you get in Australian heroines"—and although the perceptibility of this Australianness to readers is an open question, her sense of national connection to this aspect of the books is part of her double orientation to the national and the international. Campbell's international orientation is partly expressed in her choice to write Regency romance, a subgenre in which books have a consistent setting of early-nine-teenth-century England. As she describes it, Regency romance "has a world-wide audience" and cannot, by definition, be set anywhere but England. Furthermore, Campbell's publishing efforts have always been directed at the United States: as she told us, "I wouldn't say I'm not conscious of the Australian market, but the vast majority of my readership is American." Campbell began to professionalize by joining the Romance Writers of Australia (RWA) but then entered professional prizes run through American networks, and it was these that gained attention for her writing and enabled her to get an agent. American success followed: "My agent ended up setting up an auction in New York, and three of the big houses wanted to buy it. The auction went for a week, and at the end of Good Friday 2006, I was a published author and they paid me enough money to become a full-time writer."[24] Campbell went on to write five books with Avon and then moved to Hachette for a number of books. She has now moved to self-publishing, and the majority of her readership remains in the United States. Campbell exemplifies the leveraging of a large U.S. audience, developed through a career with U.S.-based publishers, into self-publishing as a rapid route to reach readers, showing the transnational possibilities of the digital change described in the previous chapter.

Campbell, like crime author Michael Robotham, is an Australian author whose work is oriented to international markets. Such authors often set their novels internationally and may adjust their spelling, idiom, and cultural references. At the Romance Writers of Australia convention in 2015 that we observed, visiting keynote speaker Deb Werksman from U.S. publisher Sourcebooks responded to a question about how popular Australian locations are for U.S. audiences. Werksman advised that for the core U.S. romance market, any location outside the U.S. Midwest or the South is unfamiliar (notwithstanding established subgenre settings such as Regency romance). That means, she said, that writers need to bring any other setting alive so the reader wants to spend time there: treat Australia like Alaska, she said—make it exotic, but not too exotic. This advice sounds a cautionary note about the limits of transnational movement and possible homogenizing effects of a global genre world dominated by U.S. publishing.

The most straightforward example of transnational movement is a book that is a success in its home market and then goes on to be acquired by publishers from other markets. But transnational careers and publishing arrangements can affect how books move in more complex ways. For example, Australian romance author Anne Gracie's primary publisher is Penguin USA, which holds world rights to her work. Her books are written for, edited for, and first published into the American market, where her Regency-set historical romances find a large readership. For Gracie, "Australia is a bonus market." Quantities of mass-market American editions of Gracie's books used to be imported by the Penguin Australia office and supplied to bookstores. Then in 2010, Sarah Fairhall, a Penguin Australia editor working in commercial fiction, acquired Australian and New Zealand rights for some of Gracie's novels. As Fairhall explains, this involved repackaging them for the Michael Joseph imprint with new covers and a larger format designed to appeal to bookshops and department stores and to reach a new Australian readership: "Often when we're publishing someone like Anne Gracie here in Australia, we're trying to reach new readers, because all of the people here at this [RWA] conference who want *The Winter Bride* would know that they could get it for eight dollars from Amazon. . . . So with the thirty-dollar edition, for example, you're reaching new readers and people who don't necessarily consider themselves part of the romance community, but who actually enjoy that fiction."[25] In an industrial sense, then, Gracie can be thought of as an American writer whose books are licensed into Australia; her residence in Australia simply helped catalyze the local marketing of those books. It is interesting to note that Gracie's most recent books are not being repackaged for Australia this way, indicating an insufficient size of the Australian market from the publisher's perspective and a corresponding difficulty for Australian readers who want to access this Australian author's print books.

Fairhall's account also points to a distinction between the core audience and fringe audience and an appreciation of how this distinction cuts transnationally—core romance readers read digitally and therefore can usually access U.S. versions, whereas the fringe audience is more nationally bound, more tied to national markets by print-distribution networks. This key point shows how globalization and digitization connect: having one's book accessible in different territories is important for writers who want to reach global markets.

Against the Flow: To the Peripheries and Lateral Movements

Against the late-capitalist tendency for talent to seek the economic resources and rewards of the center are several genre fiction authors who pursue different career trajectories. Australian crime writer Kerry Greenwood, for example, has always set her novels in Australia and has published only with Australian independent publishers, including small houses Clan Destine Press and Pulp Fiction Press, and most successfully with Allen & Unwin, Australia's largest independent publisher. As we discuss further later, the transmedia adaptations of her novels have been more vigorously taken up in international markets than the books themselves. In a different move, fantasy author Jack Dann emigrated to Australia from the United States. In Australia he became a leading figure in the national genre world, editing many anthologies and mentoring less experienced writers. As U.K. fantasy editor and anthologist Stephen Jones told us, "[Dann has] been a great lynchpin for the whole Australian genre because he's brought his knowledge—he was a best-selling genre writer in America. He's brought that to Australia; he's been a big supporter of Australian genre fiction." Author Daniel O'Malley is also an American who is an Australian citizen and was published first in Australia. In both cases, however, their moves to Australia were not intentionally related to writing-career choices. Even though Dann has become an important figure in Australian publishing, this is a by-product of his decision to marry Australian fantasy writer and academic Janeen Webb. In O'Malley's case, he works in a high-level public service position in Australia's capital, Canberra. His double orientation—part of the Australian fantasy community and part of the international publishing industry—is overlaid by a divided orientation toward his day job and toward his work as a writer, what Bernard Lahire calls "the double life of writers."[26]

In another disruption of the prevailing periphery-center movement, many significant author careers develop laterally between midsize (or small) national markets. These careers, too, are marked by power relations of different kinds. A striking example is the synergy between the German and Australian markets. Germany is one of the most significant overseas markets for Australian authors, and many of our interviewees commented on the favorable reception of Australian authors in Germany. German publishers who have published Australian authors include Heyne, Knaur, Diana Verlag, Blanvalet, Droemer Knaur, S. Fischer, Rowohlt, and Bastei Lübbe. According to data we gathered and analyzed from the German National Library (the library of deposit), five of these publishers published the following number of Australian novels in selected two-year periods, showing a steady albeit small presence for Australian fiction in Germany:

Table 1. Number of Australian titles published by selected German publishers in periods between 2000 and 2016

	2000-2001	2010-2011	2015-2016
Blanvalet	0	30	12
Diana-Verlag	0	9	1
Heyne	19	3	5
Droemer	3	0	1
Suhrkamp	0	5	7

The genre fiction authors these German companies publish include Charlotte Nash, Nicole Alexander, Rachael Treasure (all of whom write in the subgenre of Australian rural romance), Di Morrissey, Patricia Shaw, as well as fantasy authors Kim Wilkins and C. S. Pacat.[27]

As this list shows, Australian-set novels are popular in Germany—they even have a name for them, the "Australien-Roman." Australian authors are also popular in Germany even when they write novels set elsewhere. For example, both Katherine Scholes and T. M. Clark write romances set in Africa that sell well in Germany. We interviewed Hans Christian Rohr, editor for international fiction at C. Bertelsmann, Random House Germany, who has published many Australian authors. He told us that when he goes to the Frankfurt Book Fair, he is looking for connections to the German market: "If you look for special books, like, I don't know, books from Australia, then you have to think, 'What's for the German readers in there? What can travel? Is it crime fiction?' So it's category. 'Is it, is it a family story? So what is it?' You know, the big female read."[28] This editor uses genre or category as a line of connection from one nation's culture to another.

Multinational Publishers, Transnational Genre Worlds

Relations between publishers are just as important as the relations between publishers and authors when considering how transnationality works in genre worlds. A classic example of centripetal force in publishing is E. L. James's megaselling title, *Fifty Shades of Grey*. James is a U.K. author, so is not located in a peripheral place. However, her first publisher was an Australian micropress, the Writer's Coffee Shop, which then sold the rights to Random House. The publisher-to-publisher deal, based on extraordinary micropress sales, catalyzed one of the most influential global trends in early-twenty-first-century publishing.

The hub-and-spokes model of multinational publishing companies offers another productive vantage point on the transnationality of genre worlds. The dominance in romance fiction of Harlequin, which now owns its former rival, Mills & Boon, has been pursued through a specific international strategy, which involves opening local offices, sourcing local authors, and then funneling them through to the center (formerly in Canada, just to complicate things, but now in the United States, as Harlequin has been acquired by HarperCollins). Harlequin is both rigidly nationalized, with specific marketing strategies for national territories (in Australia a ribbon on a book's cover marks titles written by "Australian authors"), and fundamentally transnational. Category romance is a particularly intense example of a distribution system tilted to maximize both global reach and national sales of genre works.

Stefanie London, whose first novel was a Harlequin KISS title released in 2013, traces her initial decision to write romance to the status of Mills & Boon as a household name in Australia and childhood memories of "seeing the books at the newsagency when I used to go shopping with my mum." London, who grew up in Melbourne's northern suburbs, now lives in Canada and writes for the recently launched Dare line. London articulates her doubled experience of national connection and international location: "My agent is American, my editors are all American, and I kind of made that decision early on that I wanted to have international reach, and so—I mean, I have translations of my books, so I literally have readers all around the world and I didn't want to kind of tie myself just to one market, but I do continue to write stories set in Australia because I love my home and my culture (and that kind of stuff), but I've been told by many people I have a very international voice." Australian settings can be a trace of authors' national attachments, even in a genre where books, in romance author Carol Marinelli's words, can be set "anywhere, and everywhere" (although note Werksman's cautionary advice about this).[29]

An interesting example of a reworking of this transnational structure is offered by Tule Publishing, which was discussed in chapter 2 as an example of an author cooperative model of publishing. Tule is in some sense a rebellion against the tight control of Harlequin and its impositions on authors. But it also replicates some of the transnational power relations of Harlequin. Tule was begun by an American author, Jane Porter, but from the beginning also included Canadian and Australian authors in key roles. One of the founding authors, Barbara Dunlop, is Canadian, distanced from the publishing center of the United States, and peripheral even within Canada, located far from its publishing hub in Toronto: she says, describing the start of her career, "I lived in Yukon, so I've always lived in a very remote area." She had become friends with Porter through attending a series of workshops and RWA conferences and having similar career experiences (for example, both were finalists for the Golden Heart award, and both received publishing deals after many years of trying). Dunlop says, "We were pretty excited because we'd gone from zero to one hundred, and then as the industry started to change, Jane decided to open Tule. . . . I had too many things on the go, so Jane was patient and waited."[30] Tule adopts and adapts an established convention of a publisher in a central market, relying on the workforce of writers in a peripheral place, who are all supporting each other.

Another international appointment at Tule was Australian author Kelly Hunter, who was employed by Porter (whom she knew through Mills & Boon transnational networks) as Tule's Australia-based "headhunter" (Hunter's term) for authors and stories.[31] Hunter, who was raised in regional Australia, began writing romance novels while living in Malaysia in 2000 as a mother of young children: while they were at school, and because she had no access to romance novels in English, she wrote. First published in 2007 with Mills & Boon, she has now written more than thirty books and says that she "like[s] the tight focus of short contemporary romance."[32] Hunter is active in the Australian romance genre world; she served variously as registrar, secretary, vice president, and president of the Romance Writers of Australia. She has also pursued an international career. Hunter connected with other markets initially through her Mills & Boon contacts and second through conferences:

> Through [writing Mills & Boon titles] I met a lot of other authors who were writing similarly, and they were from the U.K. and the States. And with being an author from Australia, it's always in my best interest to travel to other conferences, to the U.K. to visit editors, meet other authors, to the U.S. to do similarly, because . . . they were the biggest English markets for the stories. The U.S., then the U.K., then Australia. And I wasn't always writing Australian-set stories. So it was always good to touch base with the markets where these books were being fed into.

Describing her role with Tule, Hunter told us that she had been part of early discussions with Porter about setting up the new publishing model, and then "Jane eventually offered me a job as an executive editor for the Holiday line, which was an international sort of arm of their brand-new company. And I promptly went about wooing authors to write for Tule, be they Australian, U.K., Spain. And they were, they were author contacts I had made during my career." Hunter explained her brokering role between Australia and the U.S. publisher: "Tule has a fairly high profile in Australia with Australian authors. There were good author connections to begin with. I did bring in authors who I had knowledge of and who I knew could write quickly and well for Tule and that I would enjoy working with."[33] For these authors turned publishers, the number of markets they have reached in their own career deepens their industry knowledge and their ability to navigate and negotiate transnational connections for themselves and their peers.

Case Study: The Multinational, Multiauthor Continuity Series, American Extreme Bull Riders Tour

A case study of one series published by Tule, the American Extreme Bull Riders Tour series, captures further dynamics of collaboration across international borders. Hunter and Dunlop have both written for this series, alongside several other authors; the series includes work by Australian, U.S., and Canadian authors. A multiauthored continuity series consists of several stand-alone novels all set in the same location—for example, a small town. The writers are in communication with one another, providing continuity across the novels. Multiauthored continuity series have been published by several companies: for example, the NASCAR series cobranded with NASCAR and Harlequin. Dunlop wrote some books for this series and described it to us: "They would go city to city, race to race; it was different authors. . . . [Y]ou looked at sort of the community and family that developed around the tour."[34] This type of continuity series is also common in fantasy fiction and has made effective use of new digital technologies in publishing.

The American Extreme Bull Riders Tour continuity series focuses on bull riders, a type of hero who is often injured, at risk, or damaged ("hard-living alphas," according to the Tule Publishing website). Dunlop told us that cowboys are "popular with readers, and they're nice heroes to write. I don't know what real cowboys might be like, but fictional cowboys make fine, strong, loyal heroes that a lot of people enjoy reading. Bull Riders, I think, was just a little bit of a twist on that, and I believe what Jane had in mind was, you know, going from city to city, you would have a variety of different settings, which would be nice, but there's also a community feeling about the bull-riding circuit." The community feeling Dunlop alludes to characterizes not only the books but also the writing process and the relationship among the authors. This relationship is founded on a highly localized, place-specific experience: a research trip undertaken by four of the authors (Jane Porter, Megan Crane, Barbara Dunlop, and Kelly Hunter). As Dunlop related, these authors "went on a trip to Montana and then did a road trip down into Deadwood and watched the bull rides together." This was an important socializing moment for the diversely located authors:

> Kelly and I hadn't met, Megan and I had met at in passing, and Jane and I knew each other quite well, and so we had a great time. It was a very, very fun trip. And I don't know if any of the others have told you this, but the second day of the bull ride we were sitting and we were watching it, and a woman came up and looked at all four of us and said, "Who are you and why are you here?" And I said, "I thought we were blending." And she's like, "No." Apparently, we were not blending, so we told her who we were and what we were doing, and she was, of course, delighted because it is kind of a fun story. And then we met briefly at the conference and we sort of discussed the bible, and beyond that I think it was very similar to working with Harlequin. I think, just sort of having that fun road trip in advance and having that baseline time together was really nice.

Dunlop explicitly links the social pleasure of bonding with fellow authors and editors with the consequent development of a "bible," that is, a document that lists facts about the shared narrative for continuity reasons. Dunlop reflected on the differences between the authors arising from their nationalities:

> You know, being a Canadian, working with Australians is actually more symbiotic than working with Americans, I think, like, we had some interestingly memorable conversations in the car driving across America. When we were talking about various political systems, and of course Kelly and I were like, "Yeah, yeah, yeah." She understands my system and I understand hers, and the Americans were

like, "What? How does it work?" So, I think as a Canadian, it's very easy working with Australians. It was great working with Kelly, and I think there's more differences between us and the Americans. . . . We represented the Commonwealth.

There are effects of this international collaboration on the page. Dunlop has had reader feedback about her similarity with Australians: "I did have someone email me once, quite a few years ago, saying, basically, 'What are you? You don't sound American, but you don't sound British?' And they were Australian and I said I'm Canadian, and they were like, 'Oh, that makes sense.'" There are Australian characters in the American Extreme Bull Riders Tour series, although this is not done simplistically. Hunter told us, "I don't come into it and say, 'I'm the Australian author; therefore, I'm going to write the Australian story.'" That said, she acknowledges that "it's often easier to make one of your characters Australian, so you have a reference point," and tells us that of all the main characters she has written, about half are Australian and half are not. Hunter sees continuity between the American cowboy and the Australian stockman, as romantic heroes: "I think there are very strong similarities in that mythological figure, you know, that, that horseman, the stockman, the long-yard stuff. The pioneer spirit, the aloneness, perhaps, of a lot of the heroes in those, in rural, Australian rural romance. So to me that, the overarching, the framework, that archetype, that mythology, is, is quite similar." But any attempts to make the Australian stockman a market equivalent to the American cowboy are subject to a power imbalance, with the American archetype and its trappings longer established in popular culture and more commercially appealing. This dynamic is mirrored in the transnational structures of bull riding itself. Hunter tells us of the wholesale adoption of American rural cultural norms in an Australian setting: "We went to the PBR [a professional bull-riding competition] in Deadwood, which is South Dakota, and the PBR finals here in Sydney. And it was exactly the same. . . . [The] show was exactly the same (interviewer: Did it feel like American import culture, though, in Australia?) I thought so . . . to the extent that PBR announcers will pray. There will be anthems. There will be thank-yous to servicemen and -women. Even in Australia."[35] U.S.-to-Australia cultural imperialism is layered here, permeating the source-inspiration material, the cultural tropes, and the industrial organization of the romance genre world. The case study of this continuity series shows, at a deep level, some of the tangled transnational connections and disconnections that characterize genre worlds.

Concluding Thoughts on Transnationality

If genre worlds are simultaneously local, national, and international, then what does this mean in industry terms? The examples discussed above show some of the complexities at play. National markets continue to shape the production and circulation of genre texts. Popular fiction is not straightforwardly international and global, even if it is bound up in a globalized, digitized publishing industry. The demands of in-person promotion, the benefits of in-person networking, and the territorial markets of the publishing industry constrain authors. The domestic U.S. market's tastes influence the production of commercial fiction on other territories; our research, focused on the peripheral market of Australia, shows the pull of that U.S. market for Australian authors.

Our research affirms the importance of transnational interactions in building genre worlds, as well as the persistent obstacles faced by genre-world participants located in regional or peripheral areas. These tensions are part of the texture of genre worlds. Our interviewees constantly weigh their national and international positions, without feeling constrained to choose between them: the challenge for them, rather, is how to navigate the movements between these positions most successfully. In genre worlds, the ambiguities of transnationality are ever present, across the textual, social, and—as this section has shown most clearly—industrial dimensions.

These tensions are also evident in, and linked to, another way in which genre worlds cross boundaries: transmedia. Transnational mobility is often facilitated by transmedia adaptations. Casanova sees Hollywood film adaptation, and the increased conglomeratization of publishing and its integration with entertainment companies, as factors in the transnational movement of commercial fiction.[36] Multinational publishing is intimately connected to other media industries, and conventionalized industry activities support movement between media formats; this is seen acutely in genre worlds. Some genre titles experience fluid movements between cultural sectors, including through adaptation, enabled by media conglomerates and mobile audiences. The industrial facilitation of cross-media movement—and transmedia storyworlds—is an important feature of genre worlds.

Transmedia Genre Worlds

An increasing convergence across media forms is one of the characteristics of twenty-first-century publishing, and, as with other publishing industry transformations, genre fiction is at the forefront of this shift. The genre-worlds model, in paying attention to the multiple dimensionality of texts, encompasses a range of different media. Evaluating genre fiction's role in the transmedia context of publishing allows us to see and understand the dynamic relationship between the content of books (the textual) and the way they are made public (the industrial).

The traditional view of literary adaptation, which might imagine a printed text written by a single author on one side and a visual medium with dispersed authorship on the other, is giving way to a new expectation that adaptation takes place across multiple media, shapes authorship practices, and is highly responsive to audiences. The publishing industry has become increasingly conscious of the adaptability of books that they acquire in a new media environment where, as Simone Murray writes, "the possibility of multipurposing any particular content package across myriad simultaneous media formats has come to underpin the structural logic of the media industries and is consciously anticipated, stage-managed and pursued at every stage of a book's pre- and post-publication life." Subsidiary rights of books—the rights to produce a book in different formats—are increasingly important to an industry operating on tightening margins. As Murray puts it, contract negotiations today are likely to focus on a book as an "IP rights bundle and potential content franchise" rather than "a singularly conceived book." Yet, at the same time, the book remains centered as an originary source of content. For one of our interviewees, television producer Fiona Eagger, it still all begins with a book: as she told us, the vision for the expanded storyworld she helped create through the *Miss Fisher's Murder Mysteries* television series was one that "evolved. . . . [O]bviously, the IP is there in the books. So it's an IP that can transform from one medium to another. So if you think about it, that's sort of the start of it. If there's enough essence in it."[37]

In some genres, especially fantasy and crime, it has become more and more common to see acquisitions announcements accompanied by news of high-profile film and television rights sales; the moment a publisher announces it will be publishing a book, it also announces that the book will be adapted.[38] Books in the most popular genres in the market may be "born convergent," positioned to take advantage of successful marketing channels established by other book-led franchises and to leverage increasingly participatory audiences across platforms.[39]

A snapshot of recent genre fiction activity across media gives a sense of emerging industry processes in bringing content and audiences together. In romance, Anna Todd's Wattpad book *After* (itself originally One Direction fan fiction) was adapted to film by Aviron Pictures after accruing more than 1.5 billion reads on its original platform. Also from Wattpad, Beth Reekles's teen romance *The Kissing Booth* was acquired directly by streaming giant Netflix. Following an association with Hallmark, Harlequin has now established its own film and television arm, Harlequin Studios. Crime has found a unique position on media platforms through true-crime podcasts—a trend so ubiquitous it has its own memes (for example, "Why I Stopped Dating Men and Married a True Crime Podcast").[40] George R. R. Martin's A Song of Ice and Fire series was adapted by television studio HBO as *A Game of Thrones* and spawned an ever-growing transmedia storyworld that spills over from the fandom into mainstream culture.[41] Young adult fantasy stories, such as works by Sarah J. Maas and Cassandra Clare, have built audiences around collectible editions, intense social media activity, and even coloring books.

The transmedia environment affects the practices of authorship. The Australian domestic noir novel *Big Little Lies,* by Liane Moriarty, was acquired for HBO by Reese Witherspoon's production company, Hello Sunshine. After the success of the first season, in an environment where one successful television season nearly always implies a second, the television production company requested Moriarty purpose-write a second-season novella for adaptation. Moriarty has written this novella, but it currently remains unpublished, even though the television series has been released.[42] Authorship becomes dispersed, too, in the case of the many fantasy writers who write novelizations for U.S. media franchises such as *Star Wars* and *The X-Files*, including Australians Garth Nix, Sean Williams, and Karen Miller.

It is important to note, however, that the whole industry is not dining out on lucrative adaptations and media tie-ins. Many books are never optioned, though an acquisition announcement in trade journals such as *Publishers Weekly* or the *Publishers Marketplace* will often trigger a cascade of requests for reading copies to be sent to production companies. The ones that are optioned may never be picked up for production. Writers may make an

income stream out of options that are renewed every few years while producers battle to interest studios and financiers. Meanwhile, option fees are
shrinking like other financial rewards in the industry. Literary agent Jenny
Darling notes that in the past, "a minimum option fee for a book was $1,500
[AUD] for a year and I regularly get offered $100 or $250 a year for options
now, and I won't even entertain them, you know? . . . A bit like advances
plummeting, the options are sort of plummeting." As the industry becomes
less predictable, too, publishers may offer contracts that lock down an ever-
expanding list of rights for adaptation to other forms—as in the example of
Mitchell Hogan that we considered in chapter 2. Just as in the early 2000s
when authors began to receive addenda to contracts that claimed e-book
rights, literary agent Selwa Anthony notes it is now becoming increasingly
difficult to sell books to publishers without audio rights included: "People
didn't believe in audiobooks twenty years ago. . . . [P]ublishers didn't even
care if they gave you the rights or not."[43] Transmedia adaptation, like other
aspects of contemporary publishing, offers high-profile examples of success
and, behind the scenes, many more examples of hustling, struggle, innovation, and stop-start progress.

Theorizing Transmedia Genre Fiction

A great deal of the cross-media activity that traverses book culture arises
from new expectations of technology, industry, and audience. Henry Jenkins conceptualizes this as convergence: not the idea that the digital has
replaced the analog, but that old and new media interact and those interactions are dynamic and productive, a conceptualization that also resonates
with recent theories of the postdigital.[44] Convergence is a product of a
number of shifts in media practice. New technologies can deliver content
differently, and new patterns of media ownership and concentration create
an imperative to maximize the value of content; as Jenkins writes, "Digitization set the conditions for convergence; corporate conglomerates created
its imperative." Convergence, then, is "the flow of content across multiple
media platforms" and "the cooperation between multiple media industries." Along with these changes, audience expectations have also changed,
creating increasingly "migratory behavior," as audiences "go almost anywhere in search of the kinds of entertainment experiences they want."[45]

This account of convergence sits well within a genre-worlds model that
encourages a broad view of the industrial conditions that shape works of

genre fiction. Genre fiction texts are primed for convergent industrial practices; the genre worlds we analyze are centered around books, but these
books are conceived of as linked to other media forms. *Big Little Lies* is a
good example, especially if compared with an earlier highly successful
international television adaptation: Colleen McCullough's *The Thorn Birds*
in 1983. McCullough's book became an international TV series, with no
other media platform involved. This one-to-one adaptation is the epitome
of the preconvergence book-televisual adaptation binary. By contrast, *Big
Little Lies* has expanded from book to television but also across into associated media. The HBO shop offers merchandise such as wineglasses, baseball
caps, and T-shirts. The official social media for the show features interactive
digital assets such as quizzes, shareable GIFs, and behind-the-scenes video
content. Content is regularly aligned with other public events such as Pride
Month (a party featuring drag queens dressed as characters) and Mother's
Day (a competition to celebrate "strong moms"). These events recognize,
reward, and include audiences, while maintaining a coherent brand (feminist, inclusive). They also proliferate the world of *Big Little Lies* beyond the
book-series dyad.

Within these multiplying storyworlds, specific media forms play a strong
role in shaping stories. If the kind of storytelling that arises in response to
media convergence is what Jenkins calls "transmedia storytelling," then, as
Marie-Laure Ryan writes, this is not simply a case of adaptation but one of
expansion, modification, and transposition. What does a medium allow?
What does it limit? How does genre fiction change in adaptation, and how
does a transformed media landscape affect the way genre fiction is written
and published? Linda Hutcheon notes that adaptations are always contingent on what "one art form or medium [can] do that another cannot." That
is, the material specifics of certain media shape the adaptation. Speaking of
the German television adaptation of his work, crime author Michael Robotham notes, "If you take a big, complex novel and turn it into ninety min-
utes of TV, something has to give."[46] This is true of adaptation into other
media forms, too. In each case, precisely what "has to give" (and what may
be added) depends on what a medium can do (its affordances and limitations) but also what that medium typically does (its conventions).

The most obvious material affordance of screen media is precisely the
visual. Visual elements are part of genre worlds even when the focus is on
the text—most particularly, through cover design—but imagery takes on

new force when genre fiction stories are augmented or adapted for visual media. When adapting from book to film or television, additional elements can be shown that enhance the story, and visually uninteresting sections of the story may be cut. Material limitations can arise from budgetary constraints or opportunities, triggering changes to setting or costumes. Daniel O'Malley's fantasy novel *The Rook* was developed for television by the production company Fickle Fish Films (co-owned by *Twilight* author Stephenie Meyer); Meyer later left her position as showrunner on the series, but it went on to stream on services including Virgin TV and Starz. Describing the communications between himself and the TV writers, O'Malley said to us: "They have to be free to make their changes. Not just according to what works for a television show, and episodes, but what resources they can get, you know? That kind of thing. If they have a really terrific actor or actress, the opportunity to work with them, well, they may need to make a character older or younger or a different race." The influence of visual media extends beyond adaptations. Trends in other media may change the way books are written and published. As Gelder has written, fantasy fiction has been a mainstay of adaptation in the twenty-first century, most often driven by large corporations with big budgets and wide reach. These adaptations have a bias toward serialization, turning a single adaptation into an ongoing franchise. The blockbuster adaptations of *The Lord of the Rings, A Game of Thrones,* and *Harry Potter* have all affected public ideas of what successful fantasy is. If we add in romance-fantasy series Twilight and dystopic fantasy series The Hunger Games, we can see a trend of serialization emerging in book-to-adaptation culture that is characteristic of twenty-first-century publishing. As Julie Bosman writes in the *New York Times,* publishers now prioritize acquisition of "story lines that can keep readers hooked for several books rather than just one," and these are usually genre books.[47]

Seriality has long been a feature of genre fiction publishing and remains important, and it intersects productively with what Dan Hassler-Forest calls the "fundamental multiplicity" of transmedia storyworlds. Reproducibility underpins industrial logic, especially in the entertainment world, where successes are rare and unpredictable; seriality, sequels, extensions, and so on are also welcomed by audiences, who may themselves extend storyworlds through practices such as fan fiction and fan art. Such extensions are a key site of pleasure in genre worlds. As Victor Watson writes, "One cannot read a series of twelve novels by chance."[48]

A shift toward serialization has been wrought not only by the economic drive of successful book-to-adaptation franchises but also by new modes of entertainment, such as streaming and bingeing. Bosman asserts, "The book business is upending its traditional timetable by encouraging a kind of binge reading, releasing new works by a single author at an accelerated pace." Jeff Bercovici writes of this new orientation toward the "instant-gratification factor" encouraging "binge buying . . . which encourages multibook series." This binge buying is supported by the capacity of digital platforms and retailers to keep backlist titles (including earlier volumes in a series) accessible for readers, which means that the publication of each new title in a multibook series can provide a sales bump across several titles, multiplying its economic impact for publisher and author. Backlist availability is in general a boon for cross-media movements and promotion of genre texts. For example, Australian romance author Miranda Lee's existing novels *The Playboy's Ruthless Pursuit, Taken Over by the Billionaire,* and *Master of Her Virtue* were repackaged and rebranded as *A Season of Seduction,* a tie-in collection for the 2018 season of *The Bachelorette Australia.*[49]

The influence of other media on the process of producing genre fiction books is manifold and extends to the shape of the stories themselves. For academic Dan Hassler-Forest, the "multidirectional proliferation" of transmedia storytelling has undermined the notion of "the single narrative as a linear and internally coherent text." Transmedia adaptations and new modes of convergent storytelling mean narrative conventions from across media are creating mutual influence. This mutual influence was pointed out by editor Shelly Shapiro, responsible for *Star Wars* books at Del Rey, in her interview with us: "I think that there is definitely an area where books/movies/videogames are drawing together"; however, she reserves the idea that merging of conventions will not be total across media: "There will (I hope!) always be novels that shine through their use of language and deep character development, for example; and there will also continue to be plenty of games that are not narrative-driven."[50]

There is a sense, in many (but not all) transmedia storytelling worlds, that the book has a primary place as the originator of content—and a corresponding hope, on the part of some genre-world participants, that transmedia adaptations and extensions may return to support the creation of more books. Author Angela Slatter characterizes the mutual influence of media forms in fantasy as "chicken and egg, but I'd say, you know, the book has to exist first, and someone who reads has to see this and go, 'I can see this on the screen,' and then share it with a larger audience."[51] This view underpins her hope, as an author, that media adaptation is "causing people to go and buy more books." That hope may be only partially realized, however: it may be only adapted texts themselves that benefit rather than the genre world as a whole. Sales patterns in publishing increasingly take the form of "comet and tail," a winner-takes-all model where the most high-profile books have sales far in excess of other titles, even in the same genre. A successful adaptation can certainly drive book sales, but the *Game of Thrones* adaptation, for example, potentially increased the market only for George R. R. Martin books and tie-ins.

Nonetheless, there can be no doubt that popular genre texts have become more visible in the twenty-first century because of the convergence across sectors enabled by media conglomerates and multimodal audiences. Contemporary genre worlds extend beyond the book, beyond the publishing industry, and beyond book cultures. This is especially true for fantasy (with its complex, big-budget, sprawling multimedia universes) and quite true for crime, which has an affinity for television and film adaptations. Historically, it has been less true for romance, because as former Momentum publisher Joel Naoum told us, "Romance readers are all about the books."[52] Netflix's recent success with *Bridgerton*, a series adapted from the Regency romance novels written by Julia Quinn, suggests that romance fiction may also productively extend into transmedia worlds via streaming services.

We now turn to two specific case studies of genre fiction that are bound up in transmedia industrial logic. Ryan distinguishes between two types of transmedia storytelling: "bottom-up," which exploits "the commercial success of a narrative originally conceived as autonomous, often a novel," and "top-down," an "operation that coordinates various media for a global experience."[53] While we would nuance the bottom-up/top-down distinction—a writer who chooses to write in a different genre under a pseudonym, for example, may do so for both top-down and bottom-up reasons—it is a useful way to conceptualize the way books and other media interact. This chapter uses two case studies to examine genre fiction's role in larger cultural and entertainment industries: the bottom-up adaptation for television of the historical crime series *Miss Fisher's Murder Mysteries* and a complex, top-down fantasy genre-world transmedia movement of a novelization in the *Star Wars* universe.

Miss Fisher's Murder Mysteries

The *Miss Fisher's Murder Mysteries* television show is an adaptation of Kerry Greenwood's series of sixteen detective novels set in 1920s Melbourne, featuring unconventional detective Phryne Fisher. The first television series aired on Australia's national public broadcaster, the ABC, in 2012, and by its third season in 2015 was attracting an average weekly audience of 1.5 million domestically (in a country with a population of fewer than 25 million). It has now sold into 160 territories and is periodically broadcast via streaming services including networks in a series of multiterritory deals. The television series has spawned other media and merchandise, from a movie to a Miss Fisher–branded version of the board game Cluedo.

This adaptation success is one milestone in the long history of the Phryne Fisher book series. The first Phryne Fisher mystery, *Cocaine Blues,* was published in 1989 by McPhee Gribble in Australia, republished in an Omnibus edition by small press Pulp Fiction in 2004, then republished again by Allen & Unwin in 2005. Greenwood credits Allen & Unwin publisher Annette Barlow with reviving the series: sales were "ordinary" until Barlow rejacketed and promoted them and "really really made a difference." *Cocaine Blues* became the first episode of the television series adaptation in 2012, just before Sisters in Crime Australia honored Greenwood with a Lifetime Achievement Award in 2013. The 2015 tie-in edition of the novel (a U.S. edition, published by crime-fiction-specific company Poisoned Pen Press) features actor Essie Davis, who plays Phryne Fisher, on the cover. Members of the genre world visible in this history include two specialist crime small presses, a committed publisher at a medium-size Australian press, and the crime community who awarded Greenwood's work. Also evident is the influence of the televisual medium, which can bolster the status of the books it adapts. Robert Stam writes of adaptation in evolutionary terms: "If mutation is the means by which the evolutionary process advances, then we can also see filmic adaptations as 'mutations' that help their source novel 'survive.'" As Jenny Darling, Greenwood's agent, notes, there were times in Greenwood's career when publishers said, "Oh, we don't know if we can publish another one."[54] The adaptation of Greenwood's series has ensured its survival, more than thirty years after Phryne Fisher was first created.

In Ryan's terms, the Miss Fisher mysteries are a bottom-up transmedia adaptation. The expanded assets are based on a book series, and with the series comes what Murray calls the "comfortingly familiar figure of the Author . . . adaptation's irrefutable point of origin—finite, individualised and conveniently open to interrogation." In our interview with Greenwood, she told us the story of how she first created the character of Phryne Fisher: "I was in the tram and she walked in and sat down, and I thought there she was; she's gorgeous." This imaginative account certainly fits with Romantic conceptions of authorial inspiration. In keeping with the role of author as the creative originator, during the production of the television series it was important for Greenwood that she retain some control over potential changes to the script. In our interview, she said that she "wouldn't have done it [sold the rights] otherwise." She was ready to "jump up and down if necessary. [But] that wasn't necessary because all of the stuff [they changed] was very good." The producers were equally happy to have Greenwood consult for the series, once again acknowledging the importance of her authorship: as Fiona Eagger told us, Greenwood was "our muse and touchstone. . . . She knows Phryne better than anyone. . . . You know, we had the oracle. So of course you've got to keep going back to it all the time."[55] The language is telling: an inspiring muse, a measuring touchstone, a knowing oracle. The Romantic idea of the author underpins the way the genre world frames this adaptation. Cross-media adaptation also, in this instance, operates as a feminist network in which creative women support other creative women, something that was particularly important to Greenwood.

At the same time, the influence of television as a medium is strongly evident in the adaptation. The conventions of a medium necessitate changes. Eagger speaks of some of the specific ways the Phryne Fisher books were adapted to television. A male character who is married in the books remains unmarried in the series: "A lot of television runs on unresolved sexual tension. We've got to have someone in that [role] here."[56] Multiple members of Phryne's family generate conflict in the books; the makers of the television series created the single character of Aunt Prudence for Phryne to rebel against, because in television, "you've got to contain your characters." While the books were "pretty much stand-alone: murder at the beginning, solved by the end," the series responded to changes in viewing habits that are now "far more binge based. So you tend to have to have a hook to get you from one episode to another." For Eagger, these conventions of the medium are also related to "audience engagement," as audiences bring expectations to a show, partly in relation to the medium of television and partly specifically in relation to the subgenre of cozy historical crime.

While she writes squarely within the genre of cozy historical crime fiction, Kerry Greenwood's heroine, Phryne Fisher, is sexually liberated. Television adaptation producer Fiona Eagger explains that there was some resistance to this characterization from within the screen industry but that others championed the character:

> There was a little bit of sexism towards Phryne as you know, too much of a dilettante, too much of a loose woman. She should sleep with people for love. . . . There were questions within organizations that you had to talk around. Sort of go, really? And even in the U.S., when she came out, there was a little bit of, she's a floozy, because she's not married and she has sort of, she's liberated in her sexuality. So there was a certain contingent in the States that found that quite distressing. And we've had some beautiful fan mail saying, "Can she please get married? I'd be so much happier." And then the Jezebel site went up in arms and said, "You don't put those sort of criteria on a male hero. Why are you giving it to a female? And James Bond doesn't get questioned." . . . I think she's definitely appealed to the feminist sort of audience out there as well. You know, the kick-arse detective we should all be. I think she's really found a following being that. And also with younger and older women.[57]

In producing Phryne Fisher, Eagger observed the ways in which cross-media adaptation can draw out progressive elements in a genre, making them more visible and focusing attention on them: here, a progressive female detective protagonist. The response to this, as mediated by Eagger, also shows how a mass audience or popular culture can splinter into a conservative core that is not ready for a particular kind of progressive character or trope but a perhaps quite sizable minority that is.

Eagger and her colleagues are experienced television producers, with long involvement in the production of crime series. This experience has evolved in a specific national context in Australia. The national broadcaster, ABC, has a tradition of importing productions from the United Kingdom (often the BBC), including its staple product of cozy crime series: from Agatha Christie adaptations through to *Midsomer Murders*. This successful tradition, along with the success of other crime-related TV shows in Australia, is what led Eagger to seek out rights to adapt the Phryne Fisher stories in the first place: these were recognizably cozy crime stories "with a twist" (the sassy young female detective and her 1920s fashion aesthetic). The synergy between book and TV genre elements speaks to the potential for these stories to operate as a transmedia storyworld.

The brand extension and engagement of a transmedia genre property are leveraged by industry across platforms to maximize marketing and, ultimately, profitability. Eagger spoke enthusiastically about the number and success of spin-off and tie-in events in the Phryne Fisher storyworld: "afternoon tea, walking tour, pop-up speakeasies (they were big). Murder Mystery dinners, high teas, meet the maker. Merchandise, after-dark jazz, garden party, live music events."[58] Other merchandise includes coloring books, mugs, bags, umbrellas, playing cards, and stationery, as well as a jewelry and clothing line. The Australian National Trust toured a costume exhibition associated with the series, which attracted nearly seventy thousand visitors. The storyworld exploited here arises from the historical setting of the books and television series. This is a strong generic element of the crime genre world, especially cozy crime, which is closely linked to the aesthetically appealing, nostalgia-tinted settings of crime's "Golden Age"—the early to mid-twentieth century.

Eagger spoke of brands like Harry Potter and Disney, telling us, "Those entrepreneurs knew how to leverage a brand. Once you've got a brand—not all television series lend themselves to it—but once you've got one, then you give the audience what they want, which is more." With words such as "leverage" and "brand," this quotation could be used as evidence that profitability and commercial calculations drive adaptation. But if we look closer, we see a clear link between that leverage and what audiences want: "more." As Eagger says, "It was only really when we realized what a passionate fan base it was and that they just, they want to be Miss Fisher. They want to own her, a bit of her, anything. They want to be, they can't get enough of the world. So then you just have to be obliging and start giving them that world."[59] The transmedia storyworld of Phryne Fisher is developed in part to service a passionate fandom.

The role of fandom in the transmedia movements of Phryne Fisher extends to directly funding it. Every Cloud Productions, the Australian production company behind the television adaptations of Kerry Greenwood's Phryne Fisher books, raised more than $700,000 internationally to make the feature film *Miss Fisher and the Crypt of Tears* (2020) via crowdfunding on the Kickstarter platform. This campaign is an example of how constraints of the medium, in this case lack of production resources, may inspire new ways of achieving transmedia goals, especially using digital platforms. Here, we see industry working with the pleasure of readers and audiences, converting that into financial investment. The transmedia storyworld is a shared space for investments, both personal and commercial. Audiences are not simply exploited, in any blunt instrumental sense; the logic of the genre world means, as Kim Wilkins argues elsewhere, that "readers have passion and purpose in their engagement . . . , and while those things can absolutely be monetised by large corporations, they can never be fully owned; nor does monetisation extinguish them entirely."[60] The *Miss Fisher's Murder Mysteries* adaptation complex offers a powerful example of how transmedia adaptation can combine pleasure and industry in the crime genre world.

The Force Unleashed and Novelizations

Fantasy is undoubtedly the genre world where transmedia movements are most evident and most complex. One of the most visible forms of transmedia movements is the franchise. Jenkins uses "franchise" to refer specifically to the "coordinated effort to brand and market fictional content" in the new conditions of transmedia synergy—with large companies in a position to own and control manifestations of a storyworld across media forms—and corresponding efforts toward extension, that is, the expansion of "potential markets by moving content across different delivery systems."[61]

Novelization is one example of brand extension within a franchise, a top-down adaptation, in Ryan's terms, that provides a distinct contrast to the Phryne Fisher example. Commissioning a tie-in book for a film is a longstanding practice in the publishing industry: *King Kong,* a novelization by Delos W. Lovelace based on the script of the film, was published in 1932 as part of "the film's advertising," explicitly linking the novelization to the marketing of an existing property.[62] In this sense, novelization is one of the earliest modes of expanding a storyworld across media for secondary profit. Novelization sometimes results in paradoxes, however, such as the novelization of Kenneth Branagh's 1994 adaptation of *Frankenstein,* impossibly titled "*Mary Shelley's Frankenstein* by Lenore Fleischer." Once the work of ghost writers, increasingly tie-ins name their authors in order to leverage the fan followings of superstar (ideally) or established writers. Most recently, YA fantasy stars Leigh Bardugo, Marie Lu, and Sarah J. Maas have produced tie-in books for the DC universe. The DC Icons book set features collect-ible novelizations about Batman, Catwoman, and Wonder Woman and joins previous and current stories told across comic books, television, film, and video games. Novelization within a franchise is not only a transmedia practice but a transnational one too. These books are industry led, which in the case of many franchises means led by the United States; authors are commissioned from a range of other countries. Authors from Australia, for example, as with authors from other "peripheral" territories, are enmeshed in the production of transmedia storyworld empires led out of the United States. From Australia, Karen Miller and Jennifer Fallon have both written in the *Stargate* universe, Garth Nix has novelized for *The X-Files* series, and Kate Orman wrote twelve novels for *Doctor Who* between 1995 and 2003. These authors, rather than being the originators of storyworlds, have a spe-cific role in fleshing out in textual form elements of a larger story. Their interactions with industry professionals and writing processes are shaped by the demands of the franchise. This limited agency is often compensated for by larger than usual advances and relatively speedy publication.

Star Wars, the focus of this case-study example, is a huge transmedia fran-chise and a cherished storyworld within the global fantasy genre world. A great deal has already been written about its vast and complex history, both pre and post its acquisition by Disney, a move that in itself served to fold the *Star Wars* universe into a global megacorporation that operates on some levels as a franchising machine.[63] Yet within that machine are creative indi-viduals, and it is that dizzying contrast between corporation and individual that we hope to capture here, particularly in terms of how creative practice may thrive (or not) in such a context. *Star Wars'* practices include commis-sioned novelizations of films and games. The first *Star Wars* novelization (*Star Wars: From the Adventures of Luke Skywalker* [1976]) was ghostwritten by Alan Dean Foster but credited to George Lucas. More recently, Disney publishing commissioned a series of children's books in the *Star Wars* uni-verse from blockbuster authors such as Tony DiTerlizzi (*The Spiderwick Chronicles*) and R. J. Palacio (*Wonder*).[64] Officially sanctioned tie-in novels for the *Star Wars* universe at the time of writing number in the hundreds (more than 160 for adults, plus movie guides, LEGO picture books, and books for children) and in 2014 passed 75 million copies sold worldwide.[65] A number of Australian fantasy authors have written novels in the *Star Wars* universe. Sean Williams (the subject of this case study) cowrote three novels with

Shane Dix in the New Jedi Order series (2003), then was commissioned to write solo three novelizations based on the *Star Wars* video games *The Force Unleashed I* and *II* and *The Old Republic* (2008–10). Our interviews relate to *The Force Unleashed I.*

The 2008 release of the video game *The Force Unleashed* (*TFU*) was a major event in the ongoing *Star Wars* franchise, filling a gap between films. The game's release was designed by official industrial channels as an opportunity to extend the *Star Wars* storyworld across strategically chosen media. Haden Blackman, the video-game designer who led the project in the United States, told us that the goal of the game *The Force Unleashed* was to "create a major *Star Wars* event, using the game as a centerpiece. . . . After I came up with the story and pitched it to Lucasfilm, the wheels were put into motion for the novelization and the comic book adaptation (which I wrote), along with a number of other tie-ins, like action figures, a LEGO starship, a 'Making Of' book, even a supplement for the official role-playing game."[66] The game thus reveals clearly the dynamics of a contemporary transmedia franchise.

Industry-led novelizations are explicitly embedded in processes of marketing, branding economics, and creative control that can seem antithetical to widely held perceptions of the purpose of creative writing. The traditional notion of the author is fundamentally disrupted by the idea of writing a novelization. As Williams himself told us regarding his work on *The Force Unleashed* novel, "I was a writer for hire, which isn't a demeaning term; it meant that I was paid to be part of a team. And these people had been working on other projects and were more deeply embedded in *Star Wars* than I was."[67] The teamwork approach is familiar from other genre-worlds scenarios, including coauthorship—such as that between James Patterson and authors such as Candice Fox, whom we discuss in chapter 4—and strong editorial direction, such as that from Mills & Boon's established norms and guidelines. In the case of novelization, this teamwork approach is very much explicit as a way to negotiate across media formats.

Even when everyone involved in a team recognizes each other's expertise, moments of creative friction related to cross-media movement can arise, and this was true during the composition of *The Force Unleashed* novelization, published in 2008 by Del Ray. In his interview with us, Haden Blackman presents the novelization process as straightforward: "The game was pretty far along when Sean started working on the novel, so I was able to pitch him the story, give him a detailed outline, and even provide him with my 'shooting scripts' for all of our in-game cinematics, which is where the bulk of the story is told in *TFU* . . . so a lot was already set in stone." In Blackman's account, the writing of the book was a practical challenge, a relatively easy path from one medium to another, as though those media are expressively similar, if not identical. "With that said," Blackman adds, "he had to flesh out some characters and fill the gaps between major events in the game." The language here is not about medium but rather implies a direct transcription with some more material added. From Williams's perspective, though, having the script in hand did not amount to a straightforward task. In fact, guidance from an expert storyteller in another medium made Williams's task more difficult in some ways: "It was made more complicated, made easier and more complicated, by the fact that I had a script, I had a story arc for the characters. But because a computer game script is not structured like a story and it's level based—it's level, level, level, level—and these were only the cut [narrative, non-game-play] scenes, so I didn't have any of the game-play scripts; they weren't written until after I finished the book."[68] The difficulties discussed here are related to medium. Novels and video games differ fundamentally in terms of narrative shape. While a novel usually follows a beginning, middle, end structure that flows in one direction with tension distributed in a rising fashion, video games like *The Force Unleashed* are more likely to be episodic, potentially iterative, sometimes repetitive, with tension distributed in short bursts at the ends of levels and then released for the start of the next level. Cut scenes, as mentioned above, are narrative scenes not controlled by the player that "cut" from the game play to fill in an overarching backstory or provide character motivation. As an aside, the traditional storytelling structure we recognize from prose, especially novels, is being disrupted by platform as well as medium. The expectations of episode-based storytelling such as Wattpad and fan-fiction sites are also reimagining narrative drive and how it is created.

Williams also tells of a late change to the script that challenged his ability to adapt the video game specifically to his medium:

> I was about halfway through it, and it was a thirteen-level game, and they emailed me to say, "We're cutting three of the levels towards the end of the game." And I said, "What are you doing to me? You know, you need this manuscript in two weeks' time, and you're telling me

you're cutting like 25 percent of the game. Twenty-five percent of the story is going, including one of the key character moments, one of the most important moments of the character; you're saying that's gone now?" And they said, "Yep." So I rang my editor and said, "Can you just let me keep this level for the book?" And she managed to win the day on that one.[69]

Again, differences between media are at play here. Williams's attachment to the idea of a "key character moment" toward the end of a novel does not fit in a level-based paradigm where levels can be removed with minimal disruption. Williams also reveals here the importance of the mediating influence of his editor, Shelly Shapiro at Del Rey, in negotiating across the divide of the medium.

In fact, writing into the *Star Wars* franchise was a highly mediated experience of authorship for Williams, as both he and Blackman reveal. Blackman's interactions with Williams went through the Lucas Licensing office, "who put us in touch a few times during his process. I remember a few Q&A sessions via phone and e-mail where I clarified things about the story and characters, and then I read each draft of the novel and provided notes, most of which went through Licensing to Sean."[70] Williams speaks of a constant round of consensus making around the novel, with changing levels of power and knowledge at work. As well as the editorial staff at Del Rey and Blackman himself, "there was the continuity people from *Star Wars,* and we all kind of needed to agree. Although depending on the situation, it might be the computer-game person who had the upper hand, or it might be my editor, or it might be the continuity people."[71] The *Star Wars* franchise is huge and wide ranging, extending well beyond novelizations. Just as Williams had to contend with control from above and mediation in his creative practice, so too did Blackman:

> I drove the creative on *TFU* from start to finish and had a great deal of freedom to tell the story I wanted to tell and craft the gameplay I personally wanted players to experience. Our biggest concerns were getting permission to: set the story in the timeframe between the prequel and classic trilogies; establish that Darth Vader had a secret apprentice; and re-envision the Force in a way that seemed more suitable for a video game. But this all turned out to be easier than we expected—a few conversations with Lucasfilm and George Lucas

about the game, and we were off and running with few limitations outside of the normal approvals (e.g., Darth Vader had to look and sound like Darth Vader, etc.).[72]

By invoking the concept of permission and approvals, Blackman alerts us to the industrial hierarchy of the franchise, where creators answer to others before innovating in the franchise. Again, the hierarchies imposed by industry practices are familiar from other genre-world scenarios but are very explicit in the case of transmedia story extensions. In the case of *Star Wars* novelizations, ultimately authorial agency traces back through the eponymous company to the franchise's ur-creator, George Lucas, named here as the person who authorized the new material and the revising of a key concept of the world to suit the video-game medium. Implied here is the idea of canon, or the inviolable laws of the franchise's storyworld. Canon is established from above, by Lucas (although now also by Disney), and spreads out across transmedia assets, with room to move negotiable in some areas and nonnegotiable in others.

Clearly, the writer in the franchise has limited creative agency. Financial and career-enhancing rewards may be part of the reason they are willing to trade their creative freedom. In addition to receiving a substantial advance, Williams knew "the book was always going to sell well because everybody who wanted to play the game would buy the book . . . , so they would get sort of cheats and stuff like that, or they'd get an idea of what the game would be like."[73] We can see here the book's embeddedness in the marketing function of the franchise, designed to generate interest before the game's release. The book debuted at number one on the *New York Times* best-seller list for hardcover fiction, the first video-game tie-in ever to do so. Williams has thereafter been able to be billed as a number-one *New York Times* best seller, a powerful marketing boost for his career.

However, it would be wrong to assume that writers undertake novelizations simply for monetary reasons. In genre worlds, pleasure in genre texts is shared. Writers are readers (and viewers). Williams's enthusiasm to write the novelization, as an avowed *Star Wars* fan himself, is clear in this quotation: "I really enjoyed writing for them and was keen to do another one. And they emailed and said, . . . 'It's about Darth Vader's secret apprentice,' and I went, 'Where do I sign?'" Like many members of the fantasy community, Williams "grew up reading *Doctor Who* novelizations and film novelizations by authors like Alan Dean Foster," the *Star Wars* novelist, and novelizing for a franchise was something "I'd always wanted to do."[74] Writing for a franchise in the genre world is, at least for Williams, a chance to extend the pleasure of the transmedia storyworld.

Because, as well as being a franchise, *Star Wars* is a fictional universe that yields creative satisfaction for fans and creators; the franchise elements discussed above can be thought of as part of the industrial conditions that constitute one layer of a genre world but also connect to the textual layer and the social layer. The fantasy genre is well known for spawning sprawling storyworlds for two reasons. First, one of the chief pleasures of fantasy fiction is the storyworld (both topographical setting and the details of lore). We know this is the case because the paratext often explicitly foregrounds these things with maps, glossaries, time lines, histories, and so on to extend the pleasure of the story beyond the written portion. Second, fantasy audiences are known for being engaged in extended storyworlds creatively through fan activities such as fan art, fan fiction, fan wikis, and so on. Tie-ins may very well be seen as a kind of commissioned fan fiction, though their relationship to canon may be more constrained than fan fiction, which can deploy the AU (alternate universe) trope without disrupting industrially established canon.[75] Fan fiction has less constraints and can play outside the rules—including through diversifying the storyworld. But both kinds of writing share the pleasure of being immersed in a particular storyworld. Hassler-Forest notes, "What most forms of sf [science fiction] and fantasy fandom have in common is an interest in world-building as a limitless and continuously expanding narrative environment." For Jenkins, that engaged activity in genre worlds is "the art of world making. To fully experience any fictional world, consumers must assume the role of hunters and gatherers, chasing down bits of the story across media channels, comparing notes with each other via online discussion groups, and collaborating to ensure that everyone who invests time and effort will come away with a richer entertainment experience."[76]

This interplay between industrial needs and participant desires is illustrated by the different *Star Wars* "bibles." In trying to control its assets, Lucas Productions has codified the *Star Wars* storyworld in an official continuity database called "The Holocron," available to all of its authors and creative designers: Sean Williams calls it an "exhaustive database of every character or thing that's ever been in *Star Wars*." The existence of such a resource aligns with Ryan's category of the "top-down" transmedia storyworld. Yet Williams admits that he did not use "The Holocron" as much as he used the fan-based wiki Wookieepedia, "because there's nothing better than obsessive fans to track absolutely everything . . . and it is humungous," an apt adjective given it contains more than 160,000 pages. Reflecting on Williams's comment earlier about how he deferred generally to others in industrial roles in the genre world because they "were more deeply embedded in *Star Wars* than I was," it is interesting to note how useful he found the knowledge of those embedded potentially more deeply ("nothing better than obsessive fans") in *Star Wars* via amateur roles in the genre world. Colin Harvey writes that transmedia extensions, "whether authorised or not, whether full stories or fragments of stories, contribute to an understanding of the fantastic storyworld in question" that may in turn lead "to a wider cultural appreciation of the storyworld."[77] Our extended case study of the novelization of *The Force Unleashed* has shown how the industrial layer of the fantasy genre world supports the creation of transmedia adaptations that produce just such appreciative engagement.

Conclusion

Genre worlds are complexes of personnel and activity, and those complexes are also located geographically in the world—in national and international configurations—and across media forms and platforms. While genre worlds are characterized by a global dimension, especially given the way they intersect with an increasingly digital and transnational publishing industry and with international transmedia storyworlds, they are also tied to smaller locales. Genre worlds are circumscribed by things such as lack of face-to-face access to personnel in the biggest publishing centers or by traditional territorial rights restrictions. On the other hand, genre worlds are enriched by things such as national pride or a desire to write about local landscapes. Movement between the local and the transnational, and between pages and screens (and other media), shows how genre worlds are at the forefront of the new economies of publishing.

Industrial personnel and practices are fundamental to these complex crossings between nations and media. Big Few publishing, which is multinational, corporate, and increasingly conglomerated, bears a privileged relationship with other large media corporations: for example, HarperCollins is owned by News Corp., part of Rupert Murdoch's media holdings, as were 21st Century Fox film studios until their 2019 merger with Disney. Genre worlds are poised to take advantage of the conventional activities that facilitate movement between platforms, but the ability to access this movement may be limited by geographical location or by size of publisher. That is, industrial logics, and particularly the structure of multinational media corporations, dictate a set of uneven power relations between centers (especially the United States) and peripheries (such as Australia). These propel some authors, publishing professionals, and readers of genre fiction toward the center, an act of mental orientation that is either American-centric or global—evident in some multimedia adaptive storyworlds, such as *Star Wars*. This is not universal, though. In other cases, genre-world participants remain local or national in their industrial practices and orientation: *Miss Fisher's Murder Mysteries* is determinedly Australian set, despite its international trade deals, and other authors and publishers of genre fiction also keep local readers in mind as a primary market. Transmedia extensions, too, are very obvious in some genre worlds, such as fantasy, and more subtle in others, such as romance.

Chapters 2 and 3 addressed how genre worlds are constituted industrially, but we have remained attuned to the idea that industry, while it sometimes seems to operate monolithically, is ultimately reducible to the people and activities within it. Power across these people is not distributed evenly: a CEO and a delivery driver have vastly different amounts of agency. However, both are implicated in the genre world, because their activities help get the work of the genre world done. A CEO and a delivery driver may have something in common, though, in that the genre books they help to bring into the world may not interest them particularly. However, within industry there are many invested parties, and social and professional relationships may converge around genre-world activity. These investments can be particularly strong at sites where genre books are created and enjoyed, and when those investments are shared, a sense of affinity may bloom. We now turn in more detail to some of the social aspects raised in the last section—including passionate engagement, shared pleasure, community, and creativity.

. . .

The road to the mountain is long, and the fellowship must hold. They start out with good cheer, but then a lone wolf joins their company, the mountain grows steep, and the sky dims with storm clouds: Are they sure they can trust each other? Read on.

CHAPTER 4

....

Community and Creativity

A genre world is fundamentally social; at its heart is the idea of the cooperative activity of people. Genre worlds catch up a range of people in different roles. These people exist not in isolation but always in relationship with one another, with the shared goal of producing and reading genre books. As we stated in the opening chapter, the various dimensions of genre worlds intertwine and traverse each other; whereas the preceding two chapters examined this with a focus on the industrial aspects of genre worlds, we now turn to their social aspects. This chapter examines in more detail the constitutive power of the social in genre worlds, showing how genre worlds are significantly formed in social interactions. Some industrial personnel are part of these formations, through either their roles or their own interests, but the social dimensions of genre worlds also encompass readers, voluntary organization staff, bloggers, and a host of other players.[1] Genre worlds feature a high level of organized connection between participants, through formal associations and events. These social relationships materially affect genre fiction texts: the words that appear on the page. The chapter gives an overview of the different social relationships that structure a genre world and create a sense of community and shows how these relationships can produce modes of criticism and collaboration that shape the creation of genre texts.

Social Infrastructure: The Formal Organizations of Genre Worlds

While publishing provides an industrial infrastructure for genre fiction, this chapter is interested in the social infrastructure of genre worlds, including formal organizations and their events and activities. This infrastructure is generated from within by writers, readers, and others invested in the genre. While it includes some industry people and can be leveraged for economic purposes, this infrastructure is fundamentally social. The difference is one of intent. While genre organizations may have aims that include professional success for their members, ultimately the central aim is celebrating and supporting the production of genre fiction texts. Each of the genre worlds we examined—crime, fantasy, and romance—provides infrastructure in this regard.

In the anglophone writing world, large organizations exist to support genre worlds. The Romance Writers of America has a membership of more than 9,000, which grew from a like-minded group of five writers who felt romance was ignored by other writers' groups. In the United Kingdom, the British Science Fiction Association presents awards and publishes journals. The Crime Writers of Canada offers a regular roster of author events. In Australia the Romance Writers of Australia is the largest genre organization, with approximately 800 members. Crime writers in Australia are represented by two organizations: the Australian Crime Writers Association (ACWA), with a membership of approximately 150, and Sisters in Crime Australia, which has 480 members. Sisters in Crime exists to support crime writing by female authors, and the Australian chapter is part of an international Sisters in Crime organization that spans fifty-one chapters across the world. The international website states that the chapters and members are "bound by our affection" for the genre, explicitly linking the infrastructure to affective investments in the texts. Unlike romance and crime, there is no central organization for fantasy writers in Australia, though the history of fandom in Australia dates back to the 1930s and is heavily tied up in the organizing of local conventions, or "cons."[2]

In fact, each of the genre worlds of romance, fantasy, and crime offers a roster of cons, both regional and international. In fantasy Worldcon and World Fantasy are the biggest international cons. In Australia cons run in most major capital cities nationally, and the various con organizers select from among them who will host the "Natcon" (or national convention) annually, which can attract up to 200 attendees, depending on its location. The Melbourne (Continuum) and Canberra (Conflux) Natcons are more likely to draw in a larger audience, whereas Perth's Swancon, despite its long history (running annually since 1976), has a smaller membership, demonstrating that the difference between the central and the regional in publishing is replicated in these events. The Romance Writers of Australia does not stage regional conventions, but its annual national convention, the RWA Conference (it has the same name as the American one), has an attendance of up to 400. An annual ARRA (Australian Romance Readers Association) conference also supports romance fiction in Australia, with up to 180 attendees. Importantly, although billed as a "readers" conference, roughly a third of attendees at the 2018 ARRA conference worked in the industry. This shows there is not an easy and clear distinction between the creators of genre fiction and its audiences. While Sisters in Crime does not have a formal convention, it organizes a range of events across the year, such as author talks, public debates, and support for writers. Some of these events can attract more than 100 attendees. Like Australia, most countries offer national conventions; the United States has dozens of regional conventions. Evocative con names abound: DragonCon, MurderCon, KissCon. The con is a central aspect of how genre-world participants interact and get the work of genre fiction done; we will return to the con in chapter 5 for a more detailed analysis.

Part of the genre-world social infrastructure also lies in the assigning of value via awards and prizes. Every major genre has its own awards that register globally, including the Rita and the Golden Heart in romance, the Hugo and the Nebula in fantasy, and the UK Crime Writers Association Daggers and the U.S.-based Edgar Awards in crime. Many of these are organized by genre associations. At the national level, Sisters in Crime Australia sponsors a yearly award ceremony, the Davitt Awards, which attracts more than one hundred entries across seven categories. The ACWA supports the Ned Kelly Awards for crime, with roughly two hundred entries annually across three categories. The Romance Writers of Australia Ruby awards run alongside the organization's conference. The Aurealis Awards for speculative fiction attract eight hundred entries annually across fifteen categories and involve forty-seven judges. Winning or being short-listed for a prize in a national genre world sometimes prefigures international prize recognition. For example, Angela Slatter's 2009 collection *Sourdough, and Other Stories* won Australia's Aurealis Award and went on to be short-listed for the World Fantasy Award, and Jane Harper's *The Dry* won two Davitt Awards (for Best Adult Novel and Reader's Choice) and a Ned Kelly Award (for Best First Novel), before going on to win the UK Crime Writers Association Gold Dagger.

Awards are increasingly important features of book culture; for genre fiction, their role includes bringing together genre communities through celebration and consecrating senior figures in the genre world as judges, shortlistees, or winners.[3] In part, genre awards are a recognition that mainstream book prizes, because of narrow definitions of literary value, are unlikely to give an award to a genre text (though there have been exceptions). Awards make a significant difference to the careers of writers and publishers. They also serve an important community function, which has been less acknowledged in research to date. Fantasy author Sean Williams told us he believes "awards exist to celebrate the community rather than individual authors." In his thinking, the awards process itself amplifies and solidifies the reputation of a genre. Enhanced reputation is particularly achieved through long lists and short lists, the use of which has increased in literary prizes. Williams believes the short lists for awards are more important than the prize: "I wish that you could just have the short list, 'These are the five' . . . , and then you can create this little statistical average of what the genre was doing or who was coming up." Fantasy author Lisa Hannett agrees: "I think short lists are the place to be. I don't know if winning is . . . I love winning, let's not mince words, winning is awesome, but being on the short list is actually, I think, as important or more than winning, because . . . ten years down the road if someone wants to go, 'What was Australian [fantasy] fiction like in 2011?' you can look at the short list to see what a judging panel deemed to be representative of really great Australian fiction."[4] Local prizes, local associations, and local communities are important conduits to international genre-world organizations, though this can be difficult to quantify. For example, Australian contingents go to Worldcon and the Romance Writers of America, and local bodies are often used to gauge interest among community members, informally organize shared accommodation and networking opportunities, and synchronize travel plans via social media beforehand. Australian genre-world members, too, have been judges on international awards and have been short-listed or won international awards. Some Australians are genre builders internationally, leveraging their contacts to recommend Australian authors to international publishers. The social infrastructure of genre worlds supports extensive networks of connections. We now turn to analysis of the nature of those connections and what kind of work they perform.

Community as a Felt Experience

In the large majority of the interviews we conducted, the concept of community was central to the accounts of genre-world participants. The term "community" was used by participants in a loose rather than a precise sense; we take it to indicate a social formation that feels voluntary and relatively stable, even if it is not always uniformly nurturing of participants. Becker's research looks for patterns of cooperation and collective activity; he presents these patterns without reference to the affective (emotional, embodied) aspects of participation, such as willingness, enjoyment, and pleasure. We want to recognize such aspects, which exist across a spectrum. For example, industrial participants in a genre world may (or may not) have a neutral relationship to the work they perform in the genre world depending on what their contribution is: Editors may be very engaged with the work, whereas warehouse workers may not. Writers and fans may have a quite intense affective investment in genre worlds, while casual readers may experience a milder form of pleasure.

Becker is almost silent on the ways in which a sense of community can be generative within the social structures of art worlds. His thinking on distribution gestures toward the way that artworks may travel between specialized "dealers" and enthusiastic audiences, but ideas such as shared pleasure, nurturing of members, and sense of belonging in an art world are not explicitly discussed by him.[5] However, they are referred to regularly in our interviews and thus are vital to our understanding of the infrastructure of genre worlds and to how genre texts are created and circulated. Invocations of community suggest that genre worlds cohere through a membership that is at least voluntary, at most passionately engaged. Communities have insiders and outsiders and through this create conditions that are often productive and sometimes exclusionary. The question of who is seen as a full or marginal participant in a genre fiction community, as well as the norms that communities foster or challenge, affects the stories and characters of genre fiction texts.

To develop the idea of the affective sociality of genre worlds, and its shaping impact, we draw on James Gee's concept of affinity spaces, which explains how social formations can support the development of shared interests. This theory allows us to be more targeted in our analysis of community, given that community feeling can take many forms. Affinity spaces are sites (which may be abstract rather than concrete) where people come together through shared interests. Social interactions on these sites determine "the (changing) universe of possible (and emergently routine) ways in which people can think about, value, act and interact about those interests."[6] Like a genre world, an affinity space includes people whose cooperative links make art, but the emphasis on community in the theory of affinity spaces allows us to ask questions about the specific complexions of those social interactions—especially around pleasurable investment, knowledge sharing, and access—and how those things affect the work a genre world produces.

Colin Lankshear and Michele Knobel have applied the concept of the affinity space to fan fiction, where they found that "practices and relationships are widely marked by generosity, reciprocity, and a sense that the more who participate the richer the experience will be." Fan fiction is an important practice within genre worlds, a source of pleasure for invested readers and of story ideas and publishing and distribution practices that influence the broader development of a genre. The ethos of sharing that Lankshear and Knobel identify in fan fiction is also one that we see celebrated in genre worlds, although whether these utopian values are realized is a separate question. Kristina Busse argues that the impulse to police borders in fan-fiction communities often arises out of the way that ascribing positive values to some members of a community may exclude others.[7] Such a dynamic is also at work in genre worlds, sometimes highly visible and controversial and sometimes low-key or not openly acknowledged.

As a theoretical model, Gee's affinity spaces provide several specific ways to talk about the social dimensions of genre worlds. Gee defines eleven features of affinity spaces, which we have grouped into three themes: common interest (which includes a sense of shared endeavor, celebration of flat hierarchy, and a generative orientation); knowledge (which includes the valuing of complementary knowledges, expectation of tacit knowledge, and the sharing of specialist knowledge); and participation (which includes tolerance of different modes of participation and status and a sense that leadership is porous and should be generous with resources).[8] These three themes—common interest, knowledge, and participation—emerge repeatedly from our interview material and show how social formations of genre worlds are linked to the production of texts.

Common Interest

Genre communities gather around a shared interest, and that interest is often spoken about with great enthusiasm and emotion. Rachael Johns, speaking of romance fiction, says, "This is my passion. I fell in love with the romance genre," while crime author Angela Savage speaks of her "love" of and "pleasure" in reading and writing crime. Fantasy author Lisa Hannett describes her attachment to fantasy fiction with a vivid image: "the feeling that I get, that I used to get as a high school kid reading until three o'clock in the morning, these fantasies where you just wish so much that this was real. This is where the pleasure is for me."[9]

Some genre-world participants openly and sometimes proudly describe themselves as "fans." Literary agent Miriam Kriss credits her influence in the urban fantasy subgenre to "being a fan," which made her aware of early trends; editor Jonathan Strahan says, "Of course [I'm] a fan . . . . I'm a fan who reads. I'm a fan of books. I'm a fan of writers."[10] Many well-known genre writers started out in fan fiction, such as Amie Kaufman, Cassandra Clare, and Lev Grossman, to name a few global best sellers. Naomi Novik, whose fantasy series Temeraire (featuring dragons in the Napoleonic Wars) began as Patrick O'Brian fan fiction, was a founding member of the Organization for Transformative Works, which is dedicated to preserving the history of fan works. Fannish love and attachments to genre, then, are not limited to audiences.

It should be said that the expressive love of genre was not apparent in every interview we conducted. Sulari Gentill, for instance, admits, "There was no epiphany or no great passion. I just thought, 'Oh, okay, that sounds all right.' And crime fiction, it suits the way I write . . . because crime fiction has a natural plot where—you know, you start with the crime or a dead body, usually, and then you spend a good part of the novel until the climax trying to figure out who made the dead body dead. And then you just tie everything off." The expectation that love for genre should be expressed in genre communities nonetheless suffused her interview, with her noting that "it seems ridiculous" that no great passion for crime existed before she began writing it. Gentill's love of genre arose more indirectly: she stayed in the genre because of the way the crime community "embraced" her. As she put it, "I often say that I like being a crime writer because I like crime writers." Gentill describes the crime community as "particularly lovely. And particularly easy to love."[11] She gestures here to how shared genre interests create an attractive social and professional network.

Genre love is shared between people, strengthening social bonds and engendering a sense of affinity that builds community. Cecilia Dart-Thornton speaks of the "absolute kinship and sisterhood and brotherhood of genre writers in Australia that's just wonderful. Everyone's just wanting to connect and wanting to share." Harlequin publisher Sue Brockhoff says of romance writers, "They're incredibly supportive of each other. They network, they workshop, they share, they collaborate, they laugh together, they cry together, they do everything." The language here describes close and affectionate bonds. These bonds are formed around genre texts. Angela Meyer says of Sisters in Crime that they are "just like a bunch of mates around some of these authors who have really helped to talk about the books and get excited about them." In surprisingly similar language, Lisa Hannett describes the Australian fantasy genre world as "a bunch of mates getting together that loved fantasy or science fiction or horror and talking about it and being really excited for each other, when they got their books published or stories published, and then going and having drinks at the bar."[12] In these quotes, connections are made between affective networks ("bunch of mates"), mutual excitement about a genre, and celebrating specific books and career milestones.

Genre communities nominally present as a flat hierarchy. This reflects Gee's point that in affinity spaces, common interest comes first, ahead of other ways of identifying oneself, including social status. This emphasis on the common interest means that a flat hierarchy is idealized and celebrated: amateurs and professionals experience little acknowledged segregation, and the contribution of all members is notionally valued.[13] As fantasy author Sean Williams says, in the fantasy genre community, "everyone's available to everybody else, more or less."[14]

Intriguingly, most of the genre-world participants we interviewed saw their own genre world as unusually inclusive. Such special claims are ways of imagining difference between genres that help define the specialness of a genre's shared interest and affinity space. So, for example, U.S. agent Amy Tannenbaum (who works across a number of genres but began her career working with romance) describes the romance community as "tight-knit" and "more supportive of each other than authors in other genres," while Harlequin marketing specialist Adam Van Roojen also suggests the romance community's supportive nature makes them "so distinctive, I think, from other genres." Crime author Angela Savage describes the crime community as "a very collegiate community" and links collegiality to lack of competition: "Like, it's a lot less competitive than a lot of us would have expected, I think. And perhaps that is a feature of genre fiction because if people read the genre, chances are they'll read your book and they'll read my book kind of thing." Sulari Gentill also makes this connection: "Crime writers as a group are very encouraging of new crime writers, so they encourage people to come and join their genre."[15]

Part of the flat hierarchy is a disavowal of competition in favor of collegiality. Gentill went on to say, "I have been told that not all genres are as welcoming or as open and that some are more competitive." Romance author Carol Marinelli claims the collegial lack of competition for the romance genre: "It's unusual in that it's not competitive. Most of my friends want me to do well and I want them to do well, and I think that's probably not the general opinion of writers and things." In both Gentill's and Marinelli's quotes, their genres are defined in contrast to writer communities that are imagined as competitive by nature (the "general opinion" of writers). A genre community's lack of competitive sentiment is presented as not just a good thing but something that defines them in a positive way. The genre of writing imagined to be brimming with hostility was literary fiction: as Gentill said, "If you try to get into literary, other authors are more likely to see you as a threat than, you know, someone joining the community."[16] We cannot ignore the long-standing, poorly defined, yet energetically policed line between genre and literary fiction and how that may condition the way writers see their communities, building a sense of belonging partly through exclusion. Genre fiction as a whole is seen as having a flatter hierarchy than literary fiction; within this, each genre world sees itself as distinctively friendly.

The fact that interviewees promoted this ideal is telling: this flat hierarchy is important to them, and it is a way that they define their outside borders. This idealization does not mean that competition and gatekeeping do not exist, of course. That so many awards and prizes are central to the functioning of genre worlds, for example, contributes to a hierarchy. Discontent and fractious relationships do exist, and we bear in mind that some interviewees would have been uncomfortable pointing out such instances to us.

Some of our interviewees gave hints of how the idealized flat hierarchy fails to materialize. As Lisa Hannett points out, the welcome and inclusion to a genre community may not be instant at all: "When I first was getting to know people, it's not that people are rude or anything at all, but it was kind of like you're an outsider, and you don't actually know them very well." She points out that "the longer you're in it, though, the more warm and welcoming it becomes." Editor Jo Fletcher suggests the flat hierarchy may have been true at one stage in the fantasy community but is not so anymore: "My peers are people like George Martin and Neil Gaiman and all these amazing writers, and we all grew up together and there didn't seem to be much of a separation between fans and writers in those days. I think as fandom has become its own thing, I think that's less the case."[17] It does seem difficult to believe that Gaiman or Martin would still be as welcoming and instantly collegiate to every participant, though they are great supporters of their community. Martin, for instance, personally pays for a lavish after-party following the Hugo Awards at Worldcon every year, and Gaiman is a reliable blurber for emerging writers' novels. Nonetheless, their market power and length of service in the community do set them apart. In a twenty-first-century publishing environment, a growing gulf exists between megaselling authors (whose books, like those of Gaiman and Martin, are often implicated in large transmedia franchises) and the rank-and-file genre writers (and readers). That these high-selling authors return to their communities to invest and encourage tells a story of the kind of routine camaraderie that exists in genre worlds, but the fact that their investment and encouragement are often notable or newsworthy also tells a story of a highly polarized market and social hierarchy.

The ideal of collegiality, then, is not uniformly realized. Commercial fiction publisher Beverley Cousins describes the active subcommunity of rural romance writers as "very competitive with each other, but they also feed off each other. . . . [O]ne minute they're, you know, stabbing each other in the back; the next minute they're really helping each other."[18] Here Cousins highlights the generative energy of competition rather than suggesting it has no place in a collegial space. Other forms of conflict, such as the clashes over diversity, inclusion, and race, can cause deep damage.

Observing behavior among genre worlds, it becomes clear that there are factions, hierarchies, and places of exclusion. Factions can be regional, generational, gendered, or subgenred. Hierarchies may be related to market success, length of experience in a community, and number of prizes won. Places of exclusion may exist around opportunity—for example, who does and doesn't get invited to contribute to an important anthology—or social bonds, where close friends at similar stages of careers may seek time away from the general membership of cons or awards nights, for room parties or dinner and drinks far from the conference hotel to avoid hangers-on.

These failures of inclusivity and the flat hierarchy are significant and produce inequities. They are often catalysts for attempts to drive change in genre worlds, as discussed in chapter 7. Simultaneously, however, the idealization of the flat hierarchy at a rhetorical level produces a sense of affinity that is enjoyed by some participants and underlies a particular set of attitudes that are supportive of texts being created. The flat hierarchy is a highly productive myth in terms of allowing each genre world to cohere and generate output.

Knowledge

In genre worlds, knowledge is one of the chief ways in which social groups are formed and maintained. Becker writes that art-world participants possess knowledge of conventions, which may change as conditions change, and these "define the outer perimeter" of an art world. According to Gee, too, specialized knowledge is used to form social bonds in affinity spaces, and enthusiasm and infrastructure exist for the transfer of knowledge between members.[19] This is true of genre worlds as well: inside the genre world there is shared knowledge, and the lack of access to that knowledge defines the outside of the genre world.

Knowledge is built and shared in a range of genre-world sites, including fan-based online forums, university courses and seminars, and public events such as writer festivals. One significant route for the transfer of knowledge in genre worlds is structured training for writers. The three genres of crime, fantasy, and romance each have structured programs and competitions aimed at helping emerging writers learn the craft and the business of their genre world. Romance Writers of Australia is particularly active in this regard, with formal workshops and sessions at conferences and other opportunities throughout the year. Author Anna Campbell tells it this way:

> I was working on my own for all those years, and the problem with that was I was just reinventing the wheel with every book. Once I joined Romance Writers of Australia, I found the contests were incredibly useful. Because what happens is, at that stage, if you got into the final, you actually got six written pieces of feedback. They don't do it quite so complicatedly now, but . . . they do a first round with three readers, they do a second round with three readers, and then . . . if you went through that to the finals, so that's seven people who aren't your mother giving you feedback.[20]

This is a demonstration of how the social infrastructure of a genre world transmits knowledge to its members—here, knowledge in the form of feedback on writing genre texts.

The fantasy community has an international workshop series called Clarion, which runs annually in San Diego (the original Clarion) and Seattle (Clarion West) and ran several iterations in Australia (Clarion South). Clarion-style workshops involve six weeks of intensive writing and workshopping, with each writer bringing in a new story every week and other participants reading it and critiquing it, following strict rules, under the facilitation of an experienced writer. Angela Slatter, who attended Clarion South in 2009, speaks highly of skills she acquired at Clarion from best-selling author of *Annihilation* Jeff VanderMeer, which she subsequently passes on to her own mentees. She also describes the value of "actually meeting the teachers and making professional connections," reminding us that knowledge is also transferred via networks, which may be built through formal training opportunities.[21]

Conventions also host formal teaching events in the form of workshops. The Australian 2017 fantasy national convention program included "The Mechanics of Short Speculative Fiction," "What Writers Must Do to Write Professional Fiction," and "Writing Other Cultures." These three titles give insight into the different kinds of knowledge that training can produce. The first workshop is solely a craft-based teaching technique, the second provides instruction on how that craft engages with industry, while the third connects craft and ethos, participating in contemporary debates about cultural appropriation and sensitive representation. The workshop titles show very clearly the link between knowledge transmission and the maintenance or disruption of conventions within a genre world. These three different forms of knowledge, transmitted through formal workshops, all contribute to the development of fantasy fiction writers and texts.

Writers and industry professionals alike are enthusiastic about the value of workshops. Former Harlequin editor Kate Cuthbert says the Romance Writers of Australia has "the best professional development" in Australia: "They know about the writing and the craft, but also the marketing and the pitching and how to deal with commercial publishers. Those things are all taught from people who've been there to people who are coming up, and it's just this constant rotation of mentor-mentee relationships." A number of romance writers spoke of specific instances where the course of their craft had been affected by an RWA workshop. Stefanie London went to her first

RWA conference in 2013 and "took a workshop with Rachel Bailey on sexual tension. . . . It changed my life and how I write." Bronwyn Parry speaks of a forensic pathologist who gave an RWA workshop: "[It was] while I was writing *Dead Heat,* and she informed a lot of that scene. Just seeing the way that she very, very sensitively talked about her work—it was clear that it always had an impact on her. It's not a very long scene, but the comments that the pathologist makes in that brief scene are informed by that session I went to at RWA." Workshops are of particular value to unpublished and emerging writers because, as Carol Marinelli tells it, "the conferences are very motivating, and you see people who are like yourself and find out they *are* published and it *can* happen. . . . You've got all these resources and this energy that happens when you've got a group of people in the room saying, 'There you go . . . You can do this,' and . . . if you need workshops, or craft, they're there." Charlotte Nash expressed a similar view: "RWA is really good, I think, for people who are prepublication, early-career writers that maybe don't have mentorship or other avenues to access information and support." Workshops may be of less value to more experienced genre-world participants; romance author Kylie Scott suggests that "once you've reached a certain level as an advanced writer/practitioner, you're not going to learn as much from those events."[22]

The ability to seek help with a manuscript is not restricted to organized events. Carol Marinelli noted that finding like-minded writers in the community can lead to informal exchange of knowledge: "There might be people I hardly see, but they might suddenly ring and say, 'Can you take a look at this . . . ?' And you could do the same with them." These lessons go beyond writing skills. Bec Sampson told us of Rachael Johns helping her with professional knowledge about the industry. Publisher with Sphere Lucy Malagoni spoke of the importance of "informal networking" in the crime community as a way for "debut authors to meet and learn from established writers, and generally speaking I've always found that, you know, that authors who are established and successful are very, very open and receptive to their support of debut writers."[23] Malagoni's quote links back to the idea of the flat hierarchy, showing how training and inclusivity operate in concert in genre worlds.

Another kind of knowledge that bonds groups is shared language. One of the quickest ways to define in-groups from out-groups is through a lexicon of shared terms that are meaningful only inside the social group, excluding those who do not understand them. Language functions as a code, and words and phrases that have specific meanings to one social group are either neutral or unintelligible outside that group.[24]

Genre worlds have key terms that are meaningful in building community. The fantasy genre's use of the word "fan" is a good example of a word that might be used to belittle outside the genre world but is deployed positively inside the genre world; for example, most fantasy awards have a "best fan art" or "best fan writer" category. Some terms are specific to genres— for example, romance's favored acronyms HEA (happily ever after), HFN (happy for now), and TSTL (too stupid to live, for implausible characters). Other coded terms are used across genres as ways of talking about writing: narrative features such as the "black moment" or the "b-plot," approaches to writing such as "plotter" or "pantser," and ways of gaining feedback on work such as "crit group" and "beta reader." Knowledge of these terms builds the affinity spaces of genre worlds, and sharing in their use is key to participation and access.

Coded language runs deep in genre worlds and has its foundation in the texts of genre fiction novels. Jayne Ann Krentz and Linda Barlow argue that certain words and phrases in romance fiction act as a hidden code "opaque to others": "Outsiders tend to be unable to interpret the conventional language of the genre or to recognise in that language the symbols, images, and allusions that are the fundamental stuff of romance."[25] Our interviewee Cuthbert gave the example of the angry alpha-male love interest:

> For a romance reader, because you understand sort of what's going on, you understand he's lashing out because he is vulnerable and because he is scared and because he can't control the way that he feels about his heroine and she is changing his life. . . . [T]hat's kind of almost the moment when you know, "Oh, well, this is the moment he realizes that he is vulnerable and has fallen in love, and that's why he is lashing out." So there is a code in there. You know, "Okay, this is the moment when . . ." and the code that can terrify the feminist readers who pick up a Mills & Boon and think that clearly all women are party to their own bondage. It's actually quite different: that's the moment when the romance reader knows that he's actually vulnerable and that the shifts of power have actually changed.[26]

Here it can be seen that romance fiction comes loaded with particular plot and character tropes that signify on the inside of the genre world but that are not readily discernible, and can be wildly misunderstood, from the out-side. As Kat Mayo says, "Until you learn how to read romance, you can't really judge its merit effectively." Similarly, Samuel R. Delany, writing of science fiction, asserts, "On the most basic level of sentence meaning, we read words differently when we read them as science fiction." Genre worlds are where the competence to decode genre is learned; elsewhere we have called this "genre competence," a type of knowledge gathered by "repeated encounters with genre texts" that equip people to "recognize, respond to, and reproduce conventions specific to genres."[27]

The lexicons of speculative fiction can be similarly opaque to outsid-ers. Passages from fantasy novels, for example, may read like a foreign lan-guage. Consider this quotation from Kate Forsyth's *The Tower of Ravens*: "Ye will find folk o' all kinds at the Theurgia. . . . Often those born o' mingled human and faery blood have the most extraordinary powers o' all. Like the Keybearer and the Banrigh who . . . are half Khan'cohban. Or the Banpri-onnsa Bronwen, whose mother was half-Fairgean. There is a Celestine in my class, a corrigan, and a girl who is a treeshifter, like my own mother."[28] For readers not versed in fantasy fiction, the estranging language here locks them out. For those on the inside of the genre world, the familiarity with the language is greater, and any residual estrangement is where the pleasure lies. The language is a portal to a genre-world experience, available only to those with shared interests. Such language is one shape that the borders of genre worlds take.

Romance author Kelly Hunter notes this coded language has an indus-trial function, too: "When you're writing back-page blurb for a particu-lar story, you're very aware . . . of coded language. Now I'm very aware of coded language and searchable language, tags, for Amazon search . . . 'Sherriff's Mail-Order Bride.' You know."[29] Here she affirms not only that choice of words triggers certain meanings in the romance genre world but that they are also helpful in the circulation of the text, for search-engine optimization, and to connect across algorithms in online bookstores (Ama-zon, for example, has a "Historical Western" subcategory of romance that does include books about sheriffs and mail-order brides). The codedness of romance fiction—and other forms of genre fiction—thus performs a dou-ble function: binding together the social layer of the romance genre world and facilitating discoverability and routes to market in the industrial layer of the romance genre world.

Participation

In the spirit of promoting the flat hierarchy, access to genre-world affinity spaces is represented as easy and open. Keri Arthur tells of attending the inaugural RWA meeting in Australia: "Even though I was never strictly romance, I never felt alienated and they were so welcoming." This idea of inclusive access is also described by Angela Savage when she speaks of Sisters in Crime: "They welcome all comers. There's not a sense of 'You've got to be a Melbourne author; you've got to be a Scarlet Stiletto winner.' All you have to do is really be a woman who writes a story with a crime theme or a thriller theme in it."[30] The term "welcoming" was used repeatedly in our interviews, suggesting a lack of thresholds to pass or gatekeepers to please in accessing a genre community. Crime author, publisher, and cofounder of Australia's Sister in Crime Lindy Cameron describes her experience as follows:

> Reading my first bit of [her novel] *Blood Guilt* out to a public audience during the St. Kilda Writer's Festival back in the dark ages, I was absolutely rigid with fear, and, so, that's one of the things that Sisters in Crime helps people get over, in a sense. We make, you know, every, the new author is welcomed into the bosom of the organization, and they're spoiled in terms of the fact that everyone's going, "Oh, I loved your book," and, you know, all that sort of stuff, and then they get interviewed by someone who's not there to pull anything apart but just to find out where they got their ideas from.[31]

The contrasting images of rigidity through fear and the bosom of an organization metaphorize a writer's entry into a genre community, from a place outside and impersonal ("public") to an insider and, in some ways, private realm. The language of family is extended through the word "spoiled" to describe support from insiders. The other contrast presented is how interest in a new writer's work can be potentially about asserting dominance (pulling it apart, or reading against the grain), which might be a traditional gatekeeper role. But in this genre community, such work is greeted with enthusiasm. Similarly, in the romance genre world, blogger Kat Mayo talked about the "protective shell of the romance writing network" that existed for some participants.[32]

Nonetheless, some genre-world participants are seen as gatekeepers because of their influence in the industry. Jonathan Strahan, a noted Australian editor and anthologist with vast and fruitful international networks in fantasy, is credited with boosting the careers of a number of Australian writers. Importantly, however, he speaks about his influence in a way that rejects hierarchy:

> I am convinced those things [that is, the successes of writers he helped] would have happened exactly the same way without my involvement anyway. Even if they don't agree, I'm absolutely convinced that it didn't take me going around. I'm unsure about the gatekeeper concept and how locked down it is as a thing. I kind of think that if you're a social person at all, there is a gatekeeper role for you to play in the world you live in. . . . There have been occasions where it will be like, "I'm going to go have drinks with my friends. You're my friend. Come along. My friends are going to like you too." And they do because you're nice and interesting. Then maybe that flows onto something else. But that's incidental.[33]

What is interesting here is that Strahan goes to great lengths to disavow his gatekeeper status in the community. For him, all sociality involves opening gates. He reorients the way he provides access to his international networks as social and informal. The influential people he has access to are friends, and his Australian genre-community peers are friends. The flat-hierarchy model sees all participants as equal, so access is simple and "flows onto something else" if the circumstances are right. Rather than see his work as a genre advocate as an exercise of the power to give or restrict access, he imagines a model of sociality in which commercial outcomes are incidental to the more important work of building networks of friends.

In a genre world, while all members are welcome and perhaps even expected to participate, some participate more actively, and from a more central position, than others.[34] Convention committee members, for example, volunteer many hours and resources to organize venues, catering, programming, and so on. Small-press publishers, for very little in the way of profits, bring writers to publication, opening up access to award short lists and greater recognition in the industry. More senior figures in the communities may perform an ambassadorial role, hosting events and promoting the work of emerging writers. Author Robyn Enlund cites key romance figures Anne Gracie and Keri Arthur in this regard:

It's the same with the Romance Writers of Australia. Like, you know, someone like Anne took on a leadership role and was the president for many years, but someone like Keri, who worked behind the scenes, was on the same committees, you know, was giving always, and so both of them have really given such a lot to the community. And I think anyone that's doing really well overseas and writing Australian genre fiction and sending it over to the U.S. is in the romance genre a lot of the time in part because of that really tight community that is there and people like Keri standing up and helping people along the way.[35]

This quote supports Gee's observation that some community members develop status and leadership via their participation, but that leadership is imagined as a resource for others in the affinity space rather than a place from which rules and hierarchies are set down.[36]

By contrast, the level of attachment to a particular genre community may be light or transient, regardless of the individual's investments in the genre itself. Mitchell Hogan tells of attending a fantasy festival at the New South Wales Writers Centre before he self-published his first novel: "There were panels there, and I met a few other people and authors and that sort of thing, but I really, and I'm still not really that involved in the community itself."[37] Hogan's lighter attachment to the community does not mean a lack of interest in him from the community, however, and he won the Aurealis Award for his self-published novel, which led to a traditional book deal with HarperCollins.

Kate Forsyth moves in and out of the fantasy community, following her switch to writing historical fiction with her 2012 novel, *Bitter Greens*. Although she is equally likely to be found at general writer festivals and historical fiction community events, in her interview with us Forsyth quoted Terry Pratchett's line "Once a fantasy writer, always a fantasy writer." Forsyth returned to fantasy writing in 2017, with a collaborative small-press publication, *The Silver Well*. Forsyth leveraged her former strong attachment with the fantasy community to attract the publishing deal and market the finished work, but it was the social aspects of the genre world that she spoke of in our interview: "One of the things I've loved about *The Silver Well* is this feeling of community, the whole community being just behind us, helping us, being connected back into that really close-knit kind of village that we have in Australia."[38] This quote exemplifies the ideal of the genre-world cohesion and does so in deeply affective language.

Genre-world participants may be central or peripheral and, like Forsyth, may feel very welcome even when their attachment is a light one. Against this, though, genre worlds can exclude. They may do this by reproducing enduring structural inequalities, on the basis of gender or race, for example, limiting some people's ability to participate or lead. This includes awards that disadvantage some genre-world members. Lindy Cameron describes how the founding of the Davitt Awards, run by the Australian chapter of Sisters in Crime, was in part a reaction to perceived bias toward male writers in the genre world through the existing Australian awards for crime fiction, the Ned Kelly Awards. Cameron noted that leading women crime writers were not being acknowledged by the Ned Kelly Awards for their novels: neither Kerry Greenwood nor Marele Day won awards for their individual crime novels, though Day was awarded the nonfiction award for her book *How to Write Crime Fiction* and Greenwood received a Lifetime Achievement Award. These exclusions sparked a more general frustration about who won the Ned Kelly Awards for best novel: "We thought, well, it's always a bloke. It's always [renowned Australian crime writer] Peter Temple, if he has a book, or another bloke if he doesn't. And it got to the stage where Peter Temple, he said, 'This is embarrassing, I'm not putting my books in any, anymore.' . . . But that's why we started the Davitt Awards because women weren't getting a look in at all." When Sisters in Crime set up the Davitt Awards for crime fiction written by women (to accompany the existing Scarlet Stiletto Awards for crime short stories written by women), its founders were proactive in approaching publishers to source nominations. They saw this as a way to counteract the informal networks that supported male crime writers:

> [Cofounder Carmel Shute] proactively goes out and attacks every single publisher, and, no matter what they'd normally publish, she'd say, "Be aware the Scarlet, the Davitt Awards are coming up, and let us know if you've got any crime novel published by a woman in this last year," whereas . . . , for the Ned Kelly Awards . . . , whoever came with their nominations that would be the pool. [The organizer] wouldn't go actively seeking anyone else. And, so, I suppose in the first couple of years it was blokes who were doing it because they were friends of his or friends of friends of his.[39]

As Cameron shows here, active steps have to be taken to expand participation in genre worlds. The sociality that produces an affective sense of community can be exclusionary: relying on networks of friends and friends of friends may reproduce disadvantage.

Cameron also acknowledged the gendered inequity of review space: "The very limited review space in very limited newspapers that exists anymore . . . [i]t still tends to be male authors that get reviewed." Our investigations bore out her sense of inequity; from 2014 to 2019 in the *Australian,* the *Sydney Morning Herald,* and the *Age* (Australia's three most-read newspapers), 58 percent of crime writers reviewed were men. This is despite crime reviewers being 67 percent female. As Cameron says, "I do still think it's uneven because, you know, everything still is uneven, and until that changes . . ."[40]

While Gentill didn't think the gender dynamics of the crime world were too disadvantageous, noting that she had a female publisher, she did observe that female authors are treated differently at writer festivals: "It's an interesting thing, and I don't find it particularly awful, but I do find that people are harder on female writers on panels than they are on men. So sitting in the audience, you hear men be rude or bolshie and so on, and everybody thinks it's funny. And if a woman were to do that, she would be scorned. . . . I have seen women scorned for being overly assertive. . . . And, interestingly enough, those audiences aren't necessarily male." She also observed that "when I'm on a panel with men they'll talk to each other," although she described this as "unconscious," "especially with high-powered men. And they will talk straight over the top of your head. And they will throw to each other." She observed that this was more likely to happen at larger festivals: "When I go to the big festivals I'm on panels with men because there just seems to be more men on panels. And when I go to the small festivals I'm on panels with women. . . . So, you know, the little country festivals and so on, it can be an all-woman panel. Never happens at the big Sydney Writers Festival and so on."[41]

One of the effects of the sexism in the crime genre world, as Cameron's and Gentill's stories point to, is a kind of gender segregation, with separate communities for male participants and female participants. Gentill describes the crime community as "warm" but qualifies, "I'm experiencing the crime community as a female crime community. . . . I don't know necessarily what the crime community is like if you, if you were just, you know, in a coed cohort." Gentill reflects that "women seem to be connected and keep up friendships much more than men. . . . So, you know, I know when I appear on panels and so on, you often sort of make a Facebook connection with the females and have relations with them afterwards, and the men you will see when you're on a panel with them next."

The feeling of being excluded is felt subjectively and not limited, of course, to gender. Gentill observed that genre fiction was less diverse in general than literary fiction. Remembering a conversation with another crime writer, she recalled:

> We were having a chat about how we were the only two writers of color in crime that we knew and how weird that was because you would think that genre was more accepting than literary fiction because literary always has that aura of elitism about it. And, you know, there could be other reasons for it. It could be that writers of color choose to write literary fiction rather than genre, rather than genre particularly excludes them, but it's just, it was just an interesting thing. And then, ever since then I've just noticed how lacking in diversity genre is for some reason.[42]

Other interviewees noted the near absence of writers of color from Australian genre fiction. It is true that the genre worlds we observed were overwhelmingly white. One effect of this is that issues of racial and cultural inclusion and representation can be sidelined by white members in a genre world. Another effect is that writers of color are sometimes forced to identify either with their genre or with writers who share their cultural background. At the time we interviewed her, Indigenous Australian author Claire G. Coleman identified herself on her Instagram account as a speculative fiction author. We asked why she hadn't identified herself as a First Nations or Indigenous author in that bio, and her reply was that "every writer gets boxed, and it's a case of choosing which box you want to get stuck in" and that "when people think of Indigenous authors they think of memoir, historical fiction, and poetry . . . and I don't write any of those."[43] At that stage of her career, Coleman wanted primarily to affiliate with the genre of speculative fiction. What we see here is the way in which writing by those from marginalized groups tends to be grouped (by readers and the public) and marketed (by the publishing industry). Such groupings have an effect on whether and how people enter, participate in, and lead the communities of genre worlds.

The Effects of Genre-World Communities

Genre-world communities exert powerful positive as well as negative effects. The generally strong communities of genre worlds produce emotional attachments, intellectual satisfactions, and meaningful networked connections for readers, writers, and publishers. The community of genre worlds is generative in that it supports the production and, especially, circulation of genre texts, as an affective complement to the industrial processes of genre worlds. Genre communities support texts through mutual admiration and willingness to talk about texts. The quotes earlier from Hannett and Meyer about the excitement that a "bunch of mates" might generate for particular books is implicated in word-of-mouth promotion, a process in which readers, publishing industry professionals, and writers all participate. This may be informal, such as sharing enthusiasm about a book online, or formal, as in providing shout quotes for peers' publications or writing blog reviews. There is a clear link between the social and the industrial in genre worlds, with social links activated in order to achieve sales.

In fact, publishers are increasingly aware of the power of genre communities to influence the success of a book and have become adept at leveraging those communities into sales. Former publisher Rochelle Fernandez gave us an example: "We did try and start up our own kind of, like, focus-group-type thing. I mean, we didn't call it a focus group; we called it, like, a salon for spec fic readers to find out what they're reading, what they like, what they don't like about books."[44] In this account, genre communities are valued even as they are mobilized for audience development and marketing purposes, what Fernandez calls "trying to fish where the fish are." A slightly more cynical example from the United States involves the fan base for Victoria Aveyard's Red Queen fantasy series. Harper Teen created a fan site inviting readers to join the Scarlet Guard (the revolutionary band from the book). These fans were charged with sharing links across their social media in order to be rewarded with previews of content and cover art. This link sharing was pitched as "our mission for the week," ironically reimagining working free for a large multinational corporation as revolutionary sentiment. Dan Hassler-Forest contends that large media corporations display "frantic and increasingly canny efforts to direct the [fan] energy that has been unleashed in directions that will maintain the existing balance of power."[45] Deep attachments to genres help books circulate more widely.

For writers, specifically, the sense of support from a genre-world community can be generative at a diffuse level as well as the level of specific support for books. Genre-world communities can have profound effects in enabling and developing careers in what is a porous and ill-defined profession with few official entry points.[46] As Katherine Giuffre notes in relation to cultural sectors, including writing, careers are "built around social networks. . . . [Artists] must make connections with other art-world members . . . in order to make a living from their work."[47] These connections are social as well as professional, and there is a real sense in which the community aspects of genre worlds underpin their sustainability by ensuring the entrance of new writers and the viability of medium- and long-term writing careers.

Genre communities can create self-belief in writers. Angela Savage reflected on the value of the Sisters in Crime organization when she told us about its impact on another writer, Cate Kennedy: they "treated her like a writer from the onset and . . . just assumed she'd be writing more, and the kind of confidence that gave her was fundamental and that's sort of what they do."[48] To be taken seriously by peers can be enabling for a writer, especially in genres that may be seen as more frivolous or easy to ridicule. The self-belief of emerging writers is fostered through a range of genre-world practices, not least fan fiction, through which millions of readers are supported to try writing by modeling stories on existing works, often leading to the development of a genre as well as the pleasure and increased skill level of readers and writers.

At the professional level, long-standing relationships between writers in communities provide opportunities to build reputations—for example, through recommendation or collaboration. Australian fantasy author Deborah Biancotti had a solid but unremarkable career as a short-story writer in small press before her relationship with award winner Margo Lanagan and U.S. best seller Scott Westerfeld resulted in a collaboration, the young adult series Zeroes, which achieved New York Times best-seller status. Writers may also improve their craft over time through peer-mentor or critical-friend relationships, either formal or informal. The next section looks more closely at these collaborative connections and their contribution to the creation of genre texts, as this is perhaps one of the clearest ways to understand how social formations shape genre worlds.

Creative Sociality

Genre worlds produce texts. Implied in that statement is the act of creative writing: conceptualizing stories and capturing them on the page. This section is particularly interested in how creative practice is situated within genre worlds and what kind of social activities interweave with creative practice. Creative sociality exists on a wide spectrum. Critical relationships can range from consulting a fellow writer for feedback on an idea to submitting a complete manuscript to a beta-reading group for multiple perspectives. Collaborations, too, differ widely. They can represent more or less equal input from writers who develop ideas together, or franchise-like enterprises, such as Tom Clancy's Op Center, where story ideas are generated by one team and written by another. The results of critical relationships and collaborations are produced through the conventions of the genre world. These conventions dictate a range of understandings about who does what, who provides which resources, who gets credit for what, and so on; these are the accepted but not indelible protocols of the genre world. These socialized practices run counter to the persistent Romantic ideal of writers as solitary and gifted individuals who exist outside society and convention. The genre-worlds view of creative practice sees it as thoroughly social, materially embedded, and subject to conventions that produce certain behaviors.

Our notion of creativity in genre worlds connects meaningfully with twenty-first-century advances in the study of creativity, particularly the much-cited work of Vlad Petre Glăveanu and Lene Tanggaard, cultural psychologists who have written widely on the sociomateriality of creativity.[49] They argue that creativity has traditionally been seen "as a system of personality traits and cognitive abilities," leading to a model centered on the creative individual and their internal traits, such as cognition and personality attributes. However, they see creativity differently, building on the growing body of scholarship that positions creative individuals in their contexts. Such work includes Glăveanu's refining of the concept of "distributed creativity," which foregrounds interactions with social relations and material things in creative processes.[50]

Glăveanu's model identifies three paradigms for analysis of creative practice. The "He-paradigm" romanticizes creative genius and emphasizes exclusivity and disconnection. Creators appear to be chosen and special, and they are imagined to have to stand outside society in order to create. In fact, society is almost depicted as hostile to creativity. One of the most famous accounts of creative practice, Coleridge's memories of writing *Kubla Khan,* blames the poem's fragmentary nature on a "gentleman on business" who called at precisely the wrong moment. Glăveanu uses the term "He" deliberately, to show us that this figure has often been conceived of as male, as the "great man," reminding us that this cultural paradigm performs the work of excluding certain people and groups. What Glăveanu calls the "I-paradigm" is a democratic ideal that sees everyone as potentially creative. This understanding grew out of a late-twentieth-century interest in personality and cognition psychology as well as an uncertain sociocultural period in U.S. history during the Cold War and is still a highly individualistic paradigm: it "replaced the genius with the 'normal' person while keeping the individual as unit of analysis." As an advance on these two understandings of creativity, he offers the model of the "We-paradigm," a relational view of creative practice that sees it as part of, and distributed across, the system and ecology in which it resides.[51] Distributed creativity reveals that creative practice is located "not within people or objects but in-between people and objects."[52] In many cases, genre worlds exemplify this "We-paradigm." Our investigations identify the conventions around the social aspects of creativity in genre worlds and analyze from there the nature of these relationships and their potential impact on texts and on the genre world more broadly. We take as our points of analysis the critical and collaborative relationships between writers.

Genre writers, like many writers, form partnerships for feedback and critique on their work. There appears to be a high level of awareness about the value of critical partnerships in genre worlds, as evidenced by the many opportunities for formal mentorship and author training and the well-developed and widely used lexicon of "crit partners," "beta readers," "spitballing," "brainstorming," and so on. While writers may eventually be edited by agents and publishers, a privileged relationship exists between writers and their peers in terms of offering critique. As romance writer Anna Campbell told us, "You actually need someone else doing it to really understand. I mean, you know, with the best will in the world and no matter how much people love you, they don't understand what it's like to have those [characters] in your head. . . . [T]here's a whole stack of stuff that only really another writer understands." Cecilia Aragon and Katie Davis's study of fan-fiction communities bears out similar findings, drawing particular attention to the way the digital tools have enabled what they call "distributed mentoring."[53]

There are several types of critical feedback that genre-world writers provide for each other on their work. Romance author Bec Sampson, who enjoys a critical partnership with Rachael Johns, indicated to us the wide range of advice they offer one another: from ideas about "upcoming books" to "I've written this paragraph. Can you think of the word that I'm missing in this sentence?" Fantasy author Angela Slatter spoke of different writers offering her different expertise when they read her drafts: "Peter Ball is my structure maven. He can tell you what beats have gone wrong, which is always very helpful. . . . Alan [Baxter] is sort of general story. He can tell me if it's fun . . . , if it's working, and more about pacing. . . . Lisa [Hannett] is, I call her my alpha reader because she can look at everything."[54]

Slatter and fantasy author Lisa Hannett became critical partners after meeting in a formal learning environment in the genre world of fantasy fiction, the Clarion South writing workshop held in 2009. Both writers were producing work that might be labeled dark fantasy, shading into horror, with historical and mythical content. It was at Clarion that they affectionately adopted the nickname "brain" for each other. As Slatter explained, "One critique morning I think I said, 'I'm sorry. I've got nothing left because . . . Lisa is using the brain today.'" The image of a shared brain highlights the model of equal partnership they enjoy, a model supported by comparable success in publication histories (after long careers in short fiction, both launched their first novels in the mid-2010s) and their ability to collaborate effectively. Hannett provided a detailed explanation of how their critical-partner process works: "My role, I've always felt, has been just to ask questions. So I'll never go, 'Oh! You should make her do "that." [Instead, I will say something like] 'If she goes there, wouldn't "this" happen?' And she'll go, 'YEAH! Because then . . . ,' and her brain'll go off in some other direction." One of the enduring and most well-loved beliefs about creativity is what David Burkus calls "the Eureka myth." He writes that "we like it when the hero is stuck and suddenly the answer just comes to her."[55] The word "eureka," Greek for "I found it," comes from the story of Archimedes in his bath, seeing water displaced around him and formulating the method for measuring volume of irregular objects. The quotation above includes a eureka moment: the emphatic "YEAH" with which Hannett characterizes Slatter's moment of creative insight. But Slatter's eureka moment was

not an individualistic moment of genius. It arose out of iterative question-
ing. Once Slatter has her "YEAH," she takes control of the creative process
again, but she would not necessarily get there without Hannett to ask her
the questions. Hannett elaborates on this further:

> Angela and I have always, for her work, gone, "Okay, let's sit down
> and talk." . . . And so we'll Skype or we'll talk on the phone, if we're
> not in the same city, and she'll just go, "I'm really thinking that I need
> to do blah . . . 'cause this is what the character wants . . . ," and half
> the time I just ask questions, and sometimes I'll say, "But that doesn't
> make sense, 'cause just before you were saying that she was sup-
> posed to do 'that.'" So it's just sort of listening and responding to it.[56]

We can see, here, how Slatter tests her ideas while Hannett "listens and
responds." Slatter feels she "needs" to write a certain idea because "that's
what the character wants," almost as though there's no arguing with these
ideas; the agency is outside of her, in the character's hands, or subject to
some kind of abstract imperative. It is Hannett's ability to push back against
those (Romantic) ideas that allows Slatter to refine or reject them. Similarly, Slatter details the feedback Hannett provided on her early draft of *Vigil*
(2016), an urban fantasy novel featuring sirens and monsters that she developed from a short story published in 2010: "I was getting very short scenes
because I was writing it like a short story. . . . [Hannett] said, 'But what's
it look like around?' You know, more words." These quotations indicate
that feedback can range from the structural (books, chapters, overarching
plots, and character development) to the line level (words, sentences, paragraphs). Feedback may be on already completed work in draft stages, either
small parts ("critique") or entire manuscripts ("beta reading"). It may also
be at the conceptual stage ("brainstorming"), when large ideas (aspects of
premise and structure) are tested: Hannett says of Slatter, "Angela gets all of
these awesome ideas by talking things through aloud."[57]

Sometimes these creative conversations are mediated by digital tools.
Hannett described brainstorming with Slatter by "talking or jotting notes
down and emailing them back and forth." Similarly, Bec Sampson spoke
to us of her digitally mediated critique relationship with Rachael Johns.
She said, "I think what we do is we probably share thirty or forty emails a
day about everything, including writing and life because, we're both being
mums, that's . . . every day . . . so when she's away on tour, or I'm rarely

away by comparison, my inbox is quite down. We also Vox, which is messaging, speech messaging."[58] Sampson's mention of "writing and life" indicates how intertwined the professional and personal can be, reminding us again of the affective sense of community in genre worlds. In some ways, Sampson's comment underscores something very important about professional relationships between genre-world participants: that they are more likely to thrive among common circumstances as well as common interests. This may be why so many of the relationships we studied were female-to-female or male-to-male, writers at similar career stages or, like Johns and Sampson, writers with children. Online tools make those relationships easier to sustain around restrictions such as geography, time, and work.

Our interviewees spoke of these creative social relationships in overwhelmingly positive terms. As always, we remain alert to the fact that writers may speak positively because they are aware that to speak negatively may expose them in some way or reveal something they may prefer remains private. At the same time, though, we recognize that these relationships likely *are* positive. Not only do they often demonstrably assist writers to be productive and improve the quality of their projects, but they can be pleasurable experiences that grow out of and forge enduring friendships: they *work* in both creative and social terms. Another reason such relationships are recounted positively is that they are entirely voluntary. The opposite of a good creative social relationship is not a bad one; it is no relationship at all, and many writers do make the choice not to engage with critical partners or groups.

Some of the reasons writers offer for opting out of critical relationships alert us to conventions around power and influence in the genre world. For example, when Cecilia Dart-Thornton told us of her long-term friendship with renowned English author Tanith Lee, she stressed it was not a critical partnership because she didn't want to be "a leech sucking the goodness out of her." Stefanie London, who writes very quickly, eschews critical relationships because the imbalance in volume of work makes her concerned she is "taking more than I'm giving." Candice Fox's level of success made her feel "distanced" from the writers club she left.[59] In these examples, what is revealed is the distinctive complexions that power imbalances bring to creative relationships.

Anna Campbell stressed to us that a critical relationship "doesn't work if there's a huge disparity between you" in terms of career stage or writing ability. Her critical partnership with Annie West, which commenced in 2003, is marked by egalitarianism. Both are writers of many romance novels, though Campbell's are usually historical and West's are usually contemporary. Their relationship has endured, according to Campbell, due to mutual respect, trust, a good match in terms of abilities, and an appreciation of each other's work: "I really liked her work, like she liked mine, which is also important if you're critiquing." In terms of how that has affected Campbell's writing, she averred that West's influence has made "a huge difference to me actually."[60] This is a model of a highly equal relationship; its promotion of the ideal of egalitarianism characterizes the way genre communities present themselves.

Mentor-mentee relationships are another common type of critical relationship in genre worlds. Many writers credited mentors—both formal and informal—for helping them achieve their goals. Writers also appreciated the value of acting as mentors. Keri Arthur spoke of Robyn Enlund, a trusted beta reader whom she had relied on for critique for many years. Our subsequent interview with Enlund revealed that the critical partnership was not straightforwardly equal, although it was clearly reciprocal. Both Arthur and Enlund agreed that Enlund's input as a beta reader was invaluable, but Arthur often served a mentoring function in Enlund's career. Enlund said:

> It's equals in that when you're critiquing someone's work, your opinion is just as valid as the next person, whether you've just started writing or whether you've been writing for ten years. But on the other hand, Keri very much is a mentor and was a mentor right from the start. I was feeling very self-conscious about my work and feeling I wasn't good enough to continue on the path I was on, and I had a few emails from her that were pretty blunt [laughing]. "Robyn, don't be stupid. I want to see you at the meeting. You have to bring work. Print it out, or I'm coming to your house and I'm going to print it out for you" [laughing]. So, she didn't take any nonsense, and she basically held my hand and pulled me along with her.[61]

This quote is, on the one hand, an articulation of the flat hierarchy that is a convention of genre worlds, where writers of varying experience are treated as equal peers. On the other, it also reveals that some writers have more influence than others: the ability to compel other people for their own good is revealed in the twinned images of holding hands (friendship) and being pulled along (external force). According to romance publisher

Kate Cuthbert, mentors often "know about the writing and the craft, but also the marketing and the pitching and how to deal with commercial."[62] Arthur's influence with Enlund arises from her greater market success, not only because such success is a kind of proof of her expert knowledge of writing and craft but also because it has given her access to knowledge and power within the industry.

With the possibility of power imbalances in critical relationships comes the potential for questions over ownership of ideas. Our research showed that genre worlds have well-established conventions for deciding ownership that arise from critical relationships. In the example above where Hannett helped Slatter achieve her eureka moment, the convention dictates that the ownership of the idea stays with Slatter. Hannett was very clear that she can feel "invested and proud" if she felt she had improved Slatter's work but that no matter how closely they work, "obviously it's her book."[63]

This clear assertion of Slatter's ownership is interesting in the context of Slatter and Hannett's many coauthored publications, where ownership is shared. The conventions for acknowledging coauthorship arise out of the creative process, and coauthoring bears similarities to the critical-partnership process but is also different in fundamental ways. While there are still talking, testing, and brainstorming in the conceptualization phase, the composition of their coauthored work is shared. Slatter described her coauthoring with Hannett this way: "Whoever starts the story, whoever's got the spark for the story, writes about two thousand words and then sends it off, and the other one edits that and then writes the next two thousand words or until their brain is empty and then sends it back." Hannett described it in almost identical terms, using the verb "handball" (a term for passing the ball in Australian Rules football) for the exchange of partial drafts, emphasizing the team-like nature of the enterprise. This sharing of creative work is iterative and results in a text that has dispersed authorship. As Slatter says: "So that's, you know, that's probably five or six goes before you get to the end of the story and then three or four passes over the top again when it's a finished product to do the editing. And the result is that it doesn't sound like either of us. . . . [I]t sounds like just the third voice." This notion of the third voice was echoed by Sean Williams, who collaborates with Garth Nix: "A collaboration is, it's like a third writer—it's not me, it's not Garth, it's something in between." This third voice is available only through the testing and refining of ideas and execution and so represents an achievement beyond the sum of its parts. It also creates what Williams called "dilution of ownership," which allows writers a new level of objectivity in evaluation and a sense of shared endeavor: "They can also stand back and go, 'That's really good; you know, we made that together.'"[64]

Coauthored collaborations are a regular feature of genre worlds and often enunciate the convention of celebrating creative sociality. The collaboration between best-selling U.S. authors Cassandra Clare and Holly Black, for example, is often marketed through the newsworthy hook of their enduring friendship. Their third voice is attributed not only to this close relationship but also to the physical proximity of their writing practice, side-by-side sharing a laptop.[65]

James Patterson is an extremely high-selling thriller author whose career has included the development of many coauthoring relationships. Australian author Candice Fox, a successful crime novelist in her own right, is one of his coauthors; they have to date jointly written five books featuring detective Harriet Blue, from *Never Never* in 2016 to *Hush Hush* in 2019. In Fox's collaborations with James Patterson, a third voice is not an aim. As Fox told us, for their coauthored books, "I had to write in his style, simply because most people will buy James Patterson collaboration books because they want the James Patterson part. So, all of his collaborators write in his style." This style, which Fox learned as a child reading Patterson's books, includes no significant subplots, avoiding mixed perspectives, short chapters with narratively propulsive endings, and "things in it like explosions, and big guns. . . . And so that was loads of fun."[66]

This quote directly connects the textual conventions of genre (short chapters, explosions) with the social and industrial conventions of genre worlds, particularly the way that social power is linked to market success. Even though those conventions belong to the genre, a particular execution of them (Patterson's style) is chosen, not least for its sales potential. Market success gives a writer power in a collaborative situation; in the case of Patterson and Fox, that power is reflected in the paratext around *Never Never,* including the different sizes of the names on the cover and where the book is shelved in stores (with Patterson's books, not Fox's). In terms of the creative process, the negotiations that characterize the voice are jointly agreed upon and, in this case, were relatively clear. As Fox noted, "I understand that he's the boss and I'm working with him, . . . whereas I think if I collaborated with somebody less powerful that the whole thing would be messier." Nonetheless, Fox still described the process in similar terms to the collaborative practice of Slatter and Hannett, including Fox and Patterson pitching ideas to test them with one another and negotiating over the gender of the protagonist. One difference is that conversations about the work (which took place over email, intercontinentally) also included a raft of industry professionals—agents, editors, and more—who were copied into the emails between the coauthors:

> I had my agent and my publisher looking in on the whole process of working with James, and then all James's people, his assistants and all that sort of thing, were cc'd in on the emails. So when we assembled *Never Never* we had all of these people watching us do it and also my publisher and my agent, privately, saying, "Before you send that off to James, make sure that it's got this; make sure that it's got that. I'm not sure about this; I'm not sure about that." That sort of thing. So, the whole experience of writing *Never Never* was very mediated.[67]

High value in the market means this collaborative creative relationship is highly mediated by industry. Genre fiction has a close relationship with industry and can openly acknowledge economic requirements alongside creative desires.[68] Overall, the conventions of coauthorship in this writing partnership do not emphasize egalitarianism but rather openly acknowledge the power certain writers have in the market.

Other collaborative relationships also require a more codified approach, and this is particularly the case when there are more than two collaborators. As we noted in chapter 3, the writers who individually write in the shared Bull Rider series for Tule Publishing have a "bible," a shared style guide and resource, which Dunlop reveals includes "a mini synopsis of each of the stories, and it has a sort of a through thread of any story line that pulls through the entire series." Dunlop explained how this continuity is not just to keep the stories logical and plausible but also to create emotional connections that create pleasure for readers and writers:

> I had a wedding in my book that the engagement had happened in the book before, so the romance had been in the book before, so I said, "Okay, this is what I am going to do for a wedding for you, and here's what the bride's going to wear, and does that work for you?" She was thrilled, and so I put her wedding in my story, so you can, without too much effort and very little compromise in what you're

doing for your own individual story, you can actually connect books up quite nicely from author to author.

Email loops, or small groups of people who email one another, also play a creative role, particularly in the romance genre world. Our case study of Harlequin's American Extreme Bull Riders Tour series in chapter 3 needs expanding here, because an email loop played an important role in developing the shared creative project that began with a road trip, extending the mutual generation of ideas into a form of collaborative writing. Several of the Bull Riders authors mentioned the email loop to us, including Megan Crane, Kelly Hunter, and Meghan Farrell. U.S.-based author Barbara Dunlop offered detailed insights:

> It's not as much communication as you would think because each story does take off on its own, and as long as you've got the core elements and anything that you do that impacts others you need to let them know, and anything that needs to happen in your book or what the time frame is or what the weather is or who, and in this case, who wins, who gets hurt, and if there's, sometimes people will come up with an interesting character that's a little bit quirky and you want to use it in your book, then you can.

Dunlop notes that she finished her book earlier than some of the others. This meant she could advise or support others: "We had an email link so people could post on, I think it was probably Facebook, I can't even remember. But we had a link that we could use, before anybody even started writing theirs, I finished mine, so I would go in and answer questions if people wanted to know, sort of, what had happened."[69]

Interestingly, the platform is not significant enough for Dunlop to mention (she is not sure whether email or Facebook was used); it was the communication itself that was important. This communication collapses the sense of geographic distance, for Dunlop:

> They could be around the world or around the block. Kelly [Hunter, an Australian author in the group] sometimes emailed us at odd times, but you know, we're quite accustomed to time-line differences. I think everybody really just takes it in stride, and I email people who are, you know, one hallway down at the office, and I email

people who are halfway around the world. It's not really that much difference. I remember when Jane used to live in Seattle and I was in Yukon and she decided to move to California, and I thought, "Oh, you're moving so far away," and then I thought, "Yeah, I'm not even going to notice the difference."[70]

Different coauthoring conventions allow work in the genre world to be done. Even for writers who are not part of explicit collaborations, the sociality of genre worlds can inform their creative work. Some writers, who are nonetheless active participants in genre events, awards, and associations, prefer not to receive peer feedback on their own writing. Crime writer Garry Disher told us he believed he "wouldn't get any nourishment" from such a situation, while Michael Robotham noted, "There are some writers that are willing to open themselves up week after week, or show their manuscript material, and have it polished; I couldn't have done that."[71] Fantasy author Cecilia Dart-Thornton, in the writing of *The Ill-Made Mute,* "thought of myself as plodding along all by myself." But the genre world of fantasy supported Dart-Thornton's creative practice in other ways. One was the acquisition of genre competence through reading and analyzing previous genre texts:

> There's one very clear time in my life. I was in my teens, I was reading Tanith Lee, and I was absolutely almost spellbound by some of her phrases and some of her paragraphs, and I said to myself, "These are so beautiful, I want to copy them out." So, somewhere in my files of teenage writings, I've got pages of little paragraphs I've copied, I've actually copied word for word from her. Partly because I thought they were so beautiful I wanted to have them, you know what I mean, to preserve them, and partly because I wanted to know what it felt like for a thought to come from my brain down my hand onto the paper the same as her thought was when she wrote it.[72]

This quote provides a compelling material expression of the concept of influence. If genre competence is a version of learning through imitation and repetition, Dart-Thornton's process of developing her craft is the apotheosis of that. In that way, it is characteristic of the conventions of genre worlds and the dynamic sociality that includes members who may never have met or interacted (although Dart-Thornton eventually became great friends with Lee). It is also characteristic of the conventions of genre worlds in that it is reverent and passionate about genre texts: words such as "spellbound" and "beautiful" underpin an impulse to "preserve" a readerly experience.

Other writers choose not to invite peer feedback on their work because they prefer to receive their formative feedback from industry professionals rather than other writers. Forsyth put it this way: "Each new editor that I worked with taught me something new, and sometimes the things that they taught me were things that I already knew dimly but had not applied in my own writing." Noongar speculative fiction writer Claire G. Coleman's early feedback came via an Indigenous Writing Fellowship via the organization black&write!, which pairs unpublished manuscripts with trainee Indigenous editors. Indigenous Editing Fellowship recipient Grace Lucas-Pennington (now director of black&write!) describes working with Coleman's manuscript, which presents as history for the first several chapters and then quickly and shockingly reveals it is in fact something else, to ensure the "twist" was preserved: "How many times can we use the word 'alien landscape' before it's too much? How much can we . . . you know, calling them 'mounts' instead of 'horses' in the early part and all that kind of thing and just putting as much description as possible in about the landscape and what's around so that people were just picturing people there and not the toads [aliens] until later on." While Lucas-Pennington and Coleman both cite *The Lord of the Rings* as a favorite book, and the work described above relates to the genre of the work, their work relationship was based on their Indigenous Australian identity (as they were both recipients of the fellowship). Coleman describes the value of Indigenous writers working with Indigenous editors simply: "You don't have to explain any of the issues because they know them."[73]

Coleman, at the time of our interview, identified as a "science fiction writer" rather than as an Indigenous writer, because "saying the word 'Indigenous' implies that . . . Indigenous is a genre, and it's not. . . . [E]very Indigenous writer's different." Yet Coleman has one of the more transient attachments to the fantasy genre world that we discussed above. While she told us she had belonged "a little bit" to the fantasy community "back in Perth like four million years ago," she had, at the time of speaking to us, not attended a fantasy con or a fantasy awards ceremony. By contrast, she had "been invited to every [Australian] capital city literary festival so far except for Canberra and Hobart." The mixed identification, both in and out of genre, that characterized the development of her manuscript carries through into the marketing of the book. Publisher Robert Watkins says, "We did market it as debut literary fiction, and I don't think even, I mean in the metadata, I think, it actually is coded towards science fiction still anyway."[74] Ultimately, *Terra Nullius* won two fantasy prizes, the Aurealis Award and the Norma K. Hemming Award, and was also short-listed in the Australian women's award for literary fiction and nonfiction, the Stella Prize. Coleman's career is a striking example of how the supportive social relationships of a genre world may intersect with other book-culture communities.

Conclusion

The chapter has examined in detail how social interactions form genre worlds. The social formations of genre worlds are constituted formally and informally and exert influence on author careers, reader experiences, and genre fiction texts themselves.

The most important formal social structures that organize genre worlds are voluntary associations, which administer awards, run conventions, provide training, and more. The associations, importantly, are generated from within genre worlds, by people with passionate investment in a genre. They are structures that arise from, and then continue to produce, an affective experience of community—if not for all participants, then for many of them—and this is their key reason for being. Features of this community include frequent expressions of shared love for the genre, an expectation of participation, and established channels for transfer of knowledge. Furthermore, genre worlds tend to idealize flat hierarchies, even though this idealization exists uneasily alongside differential levels of success and expertise.

The social aspects of genre worlds leave their traces on genre-world texts. The second part of the chapter examined how this happens by looking at the forms of relationship that undergird writers' production of genre fiction texts. Such relationships include writers' groups and courses, relationships with editors, mentorships, collaborations, and coauthorships. They also include assertions of the borders of this shared creativity and writers who choose not to share aspects of their genre-writing practice. Sociality is a layer of genre worlds, influencing how the norms and practices of genre fiction develop and how genre fiction texts are produced and circulated. The next chapter turns to an investigation of the formal and informal tools and mechanisms by which genre-world sociality is cultivated, communicated, and sustained.

. . .

Now, if only you could identify that dark figure standing at the back of the room. You approach as he lights a cigarette, the match flame momentarily illuminating his rugged face. "At last you're here," he says. "I've been trying to get a message to you . . ."

CHAPTER 5

Genre Sociality Online and in Person

Genre worlds are created through and defined by collective activity. As shown in the previous chapter, the collective activity in genre worlds is sometimes highly community minded, even when it has professional goals. The professional and the enjoyably social are difficult if not impossible to separate out in genre worlds: community and creativity intertwine. This is not to say that every professional relationship will also necessarily be a friendship but that the tools and practices of friendship and professionalism overlap significantly.

In these social interactions both private and public behavior are in play, and genre-world participants must regularly negotiate the boundaries between the private self and the public self. Two of the most interesting ways this negotiation plays out are through digitally mediated interactions and through in-person events. This chapter considers these two modes of social behavior and shows how they overlap yet each play a distinct role in the formation of genre worlds. First, we pay attention to digital communication tools and their influence on genre worlds. The rise of digital technologies has produced a host of ways in which the participants in a genre world can communicate with one another, and these communications contribute in key ways to the production and circulation of genre texts. However, genre-world professional sociality also rests significantly on in-person interaction, particularly via the genre-world major event, the convention (or con). We consider both types of sociality in turn and find ourselves a little more in the frame than we are used to.

Online Sociality and Genre Worlds

Online sociality is constituted through acts of communication that are shaped by the affordances of digital technologies, especially the platforms on which they occur.[1] José van Dijck's influential *Culture of Connectivity: A Critical History of Social Media* proposes a model for analyzing platforms as microsystems composed of technocultural components (coding technologies, users, and content) and socioeconomic elements (ownership status, governance, business models); each microsystem interacts with others in a connected media ecosystem.[2] This view of digital platforms allows for a granular and historicized analysis.

Social media is integrated into many stages of the creation and circulation of books, from writing to marketing to reception, and while not all writers or publishing professionals or readers use social media actively, for those who do it can influence their careers. A vigorous debate about a book or an amusing chat between writers might take place on Twitter; a writer's Facebook page might advertise details of their book launch; the creative writing platform Wattpad might feature thousands of reader comments on a new writer's first novel; an email loop might be the venue for a lengthy discussion about emerging trends.

Each of these platforms shapes communications, and therefore online sociality, differently. Twitter, for example, is an older social media site, launched in 2006 and widely adopted around 2008; unlike newer image- or video-based platforms such as Instagram, Snapchat, and TikTok, it focuses on words.[3] Twitter was mentioned frequently by our interviewees and is one of the most popular social media platforms for writers, publishers, and other book-culture people and institutions. It can be used in a broadcast-like way to send announcements about new books or as a forum for writers to perform success and abjection; it is also strongly oriented towards back-and-forth conversation, so that writers and readers can communicate with one another in ways that appear direct and rapid.[4] Most tweets (apart from private direct messages or those in locked accounts) are publicly visible, and hashtags can be used to group and thereby increase the visibility of discussions on different topics. Users can elect to follow one another (or not), shaping the appearance of the website on the user's device, as well as creating a visible hierarchy of popularity.

One technocultural component of each social media platform is privacy settings, which strongly influence the nature of communications.[5] In genre worlds, publicly visible social media exchanges expand genre-focused social opportunities for everyone from best-selling authors to occasional readers. Private communication options on platforms such as Facebook and everyday tools for online sociality such as email and messaging apps create opportunities for intensified genre connections that accelerate skill development and knowledge transfer for making books. Working through these two broad categories in turn—public acts of online communication and private or semiprivate acts of online communication—shows how digital affordances shape the formations of contemporary genre worlds.

Social Media as an Entry Point to Genre Worlds

For some writers, social media is a soft entry point to a professional career—a way of dipping one's toes into the waters. This was the case for crime writer Emma Viskic, the author of *Resurrection Bay* and other award-winning novels set in Melbourne and featuring deaf detective Caleb Zelic. Viskic originally wrote for pleasure and then with more serious aspirations but didn't show anyone her work for ten years. Her moment of professionalization, or entering the genre world publicly, came when she attended a crime-writing festival and was inspired by the advice of a speaker to submit short stories to competitions. This sounds like a story of traditional publishing entry points (a prize) and the importance of live events (festivals)—and it is. But Viskic learned of the festival through Twitter, demonstrating the symbiosis between live and digital events in contemporary book culture.[6] Viskic's first experience of genre-world sociality was through social media: "I didn't know anyone in the writing world at all. I wasn't in a writing group. I wasn't on social media, and I think a friend of mine, about that time had said, 'Join Twitter because you'll start meeting people who know about writing. You'll meet editors and you'll meet writers.'" Twitter has had an ongoing importance in Viskic's career and development as a writer, including directing her to resources that help her learn about the writing craft and the industry. Viskic told us that she reads a lot of articles about writing, noting that "Twitter is great for this because people post things that I put a little bookmark in and read, and so I'll just be, in a magpie-like way, I'll just dip into things." Twitter also led Viskic to one of her most significant professional and developmental relationships, with her mentor, U.K.-based editor Janette Currie:

When [*Resurrection Bay*] was almost finished, I came across a thing on Twitter called . . . Twitter is coming into this a lot . . . it's called the WoMentoring Project, which is very new and they were just setting it up, and it's basically a group of writers who wanted to give other up-and-coming writers the opportunity to be mentored, and a lot of people, from literary agents to writers and editors, offered their services, and so I applied for a mentorship through that and got a mentorship with a writer and editor called Janette Currie, and she guided me through the last draft of it. That was a writing course, yeah, just condensed. It was incredible.[7]

Currie's participation in the scheme had also come about through Twitter: when we asked her how she became involved in the WoMentoring project, Currie replied, "The short answer is I responded to a tweet from [British writer] Kerry Hudson when she was thinking about setting up a mentoring scheme for unpublished female writers."[8] After connecting via the Twitter-based program, Viskic and Currie corresponded by email, taking their public online sociality to a more private online mode.

Twitter also influenced how Viskic chose her publisher, then-new Bonnier imprint Echo; Viskic had "been following what they were looking for, you know, little statements or tweets and things, and I just thought that it feels right." Viskic's publisher, Angela Meyer of Echo Publishing, recounted her history with Viskic, describing her as an author "who I found on Twitter," elaborating that "I might have followed her and then seen that she'd won some short-story prizes."[9] Echo in its early years was notably open to online platforms as a source of manuscripts, seeking out authors on crowd-funding platforms, Twitter, and Facebook: this practice not only marks out new digital publishing industry logics but also embeds the publisher in a publicly visible online social formation.

Connections made over Twitter may flourish in person, too. Another Echo-published crime writer, Iain Ryan, found a supportive, informal professional network through an initial interaction on Twitter. As he recounted, making friends with mentor Andrew Nette over Twitter was "probably the only good thing that's ever happened to me in my life because of Twitter":

When I landed here [in Melbourne, after moving from Brisbane] I didn't know anyone. I mean, I had friends from the music industry, but

I was in a different stage of life by the time I got down here. And, actually, I think what I had was, I had that offer from Broken River to put the book out, and I think I put something on Twitter, like "Does anyone have any advice for me about how to publish books?" Or something like that, but I didn't think I'd get anything back. I thought I might get someone sending me a think piece on "five things you should know about getting published" or something. And he messaged me back and said, "I'll have a beer with you; if you buy me a beer, I'll tell you everything I know about publishing." Or something like that. And I had every intention of self-publishing the first novel, and that night on about his third or fourth pint, he was just like, "You're insane if you think that turning down this publisher is a good idea." And he was the reviews editor for *Crime Factory Journal* at that point.

Now, Ryan said, "we go to the pub all the time, it's like, I'm like, actually a friend. So. Yeah. That's the great thing about Melbourne."[10] As with Viskic's festival attendance, live and digital social interactions work symbiotically in this account. It should also be noted that the live components of these encounters also depend on the city of Melbourne's capacity to function as a literary center. Interactions may begin on Twitter but can quickly move to the physical site of a local pub, or a festival, where the concentration of writers (including crime writers) in Melbourne enables the social connection to flourish.

The important hinge between live and digital interactions is also described by fantasy author Lisa Hannett in talking about Facebook. In the early stages of her career, Facebook allowed her to both connect with others and demystify writing and writers. Hannett told us:

Facebook played a huge part in making that invisible wall go away. When you just start to see everyone on Facebook and just see them doing their regular everyday stuff, and talking about struggles with publishing and talking about not having their stories published and sort of realizing that no matter how far along you are, everybody's still going through the same sort of "I submitted my thing and it got rejected!" or "I've had a success, hooray!" And then you can use that as a platform to talk to people at conventions, face-to-face, so you don't have to do the small-talk kind of crap that I hate. Where you already know, so you don't have to go, "What are you writing?" And then you have to give the elevator pitch and synopsis. No. I already know what you're writing 'cause I've seen you on Facebook and I've met you once or twice or I've seen you on a panel at a convention, and so you can get straight into just talking to them, like a normal person, instead of having to do the awkward stuff that is just too nerve-racking.[11]

Hannett explicitly suggests that Facebook allowed her to move from being "an outsider" to an insider, with inside knowledge of other writers, which she could build on at live events such as conventions. Note, too, how discussion of professional activity—including current projects and the oft-cited "elevator pitch" for bringing commercial interest to a manuscript—is characterized here as "small talk." Hannett sees Facebook as a way to deal with the necessary and potentially nonsocial aspects of genre-world engagement; the Facebook interaction allows a kind of presocializing, where the important professional work of networking can be dealt with, so that the purely social (or performance of the social) is free to proceed in other venues without reference to the market. This presocializing highlights the blend of digital and in-person interactions that characterize genre-world sociality.

Online Sociality, Marketing, and Parasocial Relationships

There is, undeniably, a commercial aspect to public online sociality, however fuzzy, opaque, or indirect this may appear at times. As media scholars Nick Couldry and José van Dijck put it, "The social is big business."[12] Not only do social media platforms extract data from users for profit, but individual users often seek economic as well as personal benefit from their activities.[13] Marketing of both books and authors has long been a component of social media practices and is becoming increasingly refined for some genre-world participants (especially multinational publishers).[14] In general, the authors we interviewed were highly aware of the role of social media in marketing and how this has affected conventions in their genre world. Fantasy author Kate Forsyth reflected, perhaps wistfully, on the changes in the media landscape since her first publication: "The world has changed enormously since the fantasy books were published twenty years ago. So how we market our books has changed dramatically as well. So yes, I can see a distinct difference in the way that the books are being marketed, but that is as much a part of the fact that we now have social media."[15] Iain Ryan was more explicit about his love-hate relationship with Twitter:

My publicist was, "I don't need to worry about you—you've got social media sorted out," and I do teach a bit of marketing here [at a university]. So I have a very clinical relationship with [social media platforms], I suppose. I don't enjoy them like I used to. . . . It introduced me to Andrew and all of those people; there's no doubt that that has been helpful. . . . Now it's promotional. I think there's ten notifications waiting for me in Twitter every day at the moment, but it's all to do with trying to sell the book. There's no one saying, "Hi."[16]

The sense of mourning in this account is reflected in other interviews that register the loss of social media as a place for private friendship. Such loss is exacerbated by the perception that social media has shifted the task of marketing from publishers to authors. For example, romance author Kelly Hunter told us that "the move from print to digital meant that individual authors had to pick up their digital presence online and do more digital promo and social media and kick that into gear." This has positives, for some authors—such as enabling authors from peripheral markets to interact with readers from other countries, and thereby increase access to international markets. As Australian romance author Anna Campbell told us: "The other thing too that puts you on a level playing field was social media, because you can actually talk to your readers in real time. And it doesn't matter that you're in Australia; they can still talk to you in real time. So I actually think that it's a lot easier now to talk to a worldwide audience than it was ten years ago."[17] Savvy authors reflect on the strategic uses of different social media and digital platforms—which may or may not include selling books. For example, well-networked author Angela Savage recounted to us:

I was in Arizona this year, which was fascinating, with a couple of very successful writers and they were talking about social media and its utility or not to their careers, and the general gist was you don't sell books on Twitter; you can interact with your fan base if you so choose, but that's about it. Their thought was the best use of social media was around newsletters and targeted to people who've signed up to receive them and link to book releases and book signing opportunities and events and that kind of thing. Otherwise, they were pretty lukewarm on what the value of it was. . . . Twitter I tend to use also for Q&A, a little bit for promotion, and a lot for live events.

So I like tweeting live events. I really enjoy that, and I love following events when I can't be there. I think that's kind of interesting, and some interesting discussions come out of that, and some interesting resources come out of that. But I don't think, I'm not convinced that any of those things sell books.[18]

Many of our interviewees, like Savage, made use of a diffuse third-person mode to describe the impacts of social media—what Savage summarizes as the "general gist"—which shows the information gathering that is still taking place around these emerging aspects of book culture, as participants contrast their own practices and experiences with those of their peers. Discussions of social media in contemporary genre worlds are often marked by a hesitancy that suggests prevailing uncertainty, and at times discomfort, concerning social media's effects. Gathered intelligence is transformed into received wisdom and rules of thumb, as genre-world participants search for new norms to guide their behavior online.

For authors, a clear path between reader engagement on social media and the actual sale of books cannot yet be drawn. What is available, however, is a sense of connection among authors and readers that adds an intimacy to this public space. One of the effects of a heightened use of social media for book marketing is that it more closely interweaves parasocial intimacy into the marketing process.[19] An example of this is crime author Sulari Gentill, who is active online. Her publisher, Alison Green, said to us: "She's also just very responsive, and I think, on social media, she really does truly engage with people who enjoy her books. She speaks to them. She responds to everything that comes her way."[20] Social media's commerciality is enmeshed in a discourse and etiquette of intimate (para)social relations, which contributes to the overall sociality of the genre worlds.

Our research suggests that this sense of intimacy is particularly strong in the romance genre world. For example, agent Amy Tannenbaum said: "I would say probably the biggest thing that I see in the romance genres that authors have a very close relationship with their readers in a way that's uncommon in other genres. So they make them, they tend to make themselves more accessible than authors of other genre fiction. You know, they're very active on social media, and that plays a big part into their success and plays a big part into them being able to spread their word, the word about their new books, and get people excited about upcoming

releases." From the publishing industry perspective, social media marketing hinges on the connection between readers and authors. Beverley Cousins, a publisher from Penguin Random House, sums it up as follows: "I
think people . . . also feel a bit closer to the authors. I mean, we do encourage our authors to not spend all their time on social media but to have at
least one platform where they can feel—that the readers can feel that they
can interact whether we run it or whether the author runs it, but we try
and have that so that people can become more locked into a brand name
or locked into an author in a way."[21] The connection here is not directly
between engagement and sales but between engagement and brand; the
presumption is that a well-developed author brand can in time be leveraged to achieve sales. Moreover, among the language of branding, we can
also see the language of feeling. Affect is also part of social media, creating
loyalty or a sense of knowing an author, which can, of course, be leveraged
for sales.

Cousins showed a refined sense of how online sociality can support book
marketing at the multinational corporate level:

> What's been great about the merging of Penguin and Random
> House is we've now got this massive social media platform. We have
> so many people on our mailing lists and on our newsletters and our
> Facebook and our Twitter feeds that we actually think we can make
> quite a difference with our social media promotion. And because
> we've got such a large, sort of, readership now for subscribers, that
> we can actually narrow them down so we can actually see their pro-
> file and we can work out "They read crime fiction, so we won't target
> them with everything." We'll just send them, "Did you know there's
> a great thriller coming out you might want to read?" So it's going
> straight to the people who would probably pick it up.[22]

This quote shows publishers cannily targeting readers based on affinities and interests: in effect dividing a mass readership into genre worlds.
Rather than relying on the small reach and individuality of an author, this
is done via a multinational publishing company, which has large reach and
resources for social media and can target efficiently. Here, the line between
social media engagement and sales is far clearer. It is interesting to note,
too, that in some cases the publisher will step in and boost social media for
unwilling authors: as Cousins said, "Social media's brought the reader and

the author—probably less the publisher—but the author and the reader a bit closer together. And when the author doesn't want to do that, we tend to do it on their behalf," although presumably this would only be for high-selling authors with established readerships. This practice raises questions about how personal an author's voice can be online and whether this matters to readers. Social media allows the social to be performed publicly: sometimes by writers who enjoy it, sometimes by writers who do not enjoy it, and sometimes by somebody else altogether.

The Limits and Borders of Public Online Sociality

Public online sociality is not an omnipresent, ubiquitous free-for-all but has formal and informal limits between and within platforms. While genre-world participants can sometimes imagine social media as a vague morass—for example, Harlequin editor Flo Nicoll said to us that a blog we mentioned "rings bells with that sort of social media stuff that I've seen"— they also carry a sense of its borders. As Nicoll went on to tell us in another section of her interview, for example, social media marketing opportunities are often tied to national markets, because they require responses from authors who are "on the ground" and available for live events that complement digital marketing efforts. Social media cannot always substitute for offline or physical acts of sociality, either in terms of marketing or in terms of relationship building. Telling us about an author she worked with remotely, Nicoll reflected: "I knew what she looked like through kind of promo stuff, and she knew what I looked like on social media, but we've never actually met. . . . I think that can be really hard for authors because you're kind of putting all of your trust and faith in someone who you don't have that kind of face-time opportunities with."[23] In Nicoll's estimation, physical proximity can improve trust. This can be difficult when geographical distance and conflicting time zones force reliance on digital communication; even though tech giant Apple may promote an application called FaceTime, it is no substitute for actual "face time" when doing publishing business internationally.

As well as the connections and divisions between physical and digital forms of contact, there are distinct spheres of engagement online. Romance blogger Kat Mayo notes informal clusters that form, even via public online platforms:

When we get these books that are flash points, even if they're smaller flash points, the readers will find each other. So, Goodreads readers who loved *Fifty Shades* will look at other readers who reviewed *Fifty Shades* and loved them, and they'll start initiating conversations and form little groups. And so I've actually started looking more, going back to Goodreads a little bit more, because I really want to understand this new crop of readers, because I feel like I'm not connected to them, because I'm so tightly connected to the blogs that started in 2002, 2004, 2008.[24]

Mayo's account here recalls the affinity-spaces theory of Gee discussed in chapter 4 and modified there for genre worlds: social formations cluster around shared interests, with in-groups and out-groups established multiple ways, including by generational shift and preferred platform. Clusters may form around a particular website; book blogs, for example, tend to address audiences of like-minded readers. On Goodreads, the clustering of readers is encouraged through themed discussion boards and the discursive mode of addressing other readers in reviews (use of the second person to make recommendations, offer advice, or request help interpreting a book).[25] Public online platforms can thus create subcommunities within genre worlds, even at the same time as public communications allow interested outsiders to learn more about the subgroup's interests.

The multiple groups within the public online sociality of genre worlds reveal another feature of this form of activity: unequal power relations. Mayo is particularly insightful on the different roles played by authors and readers when they interact: "The author-reader relationship, I think it benefits the author a little bit more. I don't mean that it doesn't benefit the reader, because the reader loves it; it's just for many of us it's like meeting a celebrity. Even authors we don't know, it still feels like you're meeting an actor—you've just never seen their movie, but they must be good; they've been in a movie. But because there's that sense of privilege to meet an author, I think the dynamic is much different." Mayo told us that authors have "said to me, the best way to get a loyal readership is to be their friend. And they don't mean that in a sarcastic way, 'pretend to be their friend,' but actually be nice to them and treat them well" but notes, "that relationship can often be fraught with conflict of interest, and it's fine if you're just a reader, but when you start doing things like reviews, when you start doing things that

in the traditional sense would be considered publicity, it becomes really difficult and personally for me even it's really like a quagmire of ethics." For
Mayo, the commingling of roles such as friend, writer, reader, reviewer,
and blogger may result in imbalances of power and feelings of conflict. She
elaborates that, in relation to the romance genre world, "there's a culture
of niceness, I guess, which is great if you're an author, because authors, the
way RWA works, and this always really is obvious when romance authors
talk about RWA; it's a support structure it provides for authors. . . . So it
can be really confronting to read reviews of books, of your books, outside
of that sort of protective shell of the romance writing network." When
authors depend on a genre world's social dimension for support—to the
point where positivity becomes an expected norm—this can limit the com-
municative possibilities for other genre-world participants. Conversely, con-
troversies may erupt online, or public online spaces may develop critical
norms, and this can be experienced as unfriendly for authors. For authors
without genre-world community networks, such as debut writers publishing on Wattpad and other self-publishing platforms, online criticism can be
especially difficult to process. As Mayo reflects, "You go to like, for example,
Wattpad, which I'm so fascinated by. . . . I actually think a lot of self-published authors don't have the armor to kind of be distant from their books,
and when people criticize their books, they feel it very personally, which is
unfortunate but understandable. And the biggest example of this is when
you go to Goodreads: it's like a minefield of reader-author relationships."[26]
The minefield of relationships that Mayo refers to includes a spectrum of
tense interactions; one striking example is author Kathleen Hale's physical
pursuit of a Goodreads user who gave her a negative review.[27] Participating
publicly in online book talk can flare up into controversy, or just discomfort.
This discomfort can be exacerbated in tight-knit genre-world formations.
For example, writer Angela Savage told us: "I used to blog a lot. I haven't
blogged for ages, and I sort of, I used to review a lot, and I can't review
anymore because I just know everyone and it's just too undermining. . . .
It's like everyone's in the room when you're out there on social media.
It's the same with Facebook. It is a relatively small community, and we do
tend to know each other."[28] Participating in public online discussions is like
being in any social formation: the perceptions and feelings of others cannot
be ignored or discounted, and this is more intensely felt when the digital
relationships have a live counterpart, and especially in a small-to-medium

market where the chances of meeting the person you have reviewed badly are very high: "everyone's in the room." This is another way that online genre-world behavior is impossible to completely separate from in-person genre-world behavior.

Public online sociality is an important component of twenty-first-century genre worlds. It offers an entry point to genre worlds, where emerging writers or new publishers can encounter other participants in the world. For many participants, this is a sustaining and pleasurable activity. Participants are more ambivalent about the marketing aspect of public online sociality. Because it has a reader-facing element, online social behaviors also function as a kind of marketing, and this perceptibly falls on the shoulders of authors rather than publishers (even when it is mediated or undertaken by publishing professionals), as this is a realm that values parasocial intimacy. And finally, while public social media platforms are global, there are limitations to their transnational reach. Often, there is an offline element to social media conversations—a move to in-person contact—that reveals some of the hard limits to apparently unfettered online interactions. Meanwhile, public online space forms into clusters, filtered by technological affordances or behavior and based on affinities, which means that genre worlds are not completely open, even online, but can be effectively or informally closed to new entrants. Such clustering is even more acute when online communications do not take place in public.

Private or Semiprivate Online Interactions: Facebook and Email

Private or semiprivate forms of online sociality run through the social formation of genre worlds, serving a number of important functions. Emails and private messages are part of the routine business of publishing as well as ways of fostering intimacy and personal connection. Much emailing behavior consists of confidential routine transactions, such as brokering deals and communicating with agents. In this it replaces the telephone, although as editor Nicoll notes, many authors still use the phone, often combining this with email for follow-up tasks: "The communication tends to be driven by what the author prefers, and so I've worked with a lot of authors in my eight years and the bulk of them have wanted to speak on the phone, and so I would . . . , like, first thing when I got into the office and just make my cup of tea and call them, and we do a lot of email in terms of working through manuscripts." Other confidential online tools regularly used in publishing include collaboration programs such as Basecamp, where, as publisher Anna Valdinger tells us, "everyone can post up files or questions or, so there's very much joined-up communication between all the [international] teams," or Facebook Workplace, which Angela Meyer describes as "just like Facebook where you can post updates and things like that and there's different groups."[29] In these semiprivate spaces, groups are defined and limited. Writers also form semiprivate online communities, where some aspects of communication may be public, but most are not: for example, the existence of a Facebook group may be publicly available information, but the content of posts is visible only to members. These different types of private or semiprivate online communications serve a range of functions in contemporary genre worlds.

Private or Semiprivate Online Spaces as Nurturing Writers
In contrast to the sometimes confronting nature of public online sociality, private online spaces can feel far more supportive for genre-world participants. Semiprivate groups can provide a key source of social support for deprofessionalized and often isolating tasks, such as writing. As Angela Slatter put it: "as a writer sitting at home on your own, and, you know, Facebook is my only friend." That social support is linked to professional goals. For example, Sean Williams speaks of the value of an email group he belongs to, which spans the globe: "You know, it's a level playing field across the world. It used to make a huge difference if you came from Australia." Likewise, Mitchell Hogan told us, "I'm in a closed Facebook group with a lot of hybrid authors, those who both traditionally publish and self-publish."[30] This is a way in which Facebook groups can nurture professional knowledge as well as social connections.

However, private groups also have their limitations. Candice Fox speaks of a Facebook group she belongs to called "The Whine Cellar," expressly set up for professionally successful writers to "whine" about career events that may arouse envy or accusations of ingratitude in the general community.[31] Fox said:

> Already I'm finding that, even inside there, there are things that you can whinge about and things that you can't. You can't say, "I sold the TV rights to this woman, and I wanted to sell them to someone

else, and now I can't for three years." There would be other writers in there that would be like, "I *dream* of selling TV rights, or having someone interested . . ." So, I'm very careful to not sound like I'm bragging or like I'm whingeing about things that other people would desperately want.[32]

This is a delicate balancing act for an author, signaling some of the insider and outsider dynamics that can persist even in inner circles of genre worlds.

On the whole, though, private or semiprivate spaces lead to less self-censorship than public groups. This is particularly important, in blogger Mayo's account, for groups of invested genre readers, who may be unwilling to criticize authors in public:

> I think readers interacting as readers is really valuable, because when you take the author out of the discussion you have a much more honest, much more candid, interaction, but when the author is in the discussion, even as a potential observer, so when you go online there are people who will never rate a book below a three, because they feel that that will do a disservice to the author, whereas when you're talking to your friends or your book club about a book, I don't think anyone would hesitate to say, "I hated this book . . ."[33]

For readers, a private online discussion is somewhat akin to a book club, a space where a smaller group can discuss books with greater freedom than they would in public.[34] In addition to the intimacy of the small group, this is, perhaps, an instance of traditional roles reasserting themselves—even though digital technologies sometimes blur the line between author and reader, at other moments the distinction is strongly felt.

Private online groups can also be a safer place to experiment with new work and ideas, refreshing genre worlds and allowing new entrants. For example, two semiprivate online social formations were important for fantasy writer Cecilia Dart-Thornton. Dart-Thornton, who is not heavily engaged in the kind of writing relationships outlined in chapter 4 (as she says, "I can't share it [her manuscript]. . . . As soon as I do that, it shatters something"), found that she could show her work to a structured online writing group. She says:

> My other way of testing it out was when I found out about online writing workshops, and I'm talking the year 2000, well, actually, 1999

here, and the Internet was this new thing, this frontier, and there was, wow, there was actually an online writing workshop. Yeah, that's a first. Who would have thought? It was run by Del Rey. There were a few different ones, but this one seemed the most genuine. Some of them just seem to be run by who knows who. So there were actual editors looking after it, etc., and in my, in this mind here, this tool here, I thought, "Okay, I can pretend," because I often play mind tricks on myself, as I just told you. "I can pretend that these people in cyberspace aren't really real, so if any of them says something bad about my story, they're not really real, so it doesn't matter." So, that's how I got the courage to show it. Otherwise, I would not have had the courage. I had it, you know, sort of sitting there for ages not showing anyone. So I put part of it online and got this massively good response that I was actually really unprepared for, and that's how, you know, and they kind of awarded me "writer of the month" and all this kind of thing. And one of the editors emailed me privately, as you probably know, and said, "Look, you shouldn't even be on this group; you should be published." He's actually remained a very good friend of mine.[35]

In this quote, we see that it is actually the lack of a physical presence that allowed Dart-Thornton to lower her guard enough to share her work; other factors that may have contributed to her willingness to engage include the structured nature of the digital program (including its internal "writer of the month" designation) and the relationship with an established publisher that marked it out as "genuine." As well as the formative experience of this online workshop, Dart-Thornton has made use of email in her career, a kind of hidden sociality that can be perfect for introverts. Dart-Thornton says:

Basically, I typed this story in my room. I emailed to the literary agent from my room. She signed me up in my room. She sent it to Time Warner, and they bought it and said, "We'll give you a six-figure sum for all the books and publish in hardcover, which we've never done with a new author before." I got the message in my room. So basically I walked out of that room one day and said to my husband, "I've written this story, and Time Warner have bought it for a heck of a lot of money and they're going to publish it." And he's like, "What? I didn't even know you were writing a story."[36]

Dart-Thornton's physical isolation from the genre world notwithstanding, a significant and high-impact proportion of genre-world activity takes place not online but in person. These events range from large book festivals and publisher parties to author talks and library events. In genre worlds, perhaps the most significant in-person events are conventions, more lovingly known as cons.

Conventions and the Importance of Being There

Cons are in some ways physical manifestations of genre worlds. As U.K. fantasy editor Stephen Jones says, "One of the greatest pieces of advice I've always given to fans and readers on panels or in articles is it's not what you know, it's who you know in this field. And one connection leads to another connection, and leads to another connection, and that's what conventions are about; that's what events are about."[37] At conventions, the cooperative links of genre worlds may be viewed in action as participants meet and interact productively in a range of public, semiprivate, and private physical spaces. Cons support the genre world by providing professional development opportunities via calendar-based sociality; they offer structure to participants' professional lives. For example, when a writer, agent, publisher, or the like knows that Worldcon is approaching in August, they may organize other aspects of their work life around that date. While there is significant social pleasure derived from these events, their function is primarily professional, and they result in multiple professional outcomes, including knowledge transfer, enhanced networks, and the intensification of creative energy. They are also significant builders of genre-world culture, setting and upholding values and affirming and rewarding behaviors and attitudes.

Examining the convention requires us to address head-on the question around our approach as participant-observers in genre worlds. As noted, all three of us are to some extent inside the genre worlds we study; this is particularly the case for Kim Wilkins, whose long-standing genre-world participation as an author of fantasy fiction predates her work as an academic. To be in the physical space of genre worlds as academic researchers required us to think through a range of issues about objectivity, ethics, and perspective, drawing on the ideas of autoethnography and the "aca-fan." These concepts have framed our experiences but left us with questions of how, or even whether, to report the subjective in an objective, academic voice. We have settled on writing about ourselves using our given names: more familiar than the usual academic register, these names are intended to act as a reminder, not a disclaimer, of our subjectivity and invested positions.

Each of us attended a range of conventions over the duration of our research, including Romance Writers of Australia in Melbourne, Sydney, and Adelaide (2015–17); Genrecon in Brisbane (2015, 2017, 2019); the Ned Kelly Awards hosted by the Australian Crime Writers Association (2016); Romance Writers of America in Orlando (2018); Worldcon 75 in Helsinki (2017); and Continuum 13 in Melbourne (2017). What follows is an auto-ethnographic account of fantasy conventions, based mainly on Kim's comparative experiences at Continuum 13 and Worldcon 75, with these situated in relation to observations about other conventions and interviews with genre-world participants. Our observations and analysis are structured around the physical spaces of conventions—divided into public spaces and private or semiprivate spaces—showing how different spaces are purposed for different conventional behaviors.

Public Spaces: The Lobby, the Dealers Room, the Panel Rooms, and the Ballroom

Arrival at a con is a time to see or be seen, and so lobby spaces of hotels or convention centers are popular for hopeful networkers or those who favor informal, unscheduled meetings. The entrance to Helsinki Worldcon was divided into two parts. The outdoor area swarmed with people, some in cosplay, with others identifying their allegiances through T-shirts, badges, tote bags, and so on. An emblazoned T-shirt is a classic affinity-space move, interpellating other enthusiasts while actively excluding others—for example, by referencing quotes or characters from favorite fantasy films and television shows and games that may not be known to all. Kim's own mode of self-presentation was simply a toned-down version of this signaling: she was not wearing a Thor T-shirt (although she does own one), but her jewelry and clothing choices aligned her with a faux-Victorian, fairy-tale aesthetic visible in her subgenre and much of her own work. She chose to make her first appearance at Worldcon in a physical representation of her genre allegiance. A blacksmith stand had been set up outside, and two shirtless men, who resembled Vikings (and who attracted much lingering attention from female, and some male, members), sold fantasy-themed jewelry and other metal objects.

Inside, the foyer was divided into several lanes marked with ropes to funnel participants into the con. In an adjoining atrium, couches were scattered. On some of these were pairs or small groups in close conversation. It was here Kim ran into Jack Dann and Jonathan Strahan, two significant connectors of Australian and international genre worlds, saw other faces she knew (whose names she couldn't remember), and was introduced to people whose names she did know and whom she had not previously met. The occasional spectacular costume drew eyes and compliments. The much-vaunted ideal of universal acceptance was on display, as best-selling authors arrived and queued alongside the rank and file. U.S. author Robin Hobb, for example, milled about among the members.[38] In the crime genre world Iain Ryan notes a similar spread of members in the hierarchy of success, citing the Bouchercon crime convention, which welcomes "every man and his dog—it's everyone from self-published work through to, like, Lee Childs."[39]

Although participants at Worldcon were predominantly white and able-bodied, there was nonetheless a spectrum of skin colors and bodies, and the gender ratio was about equal. Even though the location was Finland, there were numerous American accents around; con members from the United States are loyal and willing to travel long distances for what is the biggest international convention in this field (in 2017, for example, 7,323 members attended). Most Worldcons attract a sizable Australian contingent, and Helsinki Worldcon had 186 members attending from Australia. These events are seen as important for Australian writers and industry professionals to make valuable international connections. Angela Slatter notes that she makes a point of traveling to an overseas convention every year, pointing out the importance of "meeting other people and meeting a different group and trying to make international links."[40]

Continuum in Melbourne, the 2017 Natcon, by contrast was a much smaller affair (134 members) with a much more local feel, although Natcons often have international guests with whom Australian writers can network on home turf. Once again, arrival at the con hotel often involves chance meetings at the check-in desk or the bar-and-food area that looks out over the hotel entrance. The arrivals are less ostentatious, mainly because the con hotel is a space shared with other hotel patrons and potentially other conferences. The chance meetings may take the form of enthusiastic greetings, catching up on happenings since the last event, and the occasional promise of "coffee" that may or may not be kept. The foyer, as a public arrival place, is implicated in the informal and socially enjoyable aspect of professional networking.

Both cons feature a dealers room, which is the name given to a convention space designated for the sale of books and merchandise. The Melbourne Continuum dealers room comprises table displays from specialist bookshops, small-press publishers, and self-published authors. Browsers in the dealers room divide into members who know the publishers and booksellers, and who may linger and "talk shop," and members who are strictly customers. However, the kind of engaged interaction seen in dealers rooms usually means that members will not stay strictly customers. The slow pace and sparse crowds of the dealers room provide opportunities for aspiring writers to network with booksellers, publishers, and established authors. Kim notes that she makes a point of always purchasing books from the dealers room, as a way of supporting the industry that supports her. While we cannot speak for others, this rationale is in keeping with the ethos of the genre world.

Worldcon's dealers room is, predictably, larger than Natcon's and includes tables from large publishing imprints. Additionally, the dealers are regionally displaced from each other, and so the sense of a national community is not felt here. Kim felt no obligation—either through national pride or concern for small businesses operated by friends—to buy books here. There was a wider range of merchandise at Worldcon, too, including the kind of merchandise one might see at mainstream pop-culture conventions such as Comic-Con: film and television tie-in toys, cups, figurines, and other collectibles. Kim ran into Jeff and Ann VanderMeer in the Helsinki dealers room. The last time she and Jeff had spoken was several years previously, when he was a guest of the Brisbane Writers Festival. Since then, Jeff had become a bona fide international best-selling author with his Southern Reach trilogy, the first of which was adapted into the film *Annihilation*. While Kim notes that he was friendly, generous, and humble, she nonetheless felt intimidated by the difference in their comparative market successes and was keen not to be seen as a hanger-on. In this way, the international scale of Worldcon deprived her of the status she had at the powerful end of the hierarchy in Australia: from big fish to little fish.

The chief location of formal knowledge transfer at any con is the panel room. These rooms, usually an event space in a large hotel or convention center, typically host a long table at the front for the panelists and multiple chairs for attendees. This room configuration concretizes the hierarchy between those who have knowledge and those who do not, but depending on the panel topic and the convention audience, that distinction can be porous (which may also result in policing of the distinction). How does this spatial hierarchy disrupt or reinforce the notion that everyone in a genre world is equal?

A panel at Melbourne Continuum titled "Fandom: Where Did We Come From?" seated at a long table several older men who were integral to the SF community in Melbourne, and thus the forefathers of the convention event. As they spoke, other "fans" of their vintage contributed freely, so that the panel resembled a large discussion group rather than a traditional writers festival panel. At another panel when the topic turned to university degrees in creative writing, one of the panelists invited Kim to speak even though she was not listed as presenting, because she was seen as having specialist knowledge in this field. In fact, some panels are designed specifically for interaction, especially in the late-evening slots on a program. For example, Continuum ran a panel called "In Defence Of . . . ," which was described as follows: "Here's the format: the moderator calls on the audience to suggest widely derided media, and the panel has to defend it. Lively discussion ensues! We hope!"

By contrast, a panel at Worldcon 75 called "High Fantasy: Is It Still Relevant?" that included best-selling authors Robin Hobb and Scott Lynch was, as one would expect, in a much larger panel room, with a stage for the panelists. From the back rows the stage was not readily visible. There were no interruptions from the audience until the mandated question time, and when one questioner took too long to ask their question (because it was, in fact, a long and detailed comment), the chair managed the interaction so the right to speak returned to the official presenters as soon as possible. Other audience members were palpably relieved. While Hobb and Lynch are very much part of their fantasy communities, their knowledge and contribution are valued in a strict hierarchy that is upheld by others in the community.

Participating in panels has value for writers and industry professionals on a number of fronts. They are a vital way to gain visibility in front of an enthusiastic and dedicated genre audience. Candice Fox tells us how "for the last three years I've attended everything that I possibly could, because I think it's good for my career, just to be seen and get my name out there and that sort of thing." Similarly, publisher Beverley Cousins regularly attends "the romance writers conventions, and I try to, sort of, get involved in things if they want me to do talks at Ned Kelly—you know, the Sisters in Crime, you know, those kinds of things I'll do . . . just to, sort of, get my name out there." Through speaking at these events, Cousins becomes known to writers, agents, and other genre-world insiders. Beyond raising visibility, Angela Slatter cites panels as a great way to engage with things of value to the community: "You get on panels and you have these discussions, and it starts the juices going and it sparks." For Slatter, there is something about the real-time interaction on specific topics important to the community that allows for the generation of ideas in a way that working in a solitary fashion cannot. Penguin publisher Sarah Fairhall sees professional development value in panels: "The industry panels are often sometimes really interesting. I mean, sometimes we're on them, but sometimes we're listening to overseas publishers talk about what's happening over there, and it's really nice to stay on top of trends, so they're really, really valuable weekends for publishers as well, I'd say."[41] Roles blur somewhat in these panels, as participants take turns to be the teacher or the enthusiastic learner, all while fostering networks and building genre-world knowledge.

Other specific professional opportunities for the unpublished and emerging writers that take place in the panel rooms include pitching sessions. Among our interviewees, publishing professionals Sarah Fairhall (Penguin), Joel Naoum (Momentum), Lindy Cameron (Clan Destine Press), and Rochelle Fernandez (HarperCollins) all spoke of taking pitches and sometimes signing authors through that process. At the 2015 Romance Writers of Australia convention, Beth and Lisa were invited to sit in on some pitching sessions; ushering people to their appointments were several male volunteers who described themselves laughingly as "the husbands." The sessions Beth and Lisa attended showed a high level of professionalism from new authors, suggesting the authors had previously attended workshops or been trained in how to pitch and providing an example of the articulated skill development offered through romance conventions. For publisher Cameron, one advantage of a pitching session is "I get an idea of the person . . . you know, what sort of person you might be working with," which emphasizes the value of in-person interaction rather than the online or email pitching opportunities some publishers provide.[42]

Worldcon 75 also provided a pitching session. Participants were promised "a feedback sheet with advice on honing your manuscript and, who knows, maybe an offer you can't refuse."[43] While there was only one pitching session, Worldcon featured dozens of workshops. Alongside professional development workshops on writing about postapocalyptic cultures, adding moral dilemmas for fiction, and how to read aloud effectively, members took part in workshops on a varied range of aspects of fan culture, including cosplay, filking (rewriting the lyrics of an existing song with fantasy lyrics), dwarven beard making, and how to explain theoretical scientific concepts to children.

Special events are often held in a ballroom. Natcons usually host a ball, called the "Maskobalo," which invites attendees to dress on a particular theme with prizes awarded for best costume. However, attendees do not necessarily dress on theme, and cosplay of all kinds is a valued activity in the fantasy genre world. One of Kim's enduring memories of a Maskobalo is a man dressed in a brown bomber jacket, jeans, and sneakers, with a whole-head latex alien mask on, shuffling alone on the dance floor to Depeche Mode's "Just Can't Get Enough." Beth thinks she may have seen this dancer at the Canongate party in Frankfurt in 2017. The audience for events such as Maskobalo includes amateur and professional members of the genre world; in fact, writer Sean Williams regularly deejays at Maskobalos, and writer Cat Sparks regularly documents them through photography.

While Worldcon hosted four dedicated dancing events, including Finnish folk dancing and Regency dancing, the largest special event was the Hugo Awards. The audience for awards ceremonies is dominated by professional writers and industry personnel. These audience members may be invited to present awards, accept awards on another winner's behalf, or accept awards for themselves. Award ceremonies are a public celebration of professional success in genre worlds and physically perform and concretize the fact that some members of the genre world are held in more esteem than others.

Private and Semiprivate Spaces: The Bar, Hallways and Other In-Between Spaces, and the Hotel Room

The Hugo Awards may be a spectacular public event, but it gives rise to one of the most interesting semiprivate events in the fantasy genre-world calendar, the Hugo Losers Party. George R. R. Martin, author of the A Song of Ice and Fire series, held the first Losers Party in 1976, and the event soon passed into the Worldcon program as an annual event, often organized by the following year's Worldcon team. In 2015 Martin, dissatisfied with the sedate and low-key nature of recent Losers Parties, resumed organizing and paying for them. On his Liveblog he writes, "I wanted to have a blast, to howl at the moon and dance till dawn and mock the winners and console the losers, the way we used to."[44] The Helsinki Worldcon Losers Party was held at a cocktail bar called Steam on Olavinkatu (now closed), steampunk themed and lavishly catered. Martin hired out the entire bar and paid for finger food and unlimited drinks, including cocktails. Martin handed out Alfies, which are a losers award. Hugo winners were able to attend this event but had to wear a "cone-head" hat. With no limit on drinks, the party became very wild and continued into the early morning. Access to the party was by guest list only, with important genre-world members such as famous authors, powerful editors, and agents in attendance. For an Australian author not on the Hugos list, the best way to get invited was to attend as somebody's "plus one." With the Losers Party, Martin presents himself as a vital and generous member of the genre world, using his position in the hierarchy to build that community's culture of genre affirmation and the importance of leveling hierarchies (embarrassing the winners and celebrating the losers). However, this is still a private event, in that only certain people are invited. Yes, those people may bring an unknown "plus one," but the system works to restrict networks. This restriction may, of course, be related to cost: with more than seven thousand members at Worldcon, even Martin could not afford to buy them all unlimited cocktails. But it is also about recognizing important members of the genre world and the inside circle of their networks. In other words, the ideal of the flat hierarchy is both celebrated and refuted by the Losers Party.

In Dublin in 2019, the Hugo Losers Party became a topic of contention when Hugo losers arrived at the overcrowded venue and were not admitted, amid complaints of cliquishness and overlooking members who were not Martin's friends or not famous. With cast members of *A Game of Thrones* on the inside and the losers on the outside, Twitter bristled with the controversy: "He needs to change the name of the party to the GRRM [George R. R. Martin] Club Party cause that's all it really seems to be." Martin devoted a long blog post to an explanation and emphasized that the party was not just for that year's Hugo losers but that all past Hugo losers were welcome: "The new losers, the guys and gals who lost for the first time this year, are certainly welcome . . . but they are joining a community, a battered brotherhood of defeat."[45] Martin offers the traditional genre-world ethos of community, welcome, and brotherhood as a refutation to accusations of inequality and favoritism.

Bars at cons play host to many private genre-world interactions. Away from panels and public events, the bar provides opportunities for professional networking between writers, agents, and publishers. This networking is not always serendipitous (though it can be), as meetings are often organized in advance, a chance for industry professionals to meet in person in a global industry that, as discussed above, is increasingly reliant on online tools for negotiations. Lisa Hannett notes that she came to World Fantasy in Toronto "to meet those publishers in person. . . . [T]here's only so much you can do over the Internet online. You don't get the sense of just finally getting to chat to the person."[46] Face-to-face meetings are important for publishers too, with Lucy Malagoni and Sarah Fairhall both citing the ways cons make it possible to talk to multiple authors they usually speak to on the phone or online.

The bar has become such an important locus of interaction that some industry professionals barely make it inside the convention. As Iain Ryan notes of the biennial NoirCon, "Half of them spend the whole conference in the bar, chatting with one another instead of going to the actual conference. Also I remember my publisher, the small-press guy, he went to Bouchercon and didn't go inside the actual conference."[47] Publisher Jo Fletcher agrees that it is difficult to attend program events but is adamant about the importance of attending cons and being open to private meetings:

> I don't think I would be doing the job I'm doing now, or any of the jobs I've done since the '80s, had I not been going [to conventions]. . . . I think that relationships you make at conventions can lead to lifelong friendships, and I think certainly for editors in this community, I think you're an idiot not to come, I really do, because chance meetings in the bar late at night are where you find the people who are going to populate your list in years to come. I do think they're really important, and you can't quite explain to people who have never been to a convention about what it is because it sounds, "Why would you spend all that money to just go and sit in a bar and not leave it? You don't get to see a program item unless you're on it."[48]

Editor Stephen Jones, too, has long used the bar as a kind of informal office: "That's where you often find Steve Jones at conventions, drinking at the bar.

I used to have offices in a bar. I used to work out of bars before the Internet. And I find I still do my best work in this kind of, sitting down with a drink, chatting to people, doing this."[49]

Writers also note the value of the bar in advancing their professional goals. During Helsinki Worldcon, Angela Slatter was courted by three international literary agents, one via email, one via Skype, and the third during a meeting in the con bar. Hannett recounted how meeting a small-press publisher at a Melbourne convention led to the publication of her story collection *Bluegrass Symphony*, which went on to be nominated for a World Fantasy Award and opened doors for her at the Worldcon in Toronto, where many of the important conversations she had were at the bar. Because *Bluegrass Symphony* was on the award short list, she told us, "people were, like, 'Oh, hello, I would like to meet you now, at the bar.' And it wasn't anything, it was just chatting, but that kind of continually going and being part of the community led to meeting other people that you like who then also liked your work and were also publishers, which led to other publication deals." In this account, we see literalized the cooperative links of genre worlds and some of the ways that they are activated: word of mouth, curiosity, validation, connection. Cons enable this kind of activation. Sean Williams also names the bar as preferable to panel rooms: "I've never been one to actually go to panels, but hanging out in the bar, going to lunch with the people, having chats with anybody in the hallway, I mean, I love catching up with my friends. And my friends just, through the process of we're the ones who didn't drop out or give up, you know, we tend to be published writers or editors now."[50] In this quote, Williams also gestures to other spaces that are nonspaces, such as hallways, as a potential place to "catch up." The language of the unintentional professional connection is also expressed in the point about his connections having held on in the industry long enough to have achieved a shared professional status. Productive friendships with the like-minded, or with those with similar career profiles, are often played out in liminal and private spaces.

Liminal spaces—waiting to enter a panel room, traveling between floors in the con venue, queuing for drinks at the bar—offer the opportunity for chance encounters and networking on the fly. At Continuum, Kim started a conversation with writer Alison Goodman in the thoroughfare outside a panel room, where she had just spoken at an event titled "Panels and Prejudice" about the influence of Jane Austen on fantasy writing. While the conversation started with the topic of the panel, it quickly ranged further afield until the panelists were planning a collective series (this project has not yet eventuated). Later, Kim lamented the state of the industry with a literary agent while waiting for a coffee. In an industry in an almost-constant state of disruption, ideas and knowledge may come from many places; being in the same physical space as individuals with shared interests provides unstructured opportunities for those ideas to be worked out.

These spaces are also regularly used as a semiprivate (private within the public) space for members of the genre world who have close personal relationships to come together between events, to share their feelings about people or events. Venting and gossip are common, as are compliments and affirmations. Sometimes the goal is simply to remove oneself from the public space for a moment and take refuge in an existing private relationship, to process thoughts and feelings before continuing. In this way, private connections run parallel to public connections at cons, as they do in other aspects of professional sociality in the genre world. This is particularly important at international cons, when writers may rely on their known communities for support. As Hannett says of Worldcon: "If you're feeling a little nervous, you'll gravitate towards the people you already know, so if all the Australians go to World Fantasy, and you're feeling like you're having kind of a down day, then you'll go and hang out with them instead of pushing yourself to meet the other international authors and things that you don't get a chance to see all the time at Natcons."[51]

Cons often require attendees to travel, which necessitates hotel rooms, and most cons offer special room rates that make the con hotel attractive to travelers. Here again are private spaces within the public space. Hotel rooms become sites of sociality when attendees stay together to contain costs, and it is common for genre-world members to broadcast for con traveling companions on social media or through word-of-mouth networks. Both people in existing social relationships and people who are open to forming new relationships take part in shared travel, though there is a hierarchical and role-based character to the pairings: generally publishing professionals will bunk with other publishing professionals, and successful authors will bunk with others around the same level of success.

The distance between Australia and Europe is immense, and Kim's journey to Worldcon required seven hours on a plane to Singapore, fourteen to London, and a further two to Helsinki. Jet lag is inevitable and takes several days to pass. For Australian writers, it makes little sense to travel that far only to return directly after the con. For that reason, a tradition has developed of Australian writers (when they can afford to do so) forming joint travel plans around Worldcon. In 2017, Juliet Marillier, Angela Slatter, and Kim flew from Worldcon to Stromness, in the Orkney Islands, for a writers retreat. They rented an old merchants cottage overlooking Scapa Flow and quickly made friends with the neighbor's cat. During the day they wrote, apart from each other; in the afternoons they walked together; and in the evenings they prepared food and talked. The conversations often revolved around the state of the publishing industry and their places in it. We cannot disclose those conversations here, because they were frank and because they were private. It is often only through that frank disclosure, however, that writers can accurately evaluate and calibrate their own professional success. As Kelly Hunter says of romance conventions:

> For me it's often in the hotel rooms and after the formal events are over that the most valuable information is shared on what publisher's doing this and, you know, who's doing that, and authors are very free I think within the romance-writing community when it comes to sharing contract information, sharing sales information, how's something going, you know, you can "rah-rah" all you like in front of a reader panel, and . . . you don't want to say this one bombed, or this one did well, or whatever. But behind closed doors, there's often some very frank discussions of what's working for you, what's not working for you, what's working within the industry, which publisher is doing good things at the moment, and which one you sort of, you know, you hear shakier things about.[52]

In private spaces, a difference emerges between the writer's public performance of genre-world habitus (the "rah-rah") and the "free" and "frank" productive and valuable professional discussions that affect professional decisions and success.

These private retreats also provide inspiration and an opportunity to advance a project rapidly. Juliet Marillier notes the inspiration available when surrounded by writers and beautiful scenery, away from the mundane duties of the world: "I think also being there with other writers who we know and love already is going to be, you know, spark the imagination. . . . I think just going somewhere different and concentrating very much on writing for a period is a magnificent thing to do." This quote buys into the myth of the Romantic artist, a myth that is equal parts inspiring and limiting (if one must always be on retreat to write, then projects will not advance quickly), but then other aspects of this chapter have likely bought into other things that are spoken about mythically, such as late-night bar deals and the power of friendships. There is truth in all of it, and there is also inspiration in believing it. Jonathan Strahan summarizes the value of conventions and the range of professional social opportunities they provide in a practical way that still allows for the "magic" to happen: "[Cons] can make a lot of difference, even though they won't be the thing that is critical. By that, I mean you won't sell a book at a convention necessarily. You won't finish that thing you were trying to do. What you'll do is you will create the conditions where it's possible."[53] It is in the realm of possibility—for improving writing, for making valuable social and professional relationships, for deepening appreciation of books and stories—that the con shines in genre worlds.

Conclusion

This chapter has sought to understand some of the mechanics and dynamics of the social dimension of genre worlds, by describing the online social formations of genre worlds alongside one of their key sites of physical togetherness: conventions. The two modes of sociality overlap, but each provide distinctive opportunities for connection that influence the formations of genre worlds.

Online social interactions are shaped by the affordances and norms of different digital platforms, in particular by the sense of privacy or public performance that each entails. Our investigation of social media use in genre worlds showed how it can provide an entry point into genre worlds, a form of networking and relationship building, and a way of marketing books and authors through parasocial interactions with readers. At the same time, social media poses its own challenges for genre-world participants: it cannot exactly replicate in-person social interactions and events, and although it is in theory accessible to all participants, it is riven with its own power dynamics that undercut the flat hierarchy that remains a genre-world ideal. Power relations also play out in private or semiprivate online spaces, such as Facebook and email. Emails undergird the everyday business of writing and publishing, as well as fostering one-on-one connections between participants. Semiprivate Facebook groups provide important support mechanisms for subsets of genre worlds, such as groups of writers.

Physical congregations of genre-world members happen alongside online interactions and also play an essential role in constituting the genre world.[54] In this chapter, we looked at conventions. These happen regularly, adding structure to a genre world, and are routes for the transfer of professional and genre-specific knowledge as well as nurturing friendships and professional networks. They set and reinforce the norms of a genre world, including what it values in texts and in practices.

In both in-person and virtual environments, genre-world participants make the most of affordances to advance professional and personal goals. As our interviews show, from readers on Goodreads to Twitter posts to convention hotel bars and parties, negotiating private space and public space is key to maximizing the social and professional benefits of genre worlds. But how does all this affect genre fiction texts? The next chapter builds on an accumulated understanding of the industrial and social dimensions of genre worlds, by turning to pay close attention to the textual dimension.

· · ·

The door to Professor Humberchurch's study creaks open. You enter and close the door to shut out the icy breeze as you gather your tattered shawl around your shoulders. Her desk is littered with papers, and ink stains the wood. In the middle of the desk is a mighty volume, pages of yellowed vellum. Your eyes run over the tightly scrawled writing, as you listen over the thump of your heart for the sound of footsteps. At last you will know the secret of Humberchurch Manor, if only you can read these strange lines . . .

CHAPTER 6

GenreWorlds on the Page

How does the theory of genre worlds ask us to treat works of fiction as objects of study? This chapter explains where reading novels fits in the project of studying genre fiction as an artistic, social, and commercial complex. Fundamentally, we hold that if popular genres are built, maintained, and transformed through the collaboration of many individuals and organizations, this must necessarily affect what appears on the page. Just as book covers, blurbs, maps, and other material aspects of books and e-books respond to and reinforce the industrial and social formulations of genre, so too do the texts: in fact, the texts do it centrally, as the objects around which those industrial and social formations coalesce. In the genre-worlds model, popular fiction texts are not read as simple windows into the ideological attitudes of a culture or industry. Rather, we look to texts for evidence of the collaborations and the conflicts that brought them into being and with an eye to the future possibilities for genre worlds that each text creates.

The first page of most genre novels signals the genre, offering textual conventions that are bound up in industry and reader expectations. Take, for example, Garry Disher's crime novel *Bitter Wash Road:*

> On a Monday morning in September, three weeks into the job, the new cop at Tiverton took a call from his sergeant: shots fired on Bitter Wash Road.
> "Know it?
> "Vaguely, Sarge," Hirsch said.
> "Vaguely. You been sitting on your arse for three weeks, or have you been poking around like I asked?"
> "Poking around, Sarge."

"You can cover a lot of ground in that time."

"Sarge."

"I told you, didn't I, no dropkicks?"

"Loud and clear, Sarge."

"No dropkicks on my watch," Sergeant Kropp said, "and no smartarses."

He switched gears, telling Hirsch that a woman motorist had called it in. "No name mentioned, tourist on her way to look at the wildflowers. Heard shots when she pulled over to photograph the Tin Hut." Kropp paused. "You with me, the Tin Hut?"

Hirsch didn't have a clue. "Sarge."

"So get your arse out there, let me know what you find."[1]

The style here is tersely procedural; the opening line reads like a police report. Disher's prose features short words with hard consonants to create a sharp rhythm and short sentences and paragraphs with limited description to increase pace; that is, even the word choice and syntax create the feel of the serious and dramatic work of policing. The characterization is concentrated into dialogue rather than introspection. In fact, we are not certain which character viewpoint we are oriented in until after this excerpt (it is Hirsch; we also learn that both characters are men). All of these textual features create narrative forward motion and increase the pace of reading, leading to the "page-turner" quality the industry uses to market crime. Moreover, the fact that a crime features in the opening line gestures toward genre pleasure: there is a mystery here that will be solved by the end of the book. The name of the road sounds unpleasant, rousing the sense of something disturbing, and the first page presents the genre trope of the new cop under pressure from their sergeant, familiar across different media formats of storytelling about police procedures. The knowledge and expectations of crime readers are implicit in every line of this brief excerpt.

By contrast, Kelly Hunter's rural romance *Maggie's Run* uses strategies that respond to different expectations:

Maggie Walker often wished she looked more intimidating. She could have taken after her late father, who'd been broad of shoulder, firm of jaw, and had cut an imposing figure no matter whose company he'd sought. She could have taken after her recently deceased great aunt, who'd been a model in her younger years—one of those aloof, impossibly leggy, aristocratic types. She could have been in possession of glacier-cut cheekbones, a piercing blue glare and enough height to make looking down on other people far too easy.

Maggie had inherited none of it.

Instead she'd topped out at five feet two, was slight of form and had a sweetness of face more commonly associated with wet kittens and baby fawns.[2]

This could not contrast more strongly with *Bitter Wash Road*. Instead of sharp, fast-paced dialogue, this opening is largely introspective, focused on the protagonist's thoughts and feelings: this style is subjective, not factual or objective. The romance reader is invited into this close third-person viewpoint to feel things alongside (through) Maggie. Analysis of the industrial and social features of the romance fiction genre world demonstrated that it is almost exclusively written by women; the fact that it is also written for women is evident in the mode of address here. Word choice such as "one of those aloof, impossible leggy, aristocratic types" creates a sense of us and them, with the reader positioned firmly on the side of us, uncool and short-legged just like Maggie. By including the reader in Maggie's self-deprecating vulnerability, the first page starts the work of creating the relatability that is valued in romance fiction.

Attention to the protagonist's appearance is especially significant for this genre's pleasures. Here, Maggie is sweet-faced and small, associating her with youth and vulnerability, a key selling point in subgenres of romance such as Harlequin's "Heartwarming" or Wild Rose Press's "Sweet Romance." Hunter's book is in American publisher Tule's Outback Brides series (all set in Australia), and the description of Maggie is consonant with the cover model of the book, who is round-faced, soft-eyed, and dimpled, dressed in bridal white. The Outback Brides covers contrast strongly with the Outback Heat series, whose covers feature sexy clinches between women and shirtless men. Alongside an assessment of Maggie's potential attractiveness, the opening to *Maggie's Run* also flags her inner fieriness (her desire to be more imposing) and a playful, self-parodying sense of humor (through the comparison to wet kittens and baby fawns). A subtype of contemporary romance heroine is invoked here, and particular pleasures can be read through the code of this opening scene.

Similarly, the social and industrial influence of genre worlds is evident in the opening scene of Sara Douglass's *Battleaxe*. The genre world of fantasy is explicitly evoked in the vast and strange setting:

> The speckled blue eagle floated high in the sky above the hopes and works of mankind. With a wingspan as wide as a man was tall, it drifted lazily through the air thermals rising off the vast inland plains of the Kingdom of Achar. Almost directly below lay the silver-blue expanse of Grail Lake, flowing into the great river Nordra as it coiled through Achar towards the Sea of Tyrre. The lake was enormous and rich in fish, and the eagle fed well there. But more than fish, the eagle fed on the refuse of the lakeside city of Carlon. Pristine as the ancient city might be with its pink and cream stone walls and gold and silver plated roofs; pretty as it might be with its tens of thousands of pennants and banners and flags fluttering in the wind, the Carlonites ate and shat like every other creature in creation, and the piles of refuse outside the city walls supported enough mice and rats to feed a thousand eagles and hawks.[3]

This scene opens with a technique borrowed from cinema: the establishing shot, where the size and scale of the world about to be entered are presented as an enticement to the reader (think of the opening scene of *Star Wars: A New Hope,* with space scrolling away and massive spaceships filling the screen). The "camera work" for Douglass's scene is performed by a familiar real-world creature, an eagle, which is given fantasy-world unfamiliarity through an unexpected color and size. The reader is immediately positioned as somewhere else, zooming in on various aspects of the created world. The ability of readers to respond to (or, indeed, pronounce) strange names is taken for granted (Nordra, Achar, Tyrre), even though these names caused one reviewer from outside the genre world to complain that "the book is nearly in code."[4]

Part of that code is provided by the convention of medieval settings, which underpin a large proportion of fantasy fiction, including staples in the genre such as *The Lord of the Rings* and *A Game of Thrones*. Douglass nods toward the heroic medieval in multiple ways: with reference to the Grail, with strong visual imagery of pennants and banners flying, with a sense of history, height, and scope. But she also represents the more "gritty" view of the medieval that began to pervade epic fantasy from the 1990s on (and which foreshadowed the rise of the grimdark fantasy subgenre), by show-ing the medieval city as smelly, wretched, and infused with a premodern sensibility that promises irrationality, fervor, and violence. The wide-angle opening shot, then, zooms down to an earthy level where the action will take place, performing perhaps the most important function in the recep-tion and circulation of fantasy texts, inviting the reader into a coherent and realistic secondary world.

As our analysis of these three opening pages shows, the genre-worlds model of reading does more than sort texts into genres. Instead, our approach looks for the mutually informing creative, social, and industrial practices that differentiate a specific genre. These practices create and rein-force the expectations of a genre's texts and are therefore visible in those texts. This chapter breaks down the various types of attention involved in a genre-worlds textual analysis. The social aspects of a genre world might be visible in the many ways a text plays to an in-crowd; the industrial aspects of a genre world might be visible in the way a text delivers or expands on genre expectations given its specific time and place in the market. A genre-worlds reading acknowledges the material embeddedness of all texts in their moment and their medium. It also acknowledges the manifold forms of pleasure and investment that people bring to genre texts.

Conceptualizing a Genre-Worlds Reading

One of the aims of a genre-world reading is to think beyond what Matt Hills terms the "decisionist" approach to popular culture, which holds that the role of scholars is to read texts or cultural practices politically, to decide where they fit on a scale from reactionary to progressive.[5] This decisionist paradigm is overwhelming in debates about popular romance, for exam-ple. Accounts of the genre—whether speaking for or against its aesthetics, pleasures, and effects—regularly begin with the question of the meanings texts produce for (or impose on) their readers, especially with regards to the texts' feminist credentials (or lack thereof).[6] Fantasy has its ideological critics, too, with Michael Moorcock famously calling out Tolkien's hidden Toryisms and Miéville labeling as "revolting" the idea that fantasy could be consolatory instead of challenging capitalist modernity.[7] Moreover, popular fiction's continued association with the marketplace, and the marketplace's continued association with exploitative neoliberalism—Adorno's capitalist popular culture—means that genre fiction is already ideologically suspect, so the decisionist game is rigged, in that it is easily decided in advance against popular fiction.

A decisionist approach (especially when it decides a text is ideologically problematic) is a version of what Rita Felski would call "reading against the grain." As contributors to the recent wave of "postcritical" literary studies have argued, research and teaching in the literary studies discipline have been stymied by entrenched habits of thinking and practice that position the critic *against* literature. As Felski writes, "Seizing the upper hand, critics read against the grain and between the lines; their self-appointed task is to draw out what a text fails—or willfully refuses—to see."[8] This approach is seen as part of the role of reading a text as an expert critical reader: to expose its biases, secrets, or crimes.

In contrast, our genre-worlds approach identifies generosity as a guiding principle. This generosity arises from our commitment to a sociologically inflected perspective that foregrounds the individual and collaborative work of participants in genre worlds. The enthusiasm of genre-world participants, in such a view, becomes an important aspect of analysis. In this, we are aligned with Felski's project to rethink literary value in ways that "do not cut it off from nonexpert readers and ordinary life." As she puts it, "One of the distinguishing marks of works of art, after all, is their ability to inspire intense responses," and critique should be "supplemented by generosity."[9] This does not rule out experiences of discomfort or unease with a text, either for critics or for nonexpert readers. Moments of change and conflict within genre worlds often include reactions against texts: for example, a text's use of rape tropes or racist character stereotypes might be decried by genre-world participants. Works from a genre world's past might be handled with circumspection in its present. It is not that there is no room in genre worlds for critique; rather, it is that a genre-worlds reading begins with generosity, reading with the grain rather than against it.

Exponents of reading with the grain in order to seek new modes of intellectual engagement with novels, such as Timothy Bewes and Rita Felski, have tended to be most interested in literary fiction. We therefore build on this line of recent work by extending it to genre fiction. It is particularly apposite as an approach here, because of the way genre books thrive in and are frequently loved by their communities. For our purposes, to read with the grain is to seek to understand the hierarchies of value and pleasure that define a popular genre for the actors who contribute to and consume its products. This means being attentive to statements made by those actors (in this research project, statements made in interviews; in other research projects, perhaps Goodreads reviews or journalistic interviews) as well as to the industrially produced paratexts and materiality of books.

Reading with the grain of genre texts involves recognition of what Felski calls, in relation to reading, "pleasures that are in plain sight," a quote that could almost function as an epithet for popular fiction.[10] The opening of this chapter showed how genre pleasures are highlighted from the first page of genre texts: terse dialogue in crime, feelings-based interior monologues in romance, epic setting in fantasy. It is those most visible pleasures that are central in the social and industrial circulation of genres. Thinking about pleasure as a marker of value in genre worlds changes the way we analyze texts. How are genre pleasures manifested in texts? Where is pleasure supplied or denied and to what effect? How might genre pleasures change over time? And how do genre pleasures become influenced or mobilized by the social and industrial activity around the text?

Pursuing answers to these questions expands both the idea of literary value and the purpose of literary criticism. In relation to any work of art, the critic's role is enriched when she imagines herself in conversation with a wide and complicated circuit of actors. From a genre-worlds perspective, narrative tropes and formal conventions are developed and sustained through the cooperative activities of many people. The people who make, distribute, read, or evaluate genre fiction—or who participate in all stages of this cycle—knowingly and often astutely activate and interpret the narrative tropes and formal conventions of popular genres and subgenres, both on and off the page. This is a model that recognizes the agency of industry professionals and readers as well as authors. The purpose and effects of textual devices—for example, the "meet cute" in romance when the hero and heroine first encounter one another, a journey through mountains in fantasy, cliffhanger chapters in the crime thriller—go beyond the production and communication of narrative and nonnarrative (ideological) meanings. Rather, as our interviews show, such conventions are central to the ecosystem of cultural, social, and economic capital that structures and sustains popular genres. Textual conventions are the source material for fans who closely analyze and dissect their favorite works. Textual conventions also offer enjoyment to more casual readers at the edges of a genre world. In short, they provide the verbal shorthand and storytelling tropes that enable the talk and the business of popular fiction.

Social and Industrial Elements of a Genre-Worlds Reading

A genre-worlds textual analysis practically applies these ideas. It looks closely at the words on the page, remaining mindful that pleasure has been a generative principle in the writing and publishing of the text and is intended to be a significant reward in the reading of it. It is also attuned to the text's embeddedness in social and industrial contexts. How the reading plays out depends, as with literary analysis, on the text in question. However, in reading a large corpus of contemporary popular fiction, we particularly noticed two elements: how texts acknowledge the genre reader's competence (linking the text to the social dimension of genre worlds) and how they reveal market influence (linking the text to the industrial dimension of genre worlds).

How Genre Texts Acknowledge Social Connections

The social aspects of a genre text may be visible in evidence that the text is playing to an "in-crowd." Across the books we read for this project, we found many examples of signposts between authors and their genre. These examples—direct quotes and subtle allusions alike—work as rewards for devoted readers who take pleasure mapping the connections between stories and find reward in building and verifying their knowledge of the genre. In Daniel O'Malley's *The Rook,* for example, a group of protesters gathers outside the Chequy, the secret government agency for supernatural matters, and characters refer to the protesters as *"X-Files* fans." In another novel, *Lost,* author Michael Robotham consciously evokes the crime genre with humorous references to Cluedo and Miss Marple—humorous because this book, as a thriller, identifies itself against the "cozy" crime tradition.[11] These overt references to the genre—pointing outside the book to characters and plots who are presented as "not real"—shore up the pleasurable feeling of reality within the book's narrative frame. They also signal to the wider genre world in which the text participates, a world built through the shared interests and passions we analyzed in chapter 4.

Another way that an in-group is signaled is through the use of parody. In genre fiction, parody is very often accepted (almost expected) rather than something that sits outside the text and critiques or works against the genre reader's pleasure. U.S. crime author Megan Abbott's *Queenpin,* for example, pushes hard-boiled tropes such as the femme fatale to the extreme while gender-flipping them. The work of Terry Pratchett deliberately sends up the tropes of fantasy (his character Rincewind is a wizard who continually runs away, to take just one example), while remaining a much-loved mainstay of the genre (Pratchett is cited as an influence by a number of our fantasy interviewees, including publisher Rochelle Fernandez and writer Claire G. Coleman). Daniel O'Malley's *The Rook* takes a comparable stance to fantasy tropes, puncturing their mystery and power with bathos. In one passage, he describes children who are strange: "Little boys with tusks. Teenage girls who could talk with clouds and get intelligible answers. Some poor youth who possessed a psychic control over flamingos."[12] This triptych of descriptions of strange children gives us first the uncanny, then the mysterious, and then plays for self-aware (and self-deprecating) laughs with a specific and mildly ridiculous image. This piece of writing works best with certain sympathetic audiences: those who not only know the tropes but also recognize that the tropes are sometimes pompous or silly.

Just as pleasure can be found in intertextuality and in-jokes, it can also be found in the use of genre code sitting squarely in its groove. Mitchell Hogan's fantasy novel *A Crucible of Souls* turns many tropes on their heads but knows when to lean into them for maximum pleasure. "Caldan leaned forward, eager to catch the words from the master. Stories held kernels of truth, and he believed any sorcery lost from before the Shattering could be discovered again. Sometimes he dreamed of discovering how to make trinkets, like most who had a talent for crafting did when they were young. It was all a fantasy, though, for in the thousands of years since the Shattering, no one had come close."[13]

Here, Hogan deploys the much-worn but much-loved image of the apprentice learning at the side of his magical master. The capitalized nominalization, the Shattering, is another staple of fantasy, generating deep history (note the mention of "thousands of years") and lore through word choice that sounds portentous and epic (see also stock fantasy words such as "stories," "sorcery," "talent"). Here, too, are the young apprentice's aspirations, suggesting narrative trajectory, provoking pleasurable expectations, and fulfilling the desires of readers to be immersed in a different world.

Sometimes, pleasure can be found in letting genre code spill over indulgently. As Anne, the heroine of Kylie Scott's romance novel *Play*, engages in foreplay with sexy drummer Mal, she notes, "The man was lucky I didn't just attack him with my vagina."[14] This quote is enjoyably over-the-top as a visceral and frank description of female desire. It is notable that this quote, along with a photograph of a hard-bodied tattooed man exposing his abdominal muscles, was used in the marketing of the book, linking the textual with the industrial. The pleasure of the text is made evident in a way that is hilarious for the romance genre's in-crowd, while its potentially controversial language makes it exclusive of, if not defiant toward, an out-crowd.

How Genre Texts Reveal Industrial Connections

The material influence of the market and other institutions in the genre world is also registered on the text. This includes the production of texts that fit market trends. Repetition is a fundamental concern of the publishing marketplace. If one book has large success, it may inspire acquisition of others that are similar. Anna Valdinger from HarperCollins describes the impact of *Fifty Shades of Grey*'s success:

> Suddenly, everyone was madly publishing their BDSM romances. And we were absolutely the same. We published *Indigo Bloom* as the first Australian answer to that, and it was a mad scramble to get that book out before any other Australian answer was published and, therefore, to get the benefit of all of those sales. And it really worked. It was a very quick turnaround, mind you. The editorial on that was like frantic. But it sold very well. . . . So I think the psychological thrillers are still going. People still really enjoy those. But I do think, I mean, *The Woman in the Window,* for example, has been going brilliantly. It's now a running joke: "girl in the whatever, woman in there, man standing peeking out from behind a bus" or whatever.[15]

This drive toward repetition of success affects which authors get published and what gets written. When Rachael Johns wanted to move away from writing rural romance, a subgenre in which she had been very successful (and a highly emulated subgenre), it helped that she had a market-friendly adjacent subgenre to go to: "So [I] went to my publisher, and I said I want to write a story about four sisters. I think I said it wasn't from the male point of view; there would be a little bit of romance. It was going to be semiset in a rural town, so it wasn't a completely different jump. And she was really supportive and said, 'Yep, give it a go; see how it goes.'" Her publisher, Sue Brockhoff, describes receiving the manuscript of *The Patterson Girls* and being confident that "there's a wider market out there now, people who might not necessarily pick up a book that has 'romance' attached to it but are looking for a great story about a family and about relationships and family issues and things that really affect all of us day-to-day." These family relationship books, often tagged as "commercial women's fiction," have a specific difference in the marketplace to rural romance. *The Patterson Girls* sold much better than Johns's rural romances because what Brockhoff intended with *The Patterson Girls* "was to position the book so that anybody going into Dymocks or into an independent bookshop or into Big W would find this book, and so that was again a deliberate strategy on our behalf to broaden the market."[16] While romance fiction's distribution channels are circumscribed (in the twenty-first century, mostly occurring through online retailers), commercial women's fiction has established channels across all types of booksellers. In this way, the content of the book—what Johns wrote—is implicated in its circulation. A genre-world reading, then, aims to recognize where the influence of industrial conditions is evident, but this isn't to say that writers are enslaved to the market who cynically write to exploit it. Rather, there is an inescapable interdependence between texts and the way they are materially made public. This is seen not only in how publishers cultivate and acquire particular titles but also in the way fan fiction and self-publishing trends shape the development of contemporary genre worlds.

When a genre trope or subgenre has been repeated too much and the market will no longer support it, texts may change to adapt to new conditions. The 1990s and early 2000s saw a boom of fantasy in Australia, and one of the stars of that boom was Fiona McIntosh. As the fantasy market softened, McIntosh reinvented herself first as a crime writer (with titles such as *Bye Bye Baby* and *Beautiful Death*) and then in commercial women's fiction, a genre in which she has become an Australian best seller. Kate Forsyth, also a fantasy writer who debuted her highly successful career in the 1990s, switched to historical fiction with her novel *Bitter Greens* in 2012. The book still featured allusions to the fantastic mode. In places, the language strongly evokes magic: "Two years after my family died, I came to Venice. It seemed like a magical city, floating on the lagoon as if conjured by an enchanter's wand." In one significant subplot, magic is a key part of the narrative. These blurred genre lines did not go unnoticed by her publishing team. Her Australian publisher, Meredith Curnow, remembers "pitching it at acquisitions and trying to explain the magic, and how it wasn't magic because it was so organic; it's just really part of the storytelling. . . . It was quite a challenge for the team to understand the concept of this historical romantic fiction that had some fantasy in it."[17] Forsyth acknowledged in a keynote speech at GenreCon in November 2019 that her U.K. and U.S. publishers did not follow her quite as readily, offering to continue publishing her fantasy fiction but not her new books, which were eventually published by another company. Different markets and organizational cultures may prioritize textual similarity or textual novelty, creating limits and opportunities for the genre texts that are produced.

The flowering and fading of niches is a feature of the evolution of texts in genre worlds. In some cases, this process tracks onto socially progressive movements within genre worlds. Lesbian crime fiction is one such instance. Crime author and publisher Lindy Cameron told us that there were fewer lesbian authors active in the Australian crime genre than in the mid-1990s. As one of the cofounders of Sisters in Crime Australia in 1991, Cameron remembers that "a lot of the [crime] fiction that was coming out of America at the time [was] . . . you know, really feminist type."

> And then around the edges was this absolute outburst of lesbian crime fiction. And, now that came out of, mostly, came out of a publisher called Naiad, and Naiad had originally gone ballistic publishing lesbian romances. . . . We lesbians who are reading them over here, because we didn't have any of our own, were reading them like, and called them lesbian Mills & Boon. . . . And then Naiad and another publisher started doing, started putting plot in, you know, hello, let's have a plot rather than just girl meets girl, girl almost loses girl, and girl gets girl in the end. . . . So, all of a sudden there's these crime series with lesbian characters and series. And, so we used to have a lot of debates and panels in the early days of Sisters in Crime that featured lesbian fiction coming out, either Val McDermid's or the stuff that was coming out of America because even all our straight members were reading it because it was different. And, so we also used to have a lot of panels with topics like, "Do lesbians do it better?" And

what we were talking about in that was, do lesbians deal with the romance better or the sex better because a lot of the contemporary straight crime writing they, the writers, didn't seem to know what to do with the men. And so we used to joke that, you know, most lesbian crime writing at the time had women who, in the first or second or third book, would get together with the person that they were going to be with forever, and they can still manage to solve crimes and they can still manage to have a relationship that was a little bit spicy or, you know, that sort of stuff, whereas all the straight writers would have a bloke who didn't know what to do with a strong female, a feminist character.[18]

This quote gives us a wonderful insight into the way that trends in publishing, often spoken about in abstract terms such as sales figures or number of titles, are experienced inside a genre world by invested participants. The trend of lesbian crime is, importantly, seen as something that the entire genre world can enjoy, rather than a niche that excludes certain readers. Cameron points out straight readers also appreciated something "different," showing that genre responsiveness to social change can invigorate texts. The rise of lesbian romance and its transition into crime fiction immediately aroused debate—about both cultural work it performed as well as the craft of the subgenre—and that debate was picked up in conventions and worked out together with other genre-world participants. When we asked Cameron what had happened to that lesbian crime-writing scene, she said: "It's still there. It's just not as big here [in Australia]. And I think it's not as big here because slowly, slowly, slowly, we got all our own writers [almost] all of whom . . . I think are straight. And, so I'm a bit sad that I'm a lone little lesbian, you know, on my rock, but we've got such good straight writers now, I don't care, but I would love as a publisher, now, to find some good lesbian writers."[19] Similar to the long quote above, the rise and fall of the trend is felt as lived experience by members of the genre world, both intellectually and affectively, and publication decisions around acquisition are very much tied to those intellectual and affective experiences. Trends emerge, grow, change, and die away, often leading to a desire for a trend to reemerge.

Related to the idea of repetition and clusters of trends is the idea of hybridity. One of the ways books are pitched at acquisitions and by sales teams to bookshops is through "comping," situating a book in relation to comparison titles. A hybridized version of this is the X-meets-Y formulation, which often makes use of high-profile texts: *Twilight* meets *Harry Potter,* for example, was used as a way of pitching Cassandra Clare's Shadowhunters series. Publishers use X-meets-Y to "predict what the text will do among readers and in the publishing industry, including how it might circulate and sell, and which existing routes to market it might exploit."[20] X-meets-Y pitches also often describe the content of texts, providing a way to understand their characterization, plots, and themes. Victoria Aveyard's young adult fantasy *Red Queen,* for example, was originally pitched as *Graceling* meets *The Selection* because it featured a physically strong and wily female character (fantasy and adventure: *Graceling*) and a competition between young women in a palace (romance and intrigue: *The Selection*).

In addition to providing a way to understand the content of texts, hybrid formulations can also illuminate cross-genre texts. Hybrids often exist because the writers and publishers hope to combine two genres in order to appeal to two audiences (although this does not always succeed). For example, Keri Arthur's *Full Moon Rising,* which combines elements of fantasy and romance, is a commercially successful hybrid text. One way to read the history of this series' success is as a story of serendipity: Arthur's genre tastes and creative proclivities aligned with a genre cycle focused on the meeting points of fantasy and romance that her agent and publishers were able to exploit. Arthur's agent, Miriam Kriss, saw the book's genre hybridity as a unique selling point in a fiction industry that trades on readers' desire to replicate their reading experience from one book (or series) to the next, while also seeking fresh characters and storyworlds. Kriss could also see the gaps in the industry where such a text might fit: "I had a good sense of who was already publishing these kinds of books and who had holes in their list who wished that they were publishing these kinds of books." Hybridity was noted in reviews of the text, including *Kirkus,* which described it as an "effective crossbreeding of romance and urban fantasy that should please fans of either genre." The novel itself represents hybridity, an issue that is so important to the story it appears on nearly every page; lead character Riley is "something that could not be—the child of a werewolf *and* a vampire."[21] In fact, the metaphorics of interbreeding is common in reviews of this novel, an interesting instance of the content of the novel and its industrial positioning overlapping.

A further way in which the industrial facets of genre worlds shape the texts of genre books is through the influence of related media products.

This influence may appear directly or indirectly. In Sean Williams's video-game novelization *The Force Unleashed,* scenes strongly evoke video-game narratives and visuals, with repetitive quests and a sense of "leveling up" narratively at chapter breaks. Cinematic scenes appear in novels across all genres—for example, the strongly visual dramatic denouement in Jane Harper's *The Dry* (now a film adaptation), in which a chase through the Australian bush, with "the crackle of dry twigs underfoot and the wind whipping through the branches," climaxes with the criminal holding a lighter and threatening to start a fire.[22]

High-concept genre tropes are entrenched by their use in multiple media, such as across crime books, films, and television shows. For example, both Michael Robotham's *Lost* and Daniel O'Malley's *The Rook* feature identity amnesia plots, which, while they might seem risible on the surface, are common enough in TV and film (think *The Bourne Identity*) to warrant their own entry on the wiki TV Tropes: "In most cases, the character has simply lost their memories, no longer remembering their name, loved ones or where they came from. This is often the cause for a Quest for Identity" (another trope with its own entry). Settings that were originally created in books—for example, urban noir settings—are now so familiar from the screen that they, in turn, inspire highly visual descriptions of city spaces in new genre books: for example, in Angela Slatter's fantasy novel, "The full moon turned the landscape silvery-ash. Everything—buildings, cars, city lights, trees, people, the river below—was washed of colour, rendered ghostly and limned with a strange sort of shine in the winter air."[23] This scene setting is firmly rooted in the sense of sight, designed to create visual images in the reader's mind, reminiscent of familiar images from the screen version of the genre. A genre-worlds reading acknowledges the multiple ways that related media influence the sociomaterial creation of genre fiction. TV and film influences, cross-genre opportunities, titles that combine features of previous best sellers, and the creation of new subgenres or writing and publishing into currently successful subgenres are, therefore, some of the ways in which the industrial dimensions of genre worlds become evident in the books themselves.

Extended Reading: *Terra Nullius* by Claire G. Coleman

To illustrate how social and industrial elements interweave with textual conventions in genre worlds, we now present an extended example of a genre-worlds approach to textual analysis. The book we have chosen for our case study is *Terra Nullius,* a work of speculative fiction published by Hachette in 2017, written by Claire G. Coleman, a Noongar woman, from the south coast of Western Australia. We acknowledge that we have chosen a work, here, that exists at the progressive end of the fantasy genre: as critics, we are therefore less gripped by the urge to unmask conservative ideologies than we might be in relation to other texts. In fact, Coleman's work is interesting to us precisely because of the way in which it mobilizes the social, industrial, and textual elements of its genre world to develop the understanding of what it is possible to achieve using the textual conventions of fantasy.

Terra Nullius is Coleman's first novel; her second, *The Old Lie,* was published by Hachette in 2019. As discussed in chapter 4, Coleman's first novel was the recipient of the black&write! grant, coadministered by the State Library of Queensland and Hachette Australia and designed to support Aboriginal and Torres Strait Islander writers and editors. In that chapter we considered the writing and editing process and Coleman's situation in the genre world; we turn now to look at the pages of her book, to see how it shows signs of cooperation in terms of genre industry and genre community, among and through the textual conventions of the fantasy genre.

Before we begin, though, we want to acknowledge one of the persistent memes of fan culture: a concern about "spoilers," revelations of hidden aspects of the plot that may spoil the reading experience for others. Coleman's text derives a great deal of its energy from a startling twist a third of the way in. As good genre citizens, we issue a "spoiler alert" here.

The Paratext of *Terra Nullius*

Paratext is the gateway to the reading experience and a key site where the industrial and the textual dimensions of genre worlds meet.[24] Paratextual elements are crucial to the marketing of a genre novel, while also shaping the interpretation of its textual elements. For example, this novel's title, *Terra Nullius,* is a Latin phrase. This sounds appropriately strange and portentous for a work of speculative fiction but is also—especially for Australian readers—a familiar term from the high-profile *Mabo* legal case of the 1990s. "Terra Nullius" means "empty land" and was the legal doctrine relied on by European settlers to claim Australian land as their own and not to compensate or negotiate with the Aboriginal people who had lived on the land for tens of thousands of years; the validity of this doctrine was overturned in the *Mabo* case.[25] The title of Coleman's novel thus performs multiple tasks. It enacts the defamiliarization of the fantasy genre through its non-English language, particularly Latin, which is often popularly associated with magic spells: think about the Latin-ish words J. K. Rowling uses for the famous spells in the Harry Potter series, for example. Like spells, which use words to make things happen, the speech acts of legal discourse also rely heavily on Latin. It is this second usage, the legal declaration of an empty land to claim for the queen, that the title also plays on, indicating the book's theme of violent colonization and foregrounding the Indigenous Australian affiliation of the book and its author.

This affiliation is also reflected in the original cover design, which recalls the Australian Aboriginal flag in its use of shape and color. Unusually for a genre fiction book, the cover design is absent of genre markers. The reason for this is in part, possibly, because depicting aliens or space ships on the cover (or in the title) would spoil the twist of the book: where what appears to be a historical account of the colonization of Aboriginal people by white settlers is revealed to be a futuristic account of the colonization of Australia (and the earth) by intergalactic settlers. But the use of abstract landscape, the colors (mostly black and white, featuring yellow or red in some editions) and the font are also quite different from other works of speculative fiction. They are still appropriate to the book: the heat of the sun and the desert landscape of Australia are absolutely integral not only as the setting of the novel but also as features that drive the plot forward because they are linked to danger and survival as experienced by Indigenous Australians, white people, and the "toads," or aliens. But one of the other effects of the cover design is that the absence of genre markers potentially positions it as literary fiction. This maximizes the book's sales across readers with different tastes, leaves award-nomination possibilities open, and enables it to secure reviews in mainstream publications. Overall, the cover effectively positions *Terra Nullius* as a work by an Indigenous Australian and about Aboriginal experience, and it is neatly ambiguous about genre while still satisfying readers that it is an accurate match for the contents of the book.

In both print and electronic versions of the original edition of the book, the cover design is used as a header for each chapter, tying this element of paratext closely to the text.

Hybridity: Combining Textual Conventions within the Book

Terra Nullius combines textual conventions from historical fiction with those from fantasy. As Coleman noted in our interview with her, this hybridity was necessary for the novel to achieve its goals, which included provoking empathy in non-Indigenous readers: "The use of speculative fiction and the tropes of historical fiction [were] absolutely fundamental because I need speculative fiction to make it work because you can't, there's no real environment in which I could . . . set the story to make the white audience feel that feeling."[26] Blending these two genres to achieve a certain effect required Coleman to choose words that worked in two lexicons: after the twist, words such as "mounts" and "ships" are repositioned by the reader from the historical genre (horses and sailing ships) to the science fiction genre (alien creatures and spaceships).

Terra Nullius is also hybridized with literary fiction. Darko Suvin's work on science fiction and cognitive estrangement holds that the work of fantasy is to make the familiar strange; Coleman's work, however, makes the strange familiar. A review of the novel by Benjamin Murphy in *Full Stop*, a journal oriented toward literary fiction (it "focuses on debuts, works in translation, and books published by small presses"), put it like this: "Coleman's point is to un-defamiliarize the genre—to render the normally defamiliarizing work of science fiction mundane within the Indigenous perspective of her telling. Her point, in other words, is to show us anew a situation that is not new but all too frequently unseen. We travel forward in time to understand a story that began centuries ago."[27] Murphy's review, which emphasizes the sophistication of Coleman's high-level manipulation of tropes, claims *Terra Nullius* at least partially for literary fiction by showing that it features some of that genre's experimental and ambiguous textual elements. Along with its prose, the book's participation in a global conversation about violence and Indigenous peoples is of interest to readers of literary fiction. This alignment is borne out by Coleman's subsequent invitations to speak at several literary festivals and the book's nomination for the Stella Prize, a literary award.

However, *Terra Nullius* also eschews some of the textual conventions of literary fiction in favor of those from fantasy. In literary accounts of the colonial Australian period, novelists tend to focus on the moral dilemmas and ambiguities of European characters: Kate Grenville's *The Secret River,* for example, imagines the inner turmoil of Grenville's own ancestor, a freed convict who may have participated in the massacre of Aboriginal Australians. Coleman, in contrast, sketches her settler characters as extremes, refusing any sympathy for them (except for Johnny Star, whom we will discuss below). Sister Bagra, for example, "hated babies" and saves special contempt for babies of "Natives": "even uglier than babies usually are, and more ugly even than older Natives." This evil-good dichotomy is a political stance that works better with some of the conventions of fantasy fiction, especially the classic epic fantasy in the style of Tolkien, where noble heroes (like hobbits and elves) take on demonic foes (like orcs and goblins). Indigenous poet and essayist Alison Whittaker highlights and grapples with this in a review of *Terra Nullius* for the prestigious literary journal the *Sydney Review of Books:* "At times, Coleman's colonial characters are didactically drawn. . . . The novel grinds itself against the Australian literary tradition of conceding moral ground to colonists (leaders of massacres, administrators and mission managers) and tending moral turbidity in their victims in the name of nuance and narrative balance. It doesn't do this without sacrifices to more conventional markers of character construction."[28] Whittaker's sensitive review, here, marks out the difference between Coleman's treatment of the violence and cruelty of white settlers and the kind of complex characters typically valued in works of literary fiction (what Whittaker terms "more conventional markers of character construction," referring to the conventions of literary fiction). This review highlights the novel's turn away from the features of literary fiction (such as an emphasis on detailed character interiority) and its utilization, instead, of the affordances of speculative fiction—particularly its nonrealist modes for starkly depicting moral issues.

Leaning in to Genre

Despite its hybridity across literary fiction and fantasy fiction, *Terra Nullius* thoroughly engages fantasy readers using craft that typically creates pleasure in the fantasy community. The staging of the twist, which is the high concept of the book and part of its word-of-mouth appeal (in both marketing and reader-enjoyment terms), creates some interesting formal effects on the page. The first section of the novel is abstract and general and deliberately withholds detail. The second section has a rush, a glut, of detail—offering exactly the kind of factual specificity to do with physiology, weaponry, and transportation systems that is a chief pleasure of speculative fiction and crucial to its imaginary world building. An example of such detail is this description of the spaceship that Sister Bagra takes home: "She would have thought that such mature technology, in use since before she was born, would have no room for improvement but clearly she was wrong. Gone was the shudder of the ship when it entered hyperspace, instead it slipped in like a hot knife through warm butter." The same chapter later notes that Sister Bagra's room on the ship was "no more than a tube with a bed in it."[29] These descriptions take place toward the end of the book, when all narrative threads have been resolved. They do not propel the plot: instead, they exist to revel in genre pleasure: the writer and the readers of this genre world share an affection for imagining spaceships. This is an example of genre as pleasure on the pages of a book, pleasure as excess to the strict requirements of the story being told. Coleman's use of detail, which is full of knowing nods to fellow fantasy fans, is a key way in which *Terra Nullius* participates in the genre world of fantasy.

Coleman also includes intertextual references, both direct and indirect, to speculative fiction works. Chapter 15 features a document written by (invented character) Professor Kalek Huss—a suitably defamiliarized name for the fantasy genre—which compares "the ancient human novel *War of the Worlds*" to the invasion of the earth by the toads: "The reality here is vastly different."[30] As well as confirming fan knowledge and providing a nod to a classic in the genre, Wells's famous fantasy scenario is overtly presented as "vastly different" from the "reality" of alien invasion. Even though *Terra Nullius*'s alien invasion is also fantastic, the comparison creates a jolt of unsettling realism.

Another example of leaning in to genre is the sympathetic alien character Johnny Star, whose name seems almost parodic but also elevates him to fantasy hero status as "Johnny from the stars." His heroic characterization is achieved through figuring him as a rebel and an outlaw, who has rejected the other alien characters. As the book progresses, his heroic outsider status is intensified, and the denouement of the novel features a shoot-out with "troopers" that echoes the death of Ned Kelly, famous Australian outlaw and folk hero, who is widely understood to have died fighting an unfair system.

Similarly, understanding his death is approaching, Johnny Star notes, "The only decision he had the power to make was how [to die], fighting to the death, fighting to stay free or public ritual execution. A blaze of gunfire or the mocking, laughing, faces of the smugly 'civilised.'" Johnny Star also enables Coleman to offer a twist on the moral extremes that are part of fantasy fiction characterization, as discussed above. Offering one character who acts differently from others of their kind is a way to introduce a more nuanced account of race relations. For Coleman, *The Lord of the Rings* is racist: "because it's like is there a good orc? . . . So therefore it's racist. . . . I think there's definitely room in fantasy fiction to tackle the complexity of racism because racism is in, well, *The Lord of the Rings* set the cultural paradigm for what modern fantasy is. And it's racist, so therefore the racism is embedded in the DNA of modern fantasy novels."[31] Coleman's reflection here shows one of the fault lines within the contemporary fantasy genre world, as it reckons with the ongoing influence of one of its most influential figures. *Terra Nullius* is an intervention in this debate. As the one sympathetic alien in the novel, Johnny Star does triple duty as fantasy hero, Australian hero, and a corrective to group stereotype-based characterization in fantastic fiction.

Invented Worlds and Histories

The most important marker of pleasure in fantasy fiction is the building of alternative worlds, and this is another convention that *Terra Nullius* embraces. Coleman adapts her fantastic setting out of the outback Australian landscape, but it is its own distinct fictional place: "The funny thing about the setting is anyone who knows those places goes, 'That environment isn't near that environment. How do they get, travel, from one to the other so quickly?' so I didn't actually use the setting at all accurately, not even slightly. . . . I just used a feel of setting instead of actual settings because I didn't put anywhere real in there." The landscape provokes strong feelings in the characters as, variously, a place to colonize, a place to feel safe, or a place to journey across on a quest. The human boy Jacky experiences a "mute awe" that is tinged with the fantastic at the sight of a rock shaped like a horse: "What beautiful, terrible magic, what history led to a rock that looked like a horse, or a giant stone horse stuck in the mud, dead, it had to be, but staring at the stars? Maybe, being a horse of rock it was merely resting; one day it would rise, shaking off the entrapping soil, climbing from its pit, running off to . . . well, Jacky had no idea where."[32]

Johnny Star, too, sees "beautiful, unbelievable magic" in the natural world when observing fauna. By contrast, the character Devil exemplifies the colonizers' view where "the alien landscape in which he found himself both frightened and sickened him."[33] In all these cases, the landscape is more than just backdrop. It is a part of the story that evokes powerful feelings and offers the fantasy reader pleasurable reading experiences.

Related to landscape is the imagined history of the fantasy world. Genre communities derive pleasure (sometimes bordering on obsession) with those elaborations of setting broadly defined as "lore." As Kim Wilkins has written, lore "refers to the codified history, cultural precedents, belief systems, traditions and knowledges of the imagined world." The codification of lore in documents that are quoted in the text can especially add a sense of a world that is too vast to appear in the narrative frame of the story, while also imparting a sense of evidentiary "truth" to the events. Such use of documents harks back to early fantastic fiction (for example, *Frankenstein*'s framing by Walton's letters) and is represented in the vast histories Tolkien wrote to support the world building of *The Lord of the Rings* (for example, *The Silmarillion*). The technique has also been used in more recent science fiction novels such as Max Brooks's *World War Z* and Christopher Priest's *The Islanders*.[34] Coleman makes use of the technique in *Terra Nullius* by heading every chapter with an excerpt from a faux document, meant to give background and add a feeling of realism to the events of the colonization of earth, including poems, songs, sayings, and historical documents from both colonizers and colonized.

Coleman's publisher at Hachette Australia, Robert Watkins, told us that at first he thought these documents were real: "I remember thinking at the time, 'Where did she find these pieces?' I thought that those bits were real, they were actually nonfiction pieces that she'd plucked from textbooks or something," demonstrating how authoritative written documents can appear to (even professional) readers. This appearance of reality adds to the sense of immersion in the fictional world. Jacky, whose viewpoint we access as readers, is also shown via the viewpoint of future alien historians in these documents: "Jacky Jerramungup will go down in history with the other outlaws, real or legendary, who have fought a more powerful enemy, one they could not really defeat. Robin Hood, Jandamarra, Yagan, Haasheh Gaarnch, all fought with whatever small resources they had, all became thorns in the sides of the administration they were fighting. All became legends in defeat. It does not matter if we capture Jacky Jerramun-gup. In allowing him to become famous, in allowing him to become a role model, we have already lost.—J. R. KAASHAKK, HISTORIAN."[35] Here, the colocated names are various levels of "real or legendary." Robin Hood is a medieval folklore character, often represented in the historical and fantasy genres. Jandamarra, or "Pigeon" as he was known to the European coloniz-ers of Australia, was a nineteenth-century Bunuba man who led guerrilla attacks on white settlers. Yagan was a nineteenth-century Noongar resis-tance leader in the 1820s and '30s. Haasheh Gaarnch is a made-up name, one that sounds like the toad names in the novel and therefore suggests a rebel alien, to round out the group. The real names here, Jandamarra and Yagan, are assertively placed alongside the mythologized white English hero. They are shown to be inspiring to a future Australia under attack from alien forces. The evidentiary authority of documents, especially those signed by a "historian" whose weight is emphasized by capital letters, gives a sense of deep and real history to the fantasy setting.

Reading *Terra Nullius* with the grain, as we have, has produced an analy-sis of a genre fiction text that is rich and multifaceted; attentive to para-textual features such as cover, book design, and positioning in the market; as well as conventional narrative features such as characterization, setting, and the use of genre tropes. We have been able to identify those elements of a text that are borne out of a genre world's debates and conflicts and its desire for progressive change. Paying attention to these facets of a text in total reveals the constant negotiations between writers, readers, publishers, marketers, agents, and editors that inform and are advanced through genre texts. *Terra Nullius* is the work of an individual of great talent and insight, and it is also a product of a cooperative social and industrial network that, directly and indirectly, leaves its mark on the text.

Conclusion

Our exploration of, and ardent advocacy for, studying the social and the industrial dimensions of popular fiction should not obscure the impor-tance—if not the centrality—of the genre fiction text itself. This chapter has shown where textual analysis and the reading of genre fiction fits in the genre-worlds model. We have argued that existing approaches to reading genre texts may fall too much into decisionist paradigms or suspicious readings. Instead, we sought to show how a generous reading—a reading with the grain—may be the most productive way of understanding how genre texts call to and satisfy their readers and how they operate in the market-place as more than just static objects that people buy (without downplaying the fact that genre texts, like all books, need to be bought in order for more books to be created). Our genre-worlds model of textual analysis recognizes moments where the social contexts of books are revealed, such as in their explicit address to genre-competent readers and the way they seek to create genre pleasures. It also illuminates how the industrial contexts of books are revealed—for example, in the way books can be situated within or against trends. We concluded by modeling a genre-worlds reading of Claire G. Coleman's *Terra Nullius* to show the kind of depth and richness that are available if we pay attention to the social and industrial inflections of genre fiction and their dynamic interplay with the textual pleasures of the book and its use of genre tropes. *Terra Nullius* reminds us that genres can be used both conventionally and unconventionally, subject to creative choices that may be influenced by social change and industrial change.

. . .

"Love isn't enough," Jess says, handing you another mojito.

You take the glass and eye it warily. It's number three since you arrived in this increasingly crowded bar, since you received the text from Simon saying he wouldn't be meeting you tonight, or any night. And that he'd already taken his toothbrush and pajamas from your apartment.

"What do you mean?" you ask.

"Relationships are like sharks. If they don't keep moving, they die."

You ponder this. Had you and Simon stagnated? Well, if that was the case, you could change. New hair, new job . . . That would bring Simon back!

Or is Jess making a bigger point? About how things are always changing, about how the smart ones keep adapting? Maybe they are the ones who don't get their hearts broken by text message.

How do you become one of those people?

CHAPTER 7

Genre Worlds and Change

A genre world is a unit of analysis for understanding how books happen. Genre books happen when genre-world participants work together—sometimes closely, sometimes distantly—with the shared goal of bringing a text into the world. This shared goal arises from a common commitment to the features of a genre—its satisfactions, pleasures, style, and attitude—which can be highly affective and bond communities or commercially instrumental (or both). Genre worlds are the interconnected networks through which genre texts are brought into being.

The research presented in this book has shown a way forward for popular fiction studies. In chapter 1, we outlined our theory of genre worlds. A genre world is a collection of people and practices that operates according to established and emerging patterns of collaborative activity to produce the texts that make popular genres recognizable. We explained how the model worked as an extension of Howard S. Becker's "art worlds," mobilizing some of his key concepts such as conventions and the cast of characters. We argued for the value of this genre-worlds model to the study of contemporary popular fiction, articulating it as a new phase and a concerted (and overdue) move away from the plethora of taxonomies and defenses that have dominated the field and celebrating the interdisciplinary location of popular fiction studies within creative writing, publishing studies and book history, and literary studies. The genre-worlds model moves away from taxonomizing one set of conventions (literary tropes) to understand a broader set of industrial and social conventions that contextualize, influence, and are influenced by those tropes. The genre-worlds model studies popular novels on their own terms: as the results of human creative collaboration, as the products of commercial negotiation and strategy, and as levers for social connection and engagement. Our model imagines a genre world as comprising three overlapping layers: the *industrial*, the *social*, and the *textual*.

In chapter 2, we introduced our focus on contemporary genre worlds through a detailed analysis of their situation in the globalized, digitized twenty-first-century publishing industry. Genre, as a process of categorizing texts, has long had an affinity with industry processes that aim to minimize risk by regularizing production and circulation, from the acquiring of new books to their arrangement in bookstores. Genre fiction is also at the forefront of industry change, as publishing's most rapidly produced, high-selling products. Using examples from our interviews, chapter 2 examined how the people, activities, and conventions of the publishing industry shape the production of genre texts. It considered editing as a professionalizing process that reinforces expectations about genre texts and distribution as a site of recent change as new pathways to readers open up. This chapter looked closely at self-publishing as a shift that is deeply reconfiguring the industry, including through the blurring of roles such as writer, reader, editor, and marketer. Genre worlds are early adopters of technology and publishing experiments and showed a rapid uptake in self- and micro-press publishing in the first two decades of the twenty-first century. Self-publishing is integral to the new economy of publishing, which is dominated by technology companies such as Amazon. A close analysis of the role of digital algorithms in shaping genre fiction texts showed the uncertain terrain authors, publishers, and readers negotiate amid the new possibilities of the twenty-first century. This chapter drew out some of the nuanced differences between contemporary genres, such as romance's greater uptake of digital technology compared to crime, but also showed their commonalities: for example, all are implicated in seriality. Genre worlds' relational structure means that there is capacity for adaptability as disruption continues in the way books are brought to readers.

Chapter 3 extended the industrial research of the book by looking at two dimensions of the publishing industry that shape genre worlds: transnational movements and transmedia movements. Each of these extends the borders of genre worlds, but the shape of each genre still holds, as it is bound together by shared conventions. Our section on transnationality in genre worlds addressed structural hierarchies in the publishing industry, including a concentration of power in New York and London. One of our key findings about genre worlds is that they are national and transnational.

Infrastructure for genre books is global, while genre communities may be local with global aspirations and connections. In all our interviews, we saw evidence of people considering their national and international positions but little evidence that anyone feels they must choose between a national and international outlook. Our section on transmedia looked at the fluidity of content across books, films, TV, and video games and how these media formats influence the texts. Our case studies, of the TV series *Miss Fisher's Murder Mysteries* and the *Star Wars* novelization *A Force Unleashed,* showed these processes at work at a granular level, including the different ways of understanding the role of the writer and diverse, industry-led forms of hierarchy and collaboration.

In chapter 4, we turned to the social dimensions of genre worlds, which influence author careers, genre fiction texts, and reader experiences. Our theorization of these social interactions drew on the concept of affinity spaces. We analyzed the social infrastructure of contemporary genre worlds, including formal voluntary associations, and how these create a felt experience of community. The awards, conventions, training, and informal networking that these social structures provide sustain the affective networks of a genre. We highlighted the expressions of shared love for a genre that arise frequently in genre worlds, their support for and expectation of participation, and their idealization of flat hierarchies in the midst of uneven success. We then looked in detail at how this sense of community is mobilized as part of creative practice, influencing the production of texts. We examined a range of different types of creative collaboration, between people of both equal and unequal status in the genre world, and looked at the ways ownership was established in genre worlds, when influence and input may come from so many different sources. The Romantic model of creativity may provide inspiration and enjoyment to writers, but creative practice as described is much more socially and materially relational.

Chapter 5 further pursued the social dimensions of genre worlds by closely examining the role of two kinds of social interactions in genre worlds: online sociality and in-person sociality at conventions. Social media platforms have become an influential means of communication among some genre-world participants, alongside the rise of other digital communications such as email, and the affordances of these technologies, from Twitter's visible follower count to a Facebook group's closed membership, affect how interactions take place. Conventions are a mainstay of genre worlds, showcasing genre affiliations and providing both structured and unstructured opportunities for participant connection and training. As numerous examples from our interviews showed, online and offline socialities are not separate, although they have distinct emphasis and character—rather, the forms of sociality interweave. Sociality in both spheres can be public (marketing announcements on social media, a panel discussion on a stage); semiprivate (a Facebook group, a small group workshop); or completely private (direct messages on Instagram, a conversation in a hotel room). This range suggests a spectrum of insiders and outsiders as well as a range of knowledges about genre worlds' industrial and social processes. We found ourselves very much in the frame in this chapter and were able to write about outsider and insider dynamics from experience.

In chapter 6, we offered an extended analysis of the textual dimensions of genre worlds, drawing together the previous chapters' work to investigate how this can reconfigure our approach to reading crime, fantasy, and romance novels. We looked to the pleasures of textual conventions and how novels may offer, withhold, or play with these. Some texts parody their own genre, while others lean in to favored tropes. We modeled a generous "reading with the grain" and considered some of the distinct textual pleasures of romance, crime, and fantasy. We considered the ways genre fiction texts are closely interwoven with industrial factors, such as the emergence and disappearance of market trends, related media formats, and bookseller demands. As an extended example of a genre-worlds textual reading, we analyzed Claire G. Coleman's *Terra Nullius*, showing how this work of fantasy operates on the page, as well as a product of the industry and of social networks. *Terra Nullius*'s paratext, use of hybrid historical and speculative fiction tropes, and reception all illustrated its position, achievement, and influence within the contemporary genre world of fantasy.

In this conclusion, chapter 7, we address the theoretical issue of change: If the preceding chapters gave a snapshot of crime, fantasy, and romance genre worlds two decades into the twenty-first century, what are the indications of how they might be changing and what the mechanisms of change might be? We look at industrial, social, and textual levers for change. A genre world makes a particular kind of text, and it does so through conventional means. Those means, however, are not neutral. They are caught up in national and transnational flow, in professional and affective relationships, and in the currents of politics and changing social norms.

Technological and Social Change in Genre Worlds

One of the directions of change we see for genre worlds is technological. Our research suggests that transmedia storytelling and media convergence will become more and more important. Internationally, China leads the way in pan-entertainment, an extreme form of vertical integration where a creative property is acquired in order to exploit rights across multiple media—for example, books, games, television, and anime. We have shown that this tendency already exists in publishing, and we expect it to intensify. Content moves fluidly between books and other media products, especially in the popular fiction sector. That fluidity flows both ways: from books to other media (for example, adaptations) and from other media to books (such as novelizations). What this means for our genre-worlds model is that it will need to maintain its focus on people as well as works. We anticipate the networks of cooperative activity to expand, as more and more different types of agents are involved in the production of works.

In general, we anticipate increased use of digital technologies in genre worlds. It is impossible to ignore the amount of change in twenty-first-century genre worlds that has been driven by digitization. Rather than stating this as a kind of technological determinism, we present it as a basic fact: humans and computers have interacted to produce new ways of doing popular fiction, which include digitally networked possibilities. For example, microgenres proliferate on Amazon, and genre-world participants connect online through the regular use of Facebook groups. These things occur alongside the continued appreciation of nondigital practices, such as browsing bookshops and attending events. As time goes on, global-platform capitalism may exercise negative effects on book culture; powerful technology companies such as Google and Amazon will certainly continue to drive innovation in genre worlds.

A second direction of change is one this concluding chapter will investigate in more depth. Questions of diversity, inclusion, representation, and inequity in genre worlds arose again and again in our interviews and have been discussed frequently in this book, from author Sulari Gentill's observations about the expectations that attended her as a writer of color to publisher Lindy Cameron's reflection on the rise and fall of lesbian crime fiction as a subgenre. We expect this debate to continue to evolve and influence genre worlds.

Many of our interviewees expressed a desire for increased diversity in genre worlds. Angela Savage, for example, expressed support for a diversified Australian crime genre world, noting that "there's so few writers of diverse backgrounds writing crime fiction or at least getting published." She pointed toward a trend of greater engagement with diversity in the pages of crime fiction, albeit written by white authors: in her words, "I totally recognize the whiteness of the publishing industry and the fact that there's heaps more space for [diverse] writers' voices to be heard, and needless to say if and when I find people writing crime fiction like that, then that's exactly who I'm going to get behind and promote." Savage shows the willingness of participants in a genre world to change and the potentially influential role of figures who support authors. Agent Miriam Kriss, too, when asked about what was changing in the genre world, observed, "You're asking about what has changed. I think now there's a real hunger for different voices. . . . Now there is a real hunger to have other non-Western voices telling their stories without compromising it, or the idea that a Western audience would be uncomfortable with that, which is an interesting and important shift, I think." In her interview with us, fantasy writer Angela Slatter reflected on her desire to support writers of color in her genre world with a very specific aim. Slatter said, "You want to see it more diverse. You want to see, you know, not just white women getting in there, but you want to see Indigenous and people of color and differently gendered people and, because fantasy is meant to be rich."[1] Here she links fantasy's ability to reach its highest quality of richness to diversity in the genre world and the texts it produces. Innovation in genre worlds depends on their ability to embrace new perspectives.

Although genre conventions may be conservative, participants may drive development in certain directions. Author Iain Ryan saw recent innovation in the crime genre as coming from female writers:

> Even though Ellroy's sort of my daddy [laughing], a lot of what I'm drawing my energy off in terms of moving my own stories outside of hard-boiled detectives and whatever else is coming from reading women, so like Gillian Flynn and Megan Abbott, Sara Gran, and people like that. I feel like it's almost obvious to say that women are doing the work. There's so much stuff about how women are doing the more interesting kind of work in the genre. I think that's certainly true because Megan Abbott's last book was about a hard-

boiled gymnast. That was amazing. I don't even understand how these tropes are working in this space, but I just remember thinking we're really into a new . . . that was the first time I'd really acknowledged . . . it's like we're in a whole other thing now.[2]

Ryan refers here to the long association of the hard-boiled crime novel with masculinity, especially through stars in the genre such as James Ellroy, whose influence is strongly felt in the community. That he sees women writers as the ones taking risks and trying new ways of writing crime is telling: in genre worlds, diversity is driving innovation.

Editor Grace Lucas-Pennington spoke to us of what she perceives as a "new wave of Indigenous speculative fiction" that is being enabled by writing fellowships like the one black&write! offers: "I think that especially now with this push for diverse books and the recognition that sci-fi and fantasy have been very white male territories that now it's like everyone is searching, seeking for this new diverse sci-fi that is around and has been written for the whole time but people just weren't picking it up. So maybe now there's more of an appetite for the publishers. I think the appetite from the audience has always been there, but there may not have been access to the books for that audience, like there is now." Importantly, Lucas-Pennington tells us that Indigenous perspectives are changing the conventions of genres and in some cases creating new genres: "I'm not sure whether that's just the breadth and prevalence of writing now that we're seeing from younger and younger people that are just making their own genres. . . . Maybe because there's less of a history of Indigenous publishing, there aren't as many rules to be laid down, so people can experiment and people can be freer to do that."[3] These interviewees indicate the will to change and the industrial, social, and textual places within genre worlds where they see the scope for that change. In addition to this general positivity toward increased diversity, there are also examples of direct action in genre worlds—revolution not evolution.

Activism and Genre Worlds

Each community of writers, readers, and industry professionals experiences internal debates about the need for change. One significant debate happening across and within genre worlds has been gender inequity, which has been countered through a series of activist projects. Prizes are perhaps the most visible kind of activism. As discussed in chapter 4, Sisters in Crime Australia runs two prizes for female crime writers: the Scarlet Stiletto Awards for short stories and the Davitt Awards for books. An article by Angela Savage recounts cofounder Carmel Shute describing the Scarlet Stilettos, launched in 1994, as "originating at a meeting over a few glasses of wine about the difficulties facing female aspiring crime writers": "The Sisters in Crime saw the Scarlet Stiletto Awards as a way of cutting through the discrimination." The Davitts were launched in 2001. Like the Stella and the Women's Prize, the Davitts responded to years of all-male short lists generated by existing awards: in this case the Ned Kelly Awards for Australian crime writing. The Davitt Awards have no prize money, cost nothing to enter, and are run thanks to the passion of this genre-based group. They have an undeniable impact. In 2017 debut author Emma Viskic won two Davitt Awards and then a Ned Kelly Award for *Resurrection Bay*, while in 2018 Sulari Gentill was short-listed for a Davitt and went on to win a Ned Kelly for *Crossing the Lines*. Prizes can be activist in terms of the authors they recognize; they can also be activist in the kinds of writing they award. The Staunch Prize is a new prize for "a thriller in which no woman is beaten, stalked, sexually exploited, raped or murdered."[4] Prizes are social actors, designed to produce reactions, are relatively straightforward to set up (although less easy to fund), and have a media impact that can travel beyond a genre world as well as prompting change within it.

Genre-world events, and particularly speeches at festivals and conventions, are another way that participants address inequality. In 2018 hundreds of romance writers and publishers gathered at the Sofitel Wentworth in Sydney for the Romance Writers of Australia Convention. Most writers and readers of romance are women, and romance fiction is a vibrant genre world in which debates about women's pleasure, relationships, careers, and finances are ever active. One of the 2018 RWA keynote presentations was given by the then managing editor of Harlequin's Escape imprint, Kate Cuthbert. Cuthbert's speech, reproduced in the industry magazine *Books + Publishing* and discussed by Jane Sullivan in the *Age,* was a moment when this genre world's internal debates became visible to literary culture more broadly.

In her speech, Cuthbert addressed the responsibilities of romance fiction writers and publishers in the #MeToo era. As Cuthbert exhorted her audience, "If we want to call ourselves a feminist genre, if we want to hold ourselves up as an example of women being centered, of representing the female gaze, of creating women heroes who not only survive but thrive, then we have to lead." For Cuthbert, this means "breaking up" with some familiar romance fiction tropes, such as the coercion of women: "Many of the behaviors that are now being called out—sexual innuendo, workplace advances, stolen kisses because the kisser couldn't resist—feel in many ways like an old friend," Cuthbert said. "They exist in the romance bubble, . . . and they readily tap into that shared emotional history over and over again in a way that feels familiar and safe." Cuthbert's compassionate acknowledgment of readers' and writers' attachment to established genre norms sits alongside her call for evolution, for renewed attention to "recognizing the heroine's bodily autonomy, her right to decide what happens to it at every point."[5] Cuthbert's speech is a call from within the heart of the romance genre to advance it in directions that are empowering for women: as characters, authors, and readers.

Race-related issues have been a particular focus for activism (and sometimes backlash) within contemporary genre worlds. One example occurred in late 2019, when the Romance Writers of America board censured prominent writer of color Courtney Milan, suspending her from the organization for a year and banning her from leadership positions for life. This decision was made following complaints by two white women, author Katherine Lynn Davis and publisher Suzan Tisdale, about statements Milan had made on Twitter, including Milan calling a specific book a "fucking racist mess." The use of the organization's formal mechanisms to censure the woman of color and validate the complaints of white women was very controversial, provoking widespread debate across social media and email lists. The debate was particularly high-profile because Milan had long been an advocate for greater inclusion and diversity within RWA and the romance genre. As the *Guardian* reported: "The choice not to discipline anyone for 'actually racist speech' made punishing someone for 'calling something racist' seem like a particularly troubling double standard, Milan said. 'People saw it as an attempt to silence marginalized people,' Milan said. 'Doing this to me seemed like a message that if it could happen to me, it could happen to anyone, and everyone needed to shut up.'"[6] The board went on to retract its decision about Milan. It is difficult, however, to calculate the damage that may have been done to writers of color within the romance genre world and the retarding effects the RWA's actions may have on the push to increase diversity in romance. Conversely, the use of Twitter to extend debate and eventually correct the RWA shows change happening, in real time.

A similar push-pull change process is evident in the fantasy genre with respect to gender and race. Romance fiction is, largely, produced by women and for women, but speculative fiction is more like crime: a noticeable gender split runs through the genre. Since it began eighty years ago, Worldcon, the World Science Fiction Convention, has featured 193 guests of honor—valued authors, artists, and fans. Of this number 154, or 80 percent, of these guests of honor have been men. The gender balance, though, looks very different in recent years. In the first sixty years of Worldcon, only 14 women were guests of honor; in contrast, 19 women were guests of honor between 2010 and 2019. The last decade of Worldcon has produced more than half of the 39 female guests of honor. This is evidence of a sharpened focus on gender inequity and rapid action within this organization, fandom, and genre world.

Such change does not happen smoothly. About the same time that the Worldcon guest-of-honor list shows an increased prominence of women in speculative fiction, the Sad Puppies / Rabid Puppies controversy erupted. It was 2013, and right-wing fantasy author Larry Correia wanted his novel short-listed for the prestigious Hugo Awards. Nominees and winners of these awards are voted on by members of Worldcon (and anyone can become a supporting member for a fee); Correia's blog post asking for votes was accompanied by a picture of a sad puppy. From here, Sad Puppies expanded into a campaign against what Correia and his allies saw as the politicization of speculative fiction; in a 2014 blog post, Correia wrote, "Message or identity politics has become far more important than entertainment or quality." The Sad Puppies campaigned online for slates of novels they wanted short-listed in the Hugo Awards in 2014 and in 2015; also in 2015, Vox Day began the more extreme Rabid Puppies. As Emily Todd VanDerWerff put it in a recap article for vox.com, "To call [Day] a controversial figure is putting it mildly. He has, at various points, suggested women should not vote, called [African American author N. K.] Jemisin half-savage, and been hugely involved in other reactionary movements, including Gamergate."[7] The Sad Puppies and Rabid Puppies were successful at getting their nominees onto the Hugo short lists, but not at securing winners—Worldcon members, instead, voted to confer "no award" in categories where the short list was composed entirely of Sad Puppies / Rabid Puppies nominees. And in 2016, just after Worldcon's board changed the rules of the Hugo Awards to inhibit bloc voting, N. K. Jemisin became the first Black author to win a Hugo Award, for her novel *The Fifth Season,* the first in her Broken Earth series. Jemisin went on to win again in 2017 and 2018, becoming the first-ever author to win three back-to-back Hugo Awards for each volume in a trilogy. In her eloquent 2018 acceptance speech, Jemisin touched on the discrimination she had experienced in her career (including her first novel being rejected because "only black people would ever possibly want to read the work of a black writer" and the "fellow panelists who tried to talk over me about my own damn life") and distilled the historical significance of her win:

> I get a lot of questions about where the themes of the Broken Earth trilogy come from. I think it's pretty obvious that I'm drawing on the human history of structural oppression, as well as my feelings about this moment in American history. What may be less obvious, though, is how much of the story derives from my feelings about science fiction and fantasy. Then again, SFF is a microcosm of the wider world, in no way rarefied from the world's pettiness or prejudice.
>
> . . . This is a year in which records have been set. A year in which even the most privilege-blindered of us has been forced to acknowledge that the world is broken and needs fixing—and that's a good thing! Acknowledging the problem is the first step toward fixing it. I look to science fiction and fantasy as the aspirational drive of the Zeitgeist: we creators are the engineers of possibility. And as this genre finally, however grudgingly, acknowledges that the dreams of the marginalized matter and that all of us have a future, so will go the world. (Soon, I hope.)

Jemisin's speech concludes by directly addressing the tone of debates around the awards: "This is the year in which I get to smile at all of those naysayers—every single mediocre insecure wannabe who fixes their mouth to suggest that I do not belong on this stage, that people like me cannot possibly have earned such an honor, that when they win it it's meritocracy but when we win it it's 'identity politics'—I get to smile at those people, and lift a massive, shining, rocket-shaped middle finger in their direction."[8] The Hugo Awards controversy, then, is an example of the fierce debates about ethics that can take place within a genre community: it shows progressive action, followed by conservative reaction, followed by progressive reaction.

The changes happening within speculative fiction include fan involvement and online debate—readers, in this genre world, are not only participants but often activists. As shown in chapter 6, these debates track onto the content of books, so that genre fiction works from previous decades bear the imprint of quite different genre-world discussion and debates than those from the contemporary period.

The Shape of the Future

Moments of friction indicate potential for change. What are some findings from our research that suggest how positive change could be encouraged—what is our research's activist potential? The list is long and includes the role of social media as a way for people to enter genre worlds, the use of training events at physical conventions, and industry schemes that support marginalized writers and editors. In chapter 2, we talked about the splintering of the market into niche subgenres—an innovation that brings potential for new texts to be published, including those that are progressive or radical. Given the changes to mediation in the publishing industry, there is no need to appeal to a majority mainstream audience anymore. Successful niches can travel into the mainstream. Marquee authors may leverage a trend, although when they do they take on more risk than self-published or small-press authors and are far more susceptible to subgenres fading.

Our research also identifies obstacles to change that will need to be overcome. For example, the high value placed on community in genre worlds, their drive toward collegiality and emphasis on shared investments, can have its dark side. Sexual harassment claims about Canadian small-press fantasy publisher ChiZine revealed that people were reluctant to report because they feared "being cut off from the community," because a "social circle centered around" ChiZine decided "who was in or out."[9] Genre worlds can feel small, making people afraid to rock the boat. Even in its positive form, community leads to a tendency to niceness in discourse, which obscures problems and can make it hard to articulate difficulties. The publishing industry and by corollary genre worlds lean toward being conservative, evolving only minimally in order to contain or balance the risk that is inherent to publishing books. Received wisdom sweeps through genre worlds, often without critical reflection. These received genre conventions—to do with texts, social interactions, and industry expectations—are self-fulfilling until interrupted by some new or dramatic event. Genre worlds are marked by forces that maintain the status quo and help the world cohere as well as by forces that drive innovation, open borders, and reach outwards. These are the push-and-pull movements of a dynamic cultural sector.

Creating the conditions of change is just one of the possible results of the myriad interactions within and between the industrial, social, and textual dimensions of genre worlds that this book has elucidated. Social and textual dimensions collide when writers offer other writers advice on creative decisions; industrial and social dimensions connect when editors and writers become friends; textual and industrial dimensions interact when paratexts emphasize genre conventions. The genre worlds of crime, fantasy, and romance pursue interactions such as these in ways that are sometimes very similar and sometimes marked by their distinctive fan cultures, histories, position in the market, and norms to do with affect and enthusiasm. Genre worlds are complexes constituted by multiple dimensions: industrial, social, and textual. Only by understanding the interactions between these dimensions do we gain a complete picture of the work of contemporary popular fiction.

. . .

Your eyes lift as the mansion comes into view. It's as you dreamed it would be: a magnificent space of possibility. Room to be creative, room to be entrepreneurial, room to be collaborative. A huge library full of every kind of book imaginable and some that nobody has imagined yet.

This is twenty-first-century publishing, and while its teetering, bat-infested gothic towers may give you pause, they also fire your imagination, inspire you, and thrill you.

"Are you ready?"

You nod and allow yourself to be lifted in strong arms and carried over the threshold. Maybe there will be a happily ever after for you here.

Acknowledgments

This research has demonstrated to us abundantly the importance of a cast of characters in completing intellectual work. We have many to thank:

Brian Halley at the University of Massachusetts Press for his enthusiasm and expertise as well as the peer reviewers of our manuscript for their generosity and insight, Page and Screen series editor Kate Eichorn, Rachael DeShano, Annette Wenda, and all at the University of Massachusetts Press who helped make the book real. Emeritus Professor David Carter from the University of Queensland for his wisdom, deep knowledge of book history, humor, and mentorship. Professor Claire Squires from the University of Stirling for illuminating new pathways and modeling outstanding academic leadership. The staff of AustLit, the Australian literature database, for working with us collaboratively to extend knowledge about popular fiction in Australia. Our highly valued research assistants, Jodi McAlister, Millicent Weber, Caitlin Francis, Claire Parnell, Eliza Murphy, Jodie Martire, Meg Vann, Caylee Tierney, Michelle Goldsmith, and Wolfram von Keesing.

This work would not have been possible without opportunities afforded us by a range of agencies and organizations. The Australian Research Council provided a generous Discovery grant for four years of fieldwork, conference travel, and writing time. The Romance Writers of America funded us for a vital seed project. The Australia Centre at the University of Melbourne, particularly Professor Ken Gelder, and genre-worlds model, particularly Peter Ball, made valuable opportunities for us to present work in progress and build the field. We also received feedback on work in progress at the International Association of Popular Romance Studies conference; the Association for Study of Australian Literature conference; the Australian Media Traditions conference; the Popular Culture Association conference;

the Society for the History of Authorship, Reading, and Publishing conference; and the University of Edinburgh Centre for the History of the Book. Some of our ideas for this monograph were developed in short monographs, journal articles, and book chapters, and we thank the editors and peer reviewers for the Cambridge Elements in Publishing and Book Culture series and the following journals and edited book collections: *Australian Literary Studies, Creative Industries Journal, First Monday, Global Media and Communication, Griffith Review, Journal of Popular Culture, Journal of Popular Romance Studies, Logos, Meanjin, Media International Australia, Mémoires du Livre / Studies in Book Culture, Post45, Interscript, Sydney Review of Books, Text, Encyclopedia of Romance Fiction* (edited by Kristin Ramsdell), *When Highbrow Meets Lowbrow* (edited by Peter Swirski and Tero Eljas Vanhanen), *New Directions in Popular Fiction* (edited by Ken Gelder), and *The Return of Print?* (edited by Aaron Mannion and Emmett Stinson).

We acknowledge the support of our respective institutions, the University of Queensland, the University of Melbourne, and the University of Tasmania, for their allocation of resources and for opportunities to present research internally. We also acknowledge the support of our partners and families, particularly during the periods of our fieldwork.

Finally, and most significantly, we extend our sincerest gratitude to the many people who participated in interviews for this project. Your time, generosity, enthusiasm, curiosity, willingness to be frank, and great good company made this research a joy. Thank you; we are so humbled to be part of your genre worlds.

Appendix

Case Studies

For each of the below case studies, we interviewed a number of people associated with the book (for example, author, agent, editor, publisher, writing mentor). We also conducted several interviews that focused on broader or contextual genre-world issues, such as the inner working of publishing houses.

Case-Study Focus	Genre
Kerry Greenwood, Phryne Fisher series of historical detective fiction (McPhee Gribble/Allen & Unwin, 1989–2020), adapted for television and a movie	Crime
American Extreme Bull Riders Tour multiauthor series (*Irresistible Cowboy, The Bull Rider's Redemption, Must Love Cowboys, Most Dangerous Cowboy, A Doctor for the Cowboy, Cowboy Takes All, Rescued by the Cowboy, Unbroken Cowboy*) (Tule, 2017)	Romance
Claire G. Coleman, *Terra Nullius* (Hachette, 2017), speculative fiction, former winner of black&write! Indigenous writing fellowship	Fantasy
Iain Ryan, *The Student* (Echo, 2017), noir thriller	Crime
Candice Fox, coauthored books with James Patterson including *Never Never* (Penguin, 2016)	Crime
Angela Slatter, *Vigil* (Hachette, 2016), urban fantasy novel, first of the Verity Fassbinder series	Fantasy
Emma Viskic, *Resurrection Bay* (Echo, 2015), thriller set in regional Australia	Crime
Anne Gracie, *The Winter Bride* (Berkley [Penguin imprint], 2014), historical romance, book 2 of the Chance Sisters series	Romance
Garry Disher, *Bitter Wash Road* (Text, 2013), police procedural	Crime
Mitchell Hogan, *Crucible of Souls* (self-published, 2013; HarperCollins, 2015)	Fantasy
Bronwyn Parry, *Darkening Skies* (Hachette, 2013), romantic suspense	Romance

Case-Study Focus (continued)	Genre
Kylie Scott, *Lick* (Pan Macmillan, 2013), first novel in the Stage Dive series	Romance
Rachael Johns, *Jilted* (HQN [Harlequin], 2012) and *The Patterson Girls* (Mira [Harlequin], 2015)	Romance
Kate Forsyth, *Bitter Greens* (Random House, 2012), fairy tale/historical fantasy	Fantasy
Daniel O'Malley, *The Rook* (HarperCollins, 2012), urban fantasy, adapted for television by Starz, premiered 2019	Fantasy
Sulari Gentill, *A Few Right Thinking Men* (Pantera Press, 2010), historical crime fiction	Crime
Sean Williams, *The Force Unleashed* (Titan Books, 2008), *Star Wars* novelization	Fantasy
Anna Campbell, *Claiming the Courtesan* (Avon, 2007), Regency romance novel	Romance
Keri Arthur, *Full Moon Rising* (Random House, 2006), paranormal romance, first in the Riley Jenson Guardian series	Romance
Michael Robotham, *Lost* (Time-Warner, 2005), psychological thriller	Crime
Cecilia Dart-Thornton, *The Ill-Made Mute* (Pan Macmillan, 2001), epic fantasy, first of the Bitterbynde trilogy	Fantasy
Sara Douglass, *Battleaxe* (HarperCollins, 1997), epic fantasy, first of the Axis trilogy	Fantasy

Notes

···

CHAPTER 1: A Theory of Genre Worlds

1. Howard S. Becker, *Art Worlds* (Berkeley: University of California Press, 1982).

2. See discussion in Beth Driscoll and DeNel Rehberg Sedo, "The Transnational Reception of Bestselling Books between Canada and Australia," *Global Media and Communication* (June 29, 2020).

3. Pascale Casanova, *World Republic of Letters* (Cambridge, MA: Harvard University Press, 2004), 169–71. For historical work on the transnational movement of popular fiction, see David Carter and Roger Osborne, who explore the history of Australian books in the U.S. and U.K. marketplace, both "serious" and popular literature, coining the term "two-sided triangle" to describe the way only the U.S. and U.K. nodes of the triangle were dynamic in the relationship. Carter and Osborne, *Australian Books and Authors in the American Marketplace, 1840s–1940s* (Sydney: Sydney University Press, 2018), 2.

4. See, for example, John Thompson, *Merchants of Culture* (Cambridge: Polity, 2010); Claire Squires, *Marketing Literature: The Making of Contemporary Literature in Britain* (Basingstoke: Palgrave Macmillan, 2007); Nick Levey, "Post-Press Literature: Self-Published Authors in the Literary Field," *Post45* (2016); and Aarthi Vadde, "Amateur Creativity: Contemporary Literature and the Digital Publishing Scene," *New Literary History* 48, no. 1 (2017): 27–51.

5. David Carter, "The Literary Field and Contemporary Trade-Book Publishing in Australia: Literary and Genre Fiction," *Media International Australia* 158, no. 1 (2016): 52.

6. David Carter, "Beyond the Antipodes: Australian Popular Fiction in Transnational Networks," in *New Directions in Popular Fiction: Genre, Distribution, Reproduction,* ed. Ken Gelder (London: Palgrave Macmillan, 2016), 349.

7. See, for example, C. Clayton Childress, "What's the Matter with Jarrettsville? Genre Classification as an Unstable and Opportunistic Construct," in *Exploring Creativity: Evaluative Practices in Innovation, Design, and the Arts,* ed. Brian Moeran and Bo T. Christensen (Cambridge: Cambridge University Press, 2013), 43–68; Thomas Franssen and Giselinde Kuipers, "Sociology of Literature and Publishing in the Early 21st Century: Away from the Centre," *Cultural Sociology* 9, no. 3 (2015): 291–95; Melanie Ramdarshan Bold, "The Return of the Social Author: Negotiating Authority and

Influence on Wattpad," *Convergence* 24, no. 2 (2018): 117–36; and Gisèle Sapiro, "The Role of Publishers in the Making of World Literature: The Case of Gallimard," *Letteratura e Letterature* 11 (2017): 81–93.

8. See discussion in Ken Gelder, "Recovering Australian Popular Fiction: Towards the End of Australian Literature," *Journal of the Association for the Study of Australian Literature* (2000): 115.

9. Kim Wilkins, "Popular Genres and the Australian Literary Community: The Case of Fantasy Fiction," *Journal of Australian Studies* 32, no. 2 (2008): 265; Kim Wilkins, Beth Driscoll, and Lisa Fletcher, "What Is Australian Popular Fiction?," *Australian Literary Studies* 33, no. 4 (2018): 1–11. See also Caylee Tierney, "An Intricate Web: Unweaving Strands of Convention in Children's Fantasy Series by Australians," *Australian Humanities Review* 66 (2020).

10. Gerard Genette, *The Artchitext: An Introduction*, trans. Jane E. Lewin (Berkeley: University of California Press, 1992); Northrop Frye, *Anatomy of Criticism* (Princeton, NJ: Princeton University Press, 1957); Tzvetan Todorov, *The Fantastic: A Structural Approach to a Literary Genre* (Cleveland, OH: Case Western Reserve University Press, 1973), 7; Hans Robert Jauss. *Toward an Aesthetic of Reception* (Minneapolis: University of Minnesota Press, 1982), 88; John Frow, *Genre* (New York: Routledge, 2006), 114.

11. Frow, *Genre*, 2, 87, 196; T. G. Pavel, "Literary Genres as Norms and Good Habits," *New Literary History* 34, no. 2 (2003): 203; Heather Dubrow, *Genre* (New York: Methuen, 1982), 2–3; Ria Cheyne, *Disability, Literature, Genre: Representation and Affect in Contemporary Fiction* (Liverpool: Liverpool University Press, 2019), 17; Kim Wilkins, "The Process of Genre," *Text* 9, no. 2 (2005), www.textjournal.com.au/oct05/wilkins.htm.

12. Steve Neale, "Questions of Genre," in *Film Genre Reader II*, ed. Barry Keith Grant (Austin: University of Texas Press, 1995), 159–83; Jason Mittell, *Genre and Television: From Cop Shows to Cartoons in American Culture* (New York: Routledge, 2004), ix.

13. Jeremy Rosen, *Minor Characters Have Their Day: Genre and the Contemporary Literary Marketplace* (New York: Columbia University Press, 2016), 4–6, vii.

14. John G. Cawelti, *Adventure, Mystery, and Romance: Formula Stories as Art and Popular Culture* (Chicago: University of Chicago Press, 1976); John Sutherland, *Bestsellers: Popular Fiction of the 1970s* (London: Routledge & Kegan Paul, 1981); Michael Butter, "Caught between Cultural and Literary Studies: Popular Fiction's Double Otherness," *Journal of Literary Theory* 4, no. 2 (2010): 201–2.

15. "Crime Fiction Studies," www.euppublishing.com/loi/cfs.

16. Janice A. Radway, *Reading the Romance: Women, Patriarchy, and Popular Literature* (Chapel Hill: University of North Carolina Press, 2009); Brian Attebery, *Strategies of Fantasy* (Bloomington: Indiana University Press, 1992); Rosemary Jackson, *Fantasy: The Literature of Subversion* (London: Methuen, 1981); Lisa Fletcher, *Historical Romance Fiction: Heterosexuality and Performativity* (Aldershot: Ashgate, 2008); Jayashree Kamblé, *Making Meaning in Popular Romance Fiction: An Epistemology* (New York: Palgrave Macmillan, 2014); Lynne Pearce, *Romance Writing* (Cambridge: Polity, 2007); Pamela Regis, *A Natural History of the Romance Novel* (Philadelphia: University of Pennsylvania Press, 2003); Hsu-Ming Teo, *Desert Passions: Orientalism and Romance Novels* (Austin: University of Texas Press, 2012); Jodi McAlister, *The Consummate Virgin Female Virginity Loss and Love in Anglophone Popular Literatures* (Cham: Palgrave Mac-

millan, 2020); Jayashree Kamblé, Eric Murphy Selinger, and Hsu-Ming Teo, eds., *The Routledge Research Companion to Popular Romance Fiction* (London: Routledge, 2020); John Clute and John Grant, eds., *The Encyclopedia of Fantasy* (London: Orbit, 1997); Farah Mendlesohn, *Rhetorics of Fantasy* (Middletown, CT: Wesleyan University Press, 2008); Brian Stableford, *Historical Dictionary of Fantasy Literature* (Lanham, MD: Scarecrow Press, 2005); Stephen Knight, *Form and Ideology in Crime Fiction* (London: Macmillan, 1980); John Scaggs, *Crime Fiction* (Abingdon: Routledge, 2005).

17. Recent edited collections giving the field weight include David Glover and Scott McCracken, eds., *The Cambridge Companion to Popular Fiction* (Cambridge: Cambridge University Press, 2012); Christine Berberich, ed., *The Bloomsbury Introduction to Popular Fiction* (London: Bloomsbury, 2014); Bernice M. Murphy and Stephen Matterson, eds., *Twenty-First-Century Popular Fiction* (Edinburgh: Edinburgh University Press, 2018); and Gelder, *New Directions in Popular Fiction*.

18. Sally R. Munt, *Murder by the Book? Feminism and the Crime Novel* (London: Routledge, 1994); Anne Cranny-Francis, *Feminist Fiction: Feminist Uses of Generic Fiction* (New York: St. Martin's Press, 1990), 9; Jackson, *Fantasy*, 2.

19. Cawelti, *Adventure, Mystery, and Romance*; Thomas J. Roberts, *An Aesthetics of Junk Fiction* (Athens: University of Georgia Press, 1990); Jerry Palmer, *Potboilers: Methods, Concepts and Case Studies in Popular Fiction* (London: Routledge, 1991); Scott McCracken, *Pulp: Reading Popular Fiction* (Manchester: Manchester University Press, 1998).

20. Pierre Bourdieu, *The Field of Cultural Production* (London: Polity, 1993); Pierre Bourdieu, *The Rules of Art: Genesis and Structure of the Literary Field* (Stanford, CA: Stanford University Press, 1996); Ken Gelder, *Popular Fiction: The Logics and Practices of a Literary Field* (Abingdon: Routledge, 2004), 11–12, 1.

21. Clive Bloom, *Bestsellers: Popular Fiction since 1900* (New York: Palgrave Macmillan, 2002); Sutherland, *Bestsellers*; Gelder, *Popular Fiction*, 1.

22. Radway, *Reading the Romance*; Frank Felsenstein and James J. Connolly, *What Middletown Read: Print Culture in an American Small City* (Amherst: University of Massachusetts Press, 2015); Danielle Fuller, *Writing the Everyday: Women's Textual Communities in Atlantic Canada* (Montreal: McGill–Queen's University Press, 2004); Nicola Humble, "The Reader of Popular Fiction," in *Cambridge Companion to Popular Fiction*, ed. Glover and McCracken, 86–102; David Carter, "Middlebrow Book Culture," in *Routledge International Handbook of the Sociology of Art and Culture*, ed. Laurie Hanquinet and Mike Savage (Abingdon: Routledge, 2016), 351–66; Beth Driscoll, *The New Literary Middlebrow: Tastemakers and Reading in the Twenty-First Century* (Basingstoke: Palgrave Macmillan, 2014); Paula Rabinowitz, *American Pulp: How Paperbacks Brought Modernism to Main Street* (Princeton, NJ: Princeton University Press, 2014); Erin Smith, "Pulp Sensations," in *Cambridge Companion to Popular Fiction*, ed. Glover and McCracken, 141–58; Michael Denning, *Mechanic Accents: Dime Novels and Working Class Culture in America* (London: Verso, 1998).

23. Kim Wilkins, *Young Adult Fantasy: Conventions, Originality, Reproducibility* (Cambridge: Cambridge University Press, 2019), 10–11.

24. Robert Darnton, "What Is the History of Books?," *Daedalus* 111, no. 3 (1982): 65–83; Padmini Ray Murray and Claire Squires, "The Digital Publishing Communications Circuit," *Book 2.0* 3, no. 1 (2013): 3–24.

25. For discussion, see Simone Murray, "Publishing Studies: Critically Mapping Research in Search of a Discipline," *Publishing Research Quarterly* 22, no. 4 (2006): 3–25; Millicent Weber and Aaron Mannion, "Discipline and Publish: Disciplinary Boundaries in Publishing Studies," in *Publishing Means Business: Australian Perspectives,* ed. Aaron Mannion, Millicent Weber, and Katherine Day (Melbourne: Monash, 2017), 182–205; and Rachel Noorda and Stevie Marsden, "Twenty-First Century Book Studies: The State of the Discipline," *Book History* 22, no. 1 (2019): 370–97.

26. Joseph McAleer, *Passion's Fortune: The Story of Mills and Boon* (Oxford: Oxford University Press, 1999); André Schiffrin, *The Business of Books: How International Conglomerates Took Over Publishing and Changed the Way We Read* (London: Verso, 2001).

27. Thompson, *Merchants of Culture;* Driscoll, *New Literary Middlebrow;* C. Clayton Childress, "Regionalism and the Publishing Class: Conflicted Isomorphism and Negotiated Identity in a Nested Field of American Publishing," *Cultural Sociology* 9, no. 3 (2015): 364–81; Squires, *Marketing Literature.*

28. Casanova, *World Republic of Letters.*

29. Gisèle Sapiro, "Translation and Symbolic Capital in the Era of Globalization: French Literature in the United States," *Cultural Sociology* 9, no. 3 (2015): 320–46; Corinna Norrick-Rühl and Melanie Ramdarshan Bold, "Crossing the Channel: Publishing Translated German Fiction in the UK," *Publishing Research Quarterly* 32, no. 2 (2016): 125–38; Gisèle Sapiro, "How Do Literary Works Cross Borders (or Not)?," *Journal of World Literature* 1, no. 1 (2016): 81–96; Driscoll and Sedo, "Transnational Reception of Bestselling Books."

30. See, for example, Joe Moran, "The Role of Multimedia Conglomerates in American Trade Book Publishing," *Media, Culture & Society* 19, no. 3 (1997): 441–55; Andrew Nash, Claire Squires, and Ian Willison, introduction to *The Cambridge History of the Book in Britain,* vol. 7, *The Twentieth Century and Beyond,* ed. Andrew Nash, Claire Squires, and Ian Willison (Cambridge: Cambridge University Press, 2019), 1–38; and Schiffrin, *Business of Books.*

31. Murray, "Publishing Studies," 7, 6.

32. See, for example, Philip G. Altbach and Edith S. Hoshino, eds., *International Book Publishing: An Encyclopedia* (London: Routledge, 2015); Giles Clark and Angus Phillips, *Inside Book Publishing,* 5th ed. (London: Routledge, 2014); Albert N. Greco, Jim Milliot, and Robert M. Wharton, *The Book Publishing Industry,* 3rd ed. (New York: Routledge, 2014); and Albert N. Greco, Clara E. Rodriguez, and Robert M. Wharton, *The Culture and Commerce of Publishing in the 21st Century* (Stanford, CA: Stanford University Press, 2007).

33. David Throsby, Jan Zwar, and Thomas Longden, "Book Authors and Their Changing Circumstances: Survey Method and Results," *Macquarie Economics Research Papers* 2 (2015).

34. Sarah Brouillette, *Literature and the Creative Economy* (Stanford, CA: Stanford University Press, 2014); Richard E. Caves, *Creative Industries: Contracts between Art and Commerce* (Cambridge, MA: Harvard University Press, 2000); Chris Gibson and Natascha Klocker, "Academic Publishing as 'Creative' Industry, and Recent Discourses of 'Creative Economies': Some Critical Reflections," *Area* 36, no. 4 (2004): 423–34; John Hartley, *Creative Industries* (New York: Wiley, 2005); David Hesmondhalgh, *The Cul-*

tural Industries (Los Angeles: SAGE, 2012); Stevie Marsden, "Positioning Publishing Studies in the Cultural Economy," *Interscript* (July 13, 2017); Erik Stam, Jeroen P. J. De Jong, and Gerard Marlet, "Creative Industries in the Netherlands: Structure, Development, Innovativeness and Effects on Urban Growth," *Geografiska Annaler: Series B, Human Geography* 90, no. 2 (2008): 119–32; Ruth Towse, ed., *A Handbook of Cultural Economics,* 2nd ed. (Cheltenham: Edward Elgar, 2011).

35. Simon Carolan and Christine Evain, "Shifting Authority: (Ex)Changing Roles in the Evolving Publishing Environment," *International Journal of the Book* 10, no. 4 (2013): 53–63; R. Matulionyte et al., "The System of Book Creation: Intellectual Property and the Self-Publishing Sector of the Creative Industries," *Creative Industries Journal* 10, no. 3 (2017): 191–210; Sara Øiestad and Markus M. Bugge, "Digitisation of Publishing: Exploration Based on Existing Business Models," *Technological Forecasting and Social Change* 83 (2014): 54–65; Joel Waldfogel and Imke Reimers, "Storming the Gatekeepers: Digital Disintermediation in the Market for Books," *Information Economics and Policy* 31 (2015): 47–58.

36. Bourdieu, *Field of Cultural Production.* See also Casanova, *World Republic of Letters;* Squires, *Marketing Literature;* and Thompson, *Merchants of Culture.*

37. Becker, *Art Worlds,* x, xv, xxiv, 25, 42.

38. Becker, *Art Worlds,* 374, 376, 378–79.

39. Howard S. Becker and Alain Pessin, "A Dialogue on the Ideas of 'World' and 'Field,'" *Sociological Forum* 21, no. 2 (2006): 285, 9; Lucy Malagoni, interview, July 26, 2017.

40. Becker, *Art Worlds,* 1; Cluley, "Art Words and Art Worlds," 209.

41. Florian Cramer, "What Is 'Post-Digital'?," *APRJA* 3, no. 1 (2014): 10–24.

42. David Barnett, "Kazuo Ishiguro Thinks His Fantasy Novel Is Not a Fantasy Novel. Are We Bothered?," *Guardian,* March 5, 2015.

43. Ken Gelder, "The Fields of Popular Fiction," in *New Directions in Popular Fiction,* ed. Gelder, 14; Bernard Lahire, *The Plural Actor,* trans. David Fernbach (Cambridge: Polity, 2011).

44. Mark McGurl, *The Program Era: Postwar Fiction and the Rise of Creative Writing* (Cambridge, MA: Harvard University Press, 2009).

45. Henry Jenkins, "Who the &%&# Is Henry Jenkins?," *Confessions of an Aca-Fan,* http://henryjenkins.org/aboutmehtml; Cécile Cristofari and Matthieu J. Guitton, "Aca-Fans and Fan Communities: An Operative Framework," *Journal of Consumer Culture* 17, no. 3 (2017): 715–16; Jenkins, "Who the &%&# Is Henry Jenkins?"; Cristofari and Guitton, "Aca-Fans and Fan Communities," 718. See Rita Felski, *The Limits of Critique* (Chicago: University of Chicago Press, 2015); and Heather Love, "Close but Not Deep: Literary Ethics and the Descriptive Turn," *New Literary History* 41, no. 2 (2010): 371–91.

46. Catherine M. Roach, *Happily Ever After: The Romance Story in Popular Culture* (Bloomington: Indiana University Press, 2016), 38, 105.

47. Cristofari and Guitton, "Aca-Fans and Fan Communities," 725.

48. Cristofari and Guitton, "Aca-Fans and Fan Communities," 719.

49. Tony E. Adams, Stacy Holman Jones, and Carolyn Ellis, *Autoethnography* (Oxford: Oxford University Press, 2014), 1–2. See also Beth Driscoll and Claire Squires, "Experiments with Book Festival People (Real and Imaginary)," *Mémoires du livre/ Studies in Book Culture* 11, no. 2 (2020): 1–41.

50. Adams, Jones, and Ellis, *Autoethnography*, 9–10, 13.

51. Becker, *Art Worlds*, 58.

52. As Becker puts it, "The term *art world*, remember, is just a way of talking about people who routinely participate in the making of an art world." Becker, *Art Worlds*, 166.

53. For a list of these case study titles, see appendix.

54. Story Factory, "Four Writers That Have Sold More than 125 Million Books and the Creator of HBO'S *True Detective* Praise a New Novel Causing It to Sell Out at Bookstores Nationwide Overnight," June 26, 2015, www.prnewswire.com; Clarisse Loughrey, "A Charity Shop Was Given *So Many Fifty Shades of Grey* Copies It Turned Them into a Fort," *Independent*, March 23, 2016, www.independent.co.uk; Adam Rowe, "Science Fiction and Fantasy Book Sales Have Doubled since 2010," *Forbes*, June 19, 2018, www.forbes.com. See also Vassiliki Veros, "The Selective Tradition, the Role of Romance Fiction Donations, and Public Library Practices in New South Wales, Australia," *Information Research* 25, no. 2 (2020), for an account of romance novels bought by volume rather than title.

55. For examples, see Danielle Fuller and DeNel Rehberg Sedo, *Reading beyond the Book: The Social Practices of Contemporary Literary Culture* (New York: Routledge, 2013); Radway, *Reading the Romance*; and Thompson, *Merchants of Culture*.

56. Danielle Fuller, "Critical Friendships: Reading Women's Writing Communities in Newfoundland," *Women's Studies International Forum* 25, no. 2 (2002): 249.

57. Anamik Saha, *Race and the Cultural Industries* (Cambridge: Polity Press, 2018), 116, 120–21, 124.

58. Alain Pessin, *The Sociology of Howard S. Becker: Theory with a Wide Horizon*, trans. Steven Rendall (Chicago: University of Chicago Press, 2017), 67.

CHAPTER 2: Genre Worlds and the Publishing Industry

1. Ann Steiner, "The Global Book: Micropublishing, Conglomerate Production, and Digital Market Structures," *Publishing Research Quarterly* 34, no. 1 (2017): 119.

2. Claire Squires, *Marketing Literature: The Making of Contemporary Writing in Britain* (Basingstoke: Palgrave Macmillan, 2007), 70–101.

3. See, for example, Julie Rak, "Genre in the Marketplace: The Scene of Bookselling in Canada," in *From Codex to Hypertext: Reading at the Turn of the Twenty-First Century*, ed. Anouk Lang, 159–73 (Amherst: University of Massachusetts Press, 2012), on genre in bookstores.

4. Thad McIlroy, "What the Big 5's Financial Reports Reveal about the State of Traditional Book Publishing," *Book Business*, August 5, 2016, www.bookbusinessmag.com.

5. Kim Wilkins, "'A Crowd at Your Back': Fantasy Fandom and Small Press," *Media International Australia* 170, no. 1 (2019): 115–25.

6. Howard S. Becker, *Art Worlds* (Berkeley: University of California Press, 1982), 161.

7. Claire Squires, "Publishing's Diversity Deficit," *CAMEo Cuts*, no. 2 (2017): 1–12. See also Claire Squires and Beth Driscoll, "The Sleaze-o-Meter: Sexual Harassment in the Publishing Industry," *Interscript*, March 8, 2018, www.interscriptjournal.com; Dave O'Brien et al., "Are the Creative Industries Meritocratic? An Analysis of the 2014

British Labour Force Survey," *Cultural Trends* 25, no. 2 (2016): 116–31; and Anamik Saha, *Race and the Cultural Industries* (Malden, MA: Polity, 2018).

8. Brigid Magner, "Behind the BookScan Bestseller Lists: Technology and Cultural Anxieties in Early-Twenty-First-Century Australia," *Script & Print* 36, no. 4 (2012): 245.

9. Becker, *Art Worlds*, 9, 11.

10. For more discussion, see Claire Parnell, "Mapping the Entertainment Ecosystem of Wattpad: Platforms, Publishing and Adaptation," *Convergence* (November 10, 2020).

11. Anna Valdinger, interview, February 18, 2019.

12. Beth Driscoll and Claire Squires, *Publishing Bestsellers: Buzz and the Frankfurt Book Fair* (Cambridge: Cambridge University Press, 2020); Jenny Darling, interview, May 10, 2018.

13. C-format is similar to U.S. standard trade paperback, with dimensions of 135mm x 216mm (5.32" x 8.51").

14. Sulari Gentill, interview, February 6, 2018.

15. Beverley Cousins, interview, April 20, 2016.

16. Mark Lucas, interview, April 28, 2017.

17. Becker, *Art Worlds*, 2.

18. "BookShots," Penguin, www.penguin.com.au/books/brands/bookshots.

19. Valdinger interview.

20. Becker, *Art Worlds*, 13; Wendy Bottero and Nick Crossley, "Worlds, Fields and Networks: Becker, Bourdieu and the Structures of Social Relations," *Cultural Sociology* 5, no. 1 (2011): 99–119; Alain Pessin, *The Sociology of Howard S. Becker: Theory with a Wide Horizon*, trans. Steven Rendall (Chicago: University of Chicago Press, 2017).

21. Stephanie Laurens, interview, July 1, 2017.

22. Becker, *Art Worlds*, 194, 198.

23. Carol Marinelli, interview, July 29, 2017.

24. Michael Robotham, interview, February 24, 2017.

25. "Write for Harlequin," Harlequin, https://harlequin.submittable.com/submit.

26. Marinelli interview.

27. Haylee Nash, interview, June 7, 2017; Sue Brockhoff, interview, June 5, 2017.

28. Bec Sampson, interview, November 3, 2017; Rachael Johns, interview, February 24, 2017.

29. Lisa Fletcher et al., "#loveyourshelfie: Mills & Boon Books and How to Find Them," *Mémoires du livre / Studies in Book Culture* 11, no. 1 (2019): 6.

30. Janice A. Radway, *Reading the Romance: Women, Patriarchy, and Popular Literature* (Chapel Hill: University of North Carolina Press, 2009), 41.

31. Becker, *Art Worlds*, 93, 94.

32. Angela Slatter, interview, April 6, 2017.

33. Becker, *Art Worlds*, 122–23.

34. Wilkins, "'Crowd at Your Back.'"

35. Bianca Bosker, "The One Direction Fan-Fiction Novel That Became a Literary Sensation," *Atlantic*, December 2018, www.theatlantic.com; Guy Kelly, "Meet Mark Dawson: The Literary Sensation You've Never Heard of," *Telegraph*, April 15, 2016, www.telegraph.co.uk.

36. Mark McGurl, "Everything and Less: Fiction in the Age of Amazon," *Modern Language Quarterly* 77, no. 3 (2016): 457; R. Lyle Skains, *Digital Authorship: Publishing in the Attention Economy* (Cambridge: Cambridge University Press, 2019), 21–22.

37. Laura Dietz, "Who Are You Calling an Author? Changing Definitions of Career Legitimacy for Novelists in the Digital Era," in *Literary Careers in the Modern Era*, ed. Guy Davidson and Nicola Evans (Basingstoke: Palgrave Macmillan, 2016), 208; Kelly, "Meet Mark Dawson"; Alexandra Alter, "Sci-Fi's Underground Hit: Authors Are Snubbing Publishers and Insisting on Keeping E-book Rights; How One Novelist Made More than $1 Million before His Book Hit Stores," *Wall Street Journal*, March 8, 2013, www.wsj.com.

38. Kylie Scott, interview, February 24, 2017.

39. Gentill interview; Scott interview.

40. Keri Arthur, interview, February 26, 2017.

41. *The Student,* Echo, July 3, 2017, www.echopublishing.com.au / titles / the-student/; Iain Ryan, interview, August 4, 2017.

42. Barbara Dunlop, interview, July 29, 2017.

43. Mitchell Hogan, interview, October 23, 2017.

44. Tarleton Gillespie, "Algorithm [Draft] [#digitalkeywords]," Culture Digitally, June 25, 2014, http://culturedigitally.org. See also Ted Striphas, "Algorithmic Culture," *European Journal of Cultural Studies* 18, nos. 4–5 (2015): 408.

45. George Packer, "Cheap Words," *New Yorker,* February 10, 2014, www.new yorker.com.

46. Kate Cuthbert, interview, November 1, 2015.

47. For a critical examination of Goodreads, see Lisa Nakamura, "'Words with Friends': Socially Networked Reading on Goodreads," *PMLA* 128, no. 1 (2013): 238–43. For consideration of readers' textual responses on Goodreads, see Beth Driscoll and DeNel Rehberg Sedo, "Faraway, So Close: Seeing the Intimacy in Goodreads Reviews," *Qualitative Inquiry* 25, no. 3 (2019): 248–59; and Emmett Stinson and Beth Driscoll, "Difficult Literature on Goodreads: Reading Alexis Wright's *The Swan Book,*" *Textual Practice* (June 26, 2020).

48. Brent Smith and Greg Linden, "Two Decades of Recommender Systems at Amazon.com," *IEEE Internet Computing* 21 (2017): 12.

49. Miriam Kriss, interview, March 22, 2018.

50. Ryan interview.

51. Ian Keith Rogers, "Without a True North: Tactical Approaches to Self-Published Fiction," *M/C Journal* 20, no. 6 (2017), http://journal.media-culture.org.au.

52. Striphas, "Algorithmic Culture," 397.

53. Antón Barba-Kay, "Data-Driven Amazon Bookstores Can't Compete with Indies," *Literary Hub,* May 4, 2018, https://lithub.com.

54. Beth Driscoll, *The New Literary Middlebrow: Tastemakers and Reading in the Twenty-First Century* (Basingstoke: Palgrave Macmillan, 2014), 5.

55. Jeremy Garner, "Is There an Algorithm for Serendipity?," *Media Avataar,* June 18, 2017, www.mediavataar.com.

CHAPTER 3: Transnational and Transmedia Genre Worlds

1. Stefanie London, interview, July 29, 2017.

2. Kelly Hunter, interview, September 4, 2017.

3. For examples of articles about the global dominance of these companies, see Jeffrey A. Trachtenberg, "'They Own the System': Amazon Rewrites Book Industry by Marching into Publishing," *Wall Street Journal*, January 16, 2019, www.wsj.com; and Brooks Barnes, "Disney Plus Racks up 28.6 Million Subscribers," *New York Times*, February 4, 2020, www.nytimes.com.

4. Kim Wilkins, "'Cutting Off the Head of the King': Sovereignty, Feudalism, Fantasy," *Australian Literary Studies* 26, nos. 3–4 (2011): 133–46.

5. For more, see Beth Driscoll, "Book Blogs as Tastemakers," *Participations: Journal of Audience and Reception Studies* 16, no. 1 (2019): 280–305.

6. Kylie Scott, interview, February 24, 2017.

7. For more detail, see "Tartan Noir 10 Top Crime Writers, and the Novels That Scared and Inspired Them," *Sunday Post*, August 15, 2015, www.sundaypost.com.

8. Jacquie Byron, "Antipodean Noir: Is Crime Melbourne's Biggest Export?," *Sydney Morning Herald*, October 18, 2019, www.smh.com.au; Garry Disher, "Our Twisted Red Heart," *Australian*, November 1, 2019, www.theaustralian.com.au; Chris Hammer, "The New Class of Australian Crime Writers: Your Guide to the Best of Outback Noir," *CrimeReads*, January 23, 2019, https://crimereads.com.

9. Michael Robotham, interview, February 24, 2017.

10. Howard S. Becker, *Art Worlds* (Berkeley: University of California Press, 1982), 35; Pascale Casanova, *The World Republic of Letters* (Cambridge, MA: Harvard University Press, 2004), 117.

11. Casanova, *World Republic of Letters*, 81.

12. See, for example, Corinna Norrick-Rühl and Melanie Ramdarshan Bold, "Crossing the Channel: Publishing Translated German Fiction in the UK," *Publishing Research Quarterly* 32, no. 2 (2016): 125–38; Gisèle Sapiro, "Globalization and Cultural Diversity in the Book Market: The Case of Literary Translations in the US and in France," *Poetics* 38, no. 4 (2010): 419–39; and Gisèle Sapiro, "How Do Literary Works Cross Borders (or Not)?," *Journal of World Literature* 1, no. 1 (2016): 81–96.

13. Beth Driscoll, *The New Literary Middlebrow: Tastemakers and Reading in the Twenty-First Century* (Basingstoke: Palgrave Macmillan, 2014); Gisèle Sapiro, "The Metamorphosis of Modes of Consecration in the Literary Field: Academies, Literary Prizes, Festivals," *Poetics* 59 (2016): 5–19.

14. Kim Wilkins, Beth Driscoll, and Lisa Fletcher, "What Is Australian Popular Fiction?," *Australian Literary Studies* 33, no. 4 (2018): 4.

15. Casanova, *World Republic of Letters*, 83, 169, 171.

16. Casanova, *World Republic of Letters*, 169–70.

17. Ann Steiner, "Serendipity, Promotion, and Literature: The Contemporary Book Trade and International Megasellers," in *Hype: Bestsellers and Literary Culture*, ed. Jon Helgason, Sara Kärrholm, and Ann Steiner (Lund: Nordic Academic Press, 2014), 55, 59.

18. See, for example, Javaria Farooqi, "The Kitchen and Beyond: The Romantic Chronotope in Pakistani Popular Fiction," *Journal of Popular Romance Studies* (August 2020).

19. C. Clayton Childress, "Regionalism and the Publishing Class: Conflicted Iso-morphism and Negotiated Identity in a Nested Field of American Publishing," *Cultural Sociology* 9, no. 3 (2015): 364–81; Wendy Griswold, *Regionalism and the Reading Class* (Chicago: University of Chicago Press, 2008).

20. Kylie Mirmohamadi, "The Federation of Literary Sympathy: The Australasian Home Reading Union," in *Republics of Letters: Literary Communities in Australia,* ed. Peter Kirkpatrick and Robert Dixon (Sydney: Sydney University Press, 2012), 17–26; David Carter and Roger Osborne, *Australian Books and Authors in the American Market-place, 1840s–1940s* (Sydney: Sydney University Press, 2018).

21. Ronald Burt, "Structural Holes and Good Ideas," *American Journal of Sociology* 110, no. 2 (2004): 349. See also Katherine Giuffre, "Cultural Production in Networks," in *International Encyclopedia of the Social and Behavioral Sciences,* ed. James D. Wright, 2nd ed. (Amsterdam: Elsevier, 2015), 467.

22. Burt, "Structural Holes and Good Ideas," 388.

23. Chris Johnston, "Bodices Ripped for Fun and Profit," *Sydney Morning Herald,* August 25, 2012, www.smh.com.au.

24. Anna Campbell, interview, November 11, 2017.

25. Anne Gracie, interview, August 23, 2015; Sarah Fairhall, interview, August 22, 2015.

26. Stephen Jones, interview, August 11, 2017; Bernard Lahire, "The Double Life of Writers," trans. Gwendolyn Wells, *New Literary History* 14, no. 2 (2010): 444.

27. For more on Australian rural romance and its growth in the early twenty-first century, see Beth Driscoll, Lisa Fletcher, and Kim Wilkins, "Women, Akubras and Ereaders: Romance Fiction and Australian Publishing," in *The Return of Print? Con-temporary Australian Publishing,* ed. Aaron Mannion and Emmett Stinson (Clayton, Victoria: Monash University, 2016), 67–88.

28. Hans Christian Rohr, interview, October 12, 2018.

29. London interview; Carol Marinelli, interview, July 29, 2017.

30. Barbara Dunlop, interview, July 29, 2017.

31. Hunter interview.

32. Kelly Hunter, "Bio," *Kelly Hunter* (blog), https://kellyhunter.net/bio/.

33. Hunter interview.

34. Dunlop interview.

35. Dunlop interview; Hunter interview.

36. Casanova, *World Republic of Letters,* 171.

37. Simone Murray, *The Adaptation Industry: The Cultural Economy of Contemporary Lit-erary Adaptation* (New York: Routledge, 2012), 26, 36; Fiona Eagger, interview, May 5, 2017.

38. For example, "HarperCollins to Publish 'Electrifying' Debut Novel; UK, Film Rights Sold," *Books + Publishing,* July 10, 2019, www.booksandpublishing.com.au.

39. Kim Wilkins, *Young Adult Fantasy Fiction: Conventions, Originality, Reproducibility* (Cambridge: Cambridge University Press, 2019), 47.

40. "Why I Stopped Dating Men and Married a True Crime Podcast," *Reductress,* https://reductress.com.

41. For more on this, see Ken Gelder, *Adapting Bestsellers: Fantasy, Franchise and the Afterlife of Storyworlds* (Cambridge: Cambridge University Press, 2019); and Tobi

Evans, "Some Knights Are Dark and Full of Terror: The Queer Monstrous Feminine, Masculinity, and Violence in the Martinverse," *Journal of Language, Literature and Culture* 66, no. 3 (2019): 134–56.

42. Maria Vultaggio, *"Big Little Lies* Author Liane Moriarty Wrote Season 2 Just for Meryl Streep," *Newsweek,* June 10, 2019, www.newsweek.com.

43. Jenny Darling, interview, May 10, 2018; Selwa Anthony, interview, October 24, 2017. We note that Selwa Anthony is the agent of Kim Wilkins, one of the authors of this book.

44. Henry Jenkins, *Convergence Culture: Where Old and New Media Collide* (New York: New York University Press, 2008). On the postdigital, see Christian Ulrik Andersen and Søren Bro Pold, *Post-digital Books and Disruptive Literary Machines* (Formules, 2014); Alessandro Ludovico, *Post-digital Print: The Mutation of Publishing since 1894* (Onomatopee, 2013).

45. Henry Jenkins, *Convergence Culture,* 11, 2.

46. Henry Jenkins, *Convergence Culture,* 21; Marie-Laure Ryan, "Transmedia Storytelling: Industry Buzzword or New Narrative Experience?," *Storyworlds: A Journal of Narrative Studies* 7, no. 2 (2015): 2; Linda Hutcheon, *A Theory of Adaptation* (London: Routledge, 2013), 35; Robotham interview.

47. Daniel O'Malley, interview, May 21, 2018; Gelder, *Adapting Bestsellers,* 2; Julie Bosman, "Impatience Has Its Reward: Books Are Rolled Out Faster," *New York Times,* February 11, 2014, 1.

48. Dan Hassler-Forest, *Science Fiction, Fantasy, and Politics: Transmedia World-Building beyond Capitalism* (London: Rowman and Littlefield, 2017), 8; Victor Watson, *Reading Series Fiction: From Arthur Ransome to Gene Kemp* (London: Routledge, 2000), 1.

49. Bosman, "Impatience Has Its Reward," 1; Jeff Bercovici, "The Hunger Games Economy," *Forbes,* July 20, 2013, www.forbesindia.com/printcontent/35629; "Mills & Boon Teams up with *The Bachelorette!*," *The Booktopian* (blog), October 12, 2018, www.booktopia.com.

50. Hassler-Forest, *Science Fiction, Fantasy, and Politics,* 8; Shelly Shapiro, email, August 1, 2017.

51. Angela Slatter, interview, April 6, 2017.

52. Joel Naoum, interview, June 5, 2017.

53. Ryan, "Transmedia Storytelling," 5.

54. Kerry Greenwood, interview, March 24, 2017; Robert Stam, "The Theory and Practice of Adaptation," in *Literature and Film: A Guide to the Theory and Practice of Film Adaptation,* ed. Robert Stam and Alessandra Raengo (Malden, MA: Blackwell, 2005), 3; Darling interview.

55. Murray, *Adaptation Industry,* 25; Greenwood interview; Eagger interview.

56. Eagger interview.

57. Eagger interview.

58. Eagger interview.

59. Eagger interview.

60. Wilkins, *Young Adult Fantasy Fiction,* 63.

61. Jenkins, *Convergence Culture,* 19.

62. *"King Kong* (1932 Novelization)," *Wikizilla,* April 30, 2019, https://wikizilla.org; Ryan, "Transmedia Storytelling," 2.

63. Sean Guynes and Dan Hassler-Forest, eds., *"Star Wars" and the History of Transmedia Storytelling* (Amsterdam: Amsterdam University Press, 2018); William Proctor and Richard McCulloch, eds., *Disney's "Star Wars": Forces of Production, Promotion, and Reception* (Iowa City: University of Iowa Press, 2019).

64. Karen Raugust, "Disney Partners with Bestselling Children's Authors for New *Star Wars* Adaptations," *Publishers Weekly,* April 17, 2014, www.publishersweekly.com.

65. Molly Driscoll, *"Star Wars* Novels: Still on Bestseller lists," *Christian Science Monitor,* March 26, 2012, www.csmonitor.com; "Disney Publishing Worldwide and Random House Announce Relaunch of *Star Wars* Adult Fiction Line," *Star Wars,* April 25, 2014, www.starwars.com.

66. Haden Blackman, email, July 21, 2017.

67. Sean Williams, interview, April 11, 2017.

68. Blackman email; Williams interview.

69. Williams interview.

70. Blackman email.

71. Williams interview.

72. Blackman email.

73. Williams interview.

74. Williams interview.

75. *TWC* editor, interview with Jo Graham, Melissa Scott, and Martha Wells, *Transformative Works and Cultures,* no. 5, https://doi.org/10.3983/twc.2010.0239.

76. Hassler-Forest, *Science Fiction, Fantasy, and Politics,* 3; Jenkins, *Convergence Culture,* 21.

77. Williams interview; Colin B. Harvey, *Fantastic Transmedia* (London: Palgrave Macmillan, 2015), 182–83.

CHAPTER 4: Community and Creativity

1. See, for example, Wilkins's research on the small-press publishers that started out in fantasy fandom. Kim Wilkins, "'A Crowd at Your Back': Fantasy Fandom and Small Press," *Media International Australia* 170, no. 1 (2019): 115–25.

2. "RWA's Origin Story," Romance Writers of America, www.rwa.org/Online/About /History.aspx; "Who We Are," Sisters in Crime, www.sistersincrime.org/page/ABOUT; Vol Molesworth, *A History of Australian Fandom, 1935–1963* (Faulconbridge: R. & S. Clarke, 1980).

3. See James F. English, *The Economy of Prestige: Prizes, Awards, and the Circulation of Cultural Value* (Cambridge, MA: Harvard University Press, 2009).

4. Sean Williams, interview, April 11, 2017; Lisa Hannett, interview, April 10, 2017.

5. Howard S. Becker, *Art Worlds* (Berkeley: University of California Press, 1982), 111.

6. James Paul Gee, "Semiotic Social Spaces and Affinity Spaces," in *Beyond Communities of Practice: Language, Power and Social Context,* ed. David Barton and Karin Tusting (Cambridge: Cambridge University Press, 2005), 228.

7. Colin Lankshear and Michele Knobel, "Researching New Literacies: Web 2.0

Practices and Insider Perspectives," *E-Learning and Digital Media* 4, no. 3 (2007): 227–28; Kristina Busse, *Framing Fanfiction: Literary and Social Practices in Fanfiction Communities* (Iowa City: University of Iowa Press, 2017), 179.

8. Gee, "Semiotic Social Spaces," 225–29.

9. Rachael Johns, interview, February 24, 2017; Angela Savage, interview, December 1, 2017; Hannett interview.

10. Miriam Kriss, interview, March 22, 2018; Jonathan Strahan, interview, August 10, 2017.

11. Sulari Gentill, interview, February 6, 2018.

12. Cecilia Dart-Thornton, interview, June 3, 2017; Sue Brockhoff, interview, June 5, 2017; Angela Meyer, interview, July 28, 2017; Hannett interview.

13. Gee, "Semiotic Social Spaces," 225–26.

14. Williams interview.

15. Amy Tannenbaum, interview, June 10, 2017; Adam van Roojen, interview, June 5, 2017; Savage interview; Gentill interview.

16. Gentill interview; Carol Marinelli, interview, July 29, 2017; Gentill interview.

17. Hannett interview; Jo Fletcher, interview, August 10, 2017.

18. Beverley Cousins, interview, April 20, 2016.

19. Becker, *Art Worlds*, 59, 46; Gee, "Semiotic Social Spaces," 226–27.

20. Anna Campbell, interview, November 11, 2017.

21. Angela Slatter, interview, April 6, 2017.

22. Kate Cuthbert, interview, November 1, 2015; Stefanie London, interview, July 29, 2017; Bronwyn Parry, interview, October 17, 2015; Marinelli interview; Charlotte Nash, interview, October 31, 2015; Kylie Scott, interview, February 24, 2017.

23. Marinelli interview; Lucy Malagoni, interview, July 26, 2017.

24. Kim Wilkins, "Valhallolz: Medievalist Humour on the Internet," *Postmedieval* 5, no. 2 (2014): 200.

25. Jayne Ann Krentz and Linda Barlow, "Beneath the Surface: The Hidden Codes of Romance," in *Dangerous Men and Adventurous Women: Romance Writers on the Appeal of the Romance,* ed. Jayne Ann Krentz (Philadelphia: University of Pennsylvania Press, 1992), 15.

26. Cuthbert interview.

27. Wheeler Centre, "The F-Word: Romance," June 25, 2015, www.wheelercentre.com /events/women-and-romance-fiction; Samuel R. Delany, *Starboard Wine* (Kindle: Gollancz, 2013); Lisa Fletcher, Beth Driscoll and Kim Wilkins, "Genre Worlds and Popular Fiction: The Case of Twenty-First-Century Australian Romance," *Journal of Popular Culture* 51, no. 4 (2018): 1007.

28. Kate Forsyth, *The Tower of Ravens* (North Sydney: Arrow, 2004), 238.

29. Kelly Hunter, interview, September 4, 2017.

30. Keri Arthur, interview, February 26, 2017; Savage interview.

31. Lindy Cameron, interview, September 18, 2017.

32. Kat Mayo, interview, October 27, 2016.

33. Strahan interview.

34. Gee's work on affinity spaces also expresses this view. See "Semiotic Social Spaces," 228.

35. Robyn Enlund, interview, July 1, 2017.

36. Gee, "Semiotic Social Spaces," 228.

37. Mitchell Hogan, interview, October 23, 2017.

38. Kate Forsyth, interview, November 30, 2017. The anthology *The Silver Well* was cowritten with Kim Wilkins, one of the team behind *Genre Worlds*.

39. Cameron interview.

40. Cameron interview.

41. Gentill interview.

42. Gentill interview.

43. Claire G. Coleman, interview, May 14, 2018. Note that now Coleman does write literary fiction and poetry.

44. Rochelle Fernandez, interview, February 19, 2019.

45. Sue Corbett, "Red Queen Rising: Victoria Aveyard's Expanding YA Empire," *Publishers Weekly,* February 2, 2016, www.publishersweekly.com; Dan Hassler-Forest, *Science Fiction, Fantasy, and Politics: Transmedia World-Building beyond Capitalism* (London: Rowman and Littlefield, 2017), 17.

46. See Bernard Lahire, "The Double Life of Writers," trans. Gwendolyn Wells, *New Literary History* 14, no. 2 (2010), 443–65.

47. Katherine Giuffre, "Cultural Production in Networks," in *International Encyclopedia of the Social and Behavioral Sciences,* ed. James D. Wright, 2nd ed. (Amsterdam: Elsevier, 2015), 5:466–70.

48. Savage interview.

49. See also Sophie Hennekam and Dawn Bennett, "Involuntary Career Transition and Identity within the Artist Population," *Personnel Review* 45, no. 6 (2016): 1114–31; Stephen J. Dollinger and Stephanie Clancy Dollinger, "Creativity and Identity," in *The Creative Self: Effect of Beliefs, Self-Efficacy, Mindset, and Identity,* ed. Maciej Karwowski and James C. Kaufman (London: Elsevier, 2017), 49–64; Izabela Lebuda and Mihaly Csikzentmihalyi, "Me, Myself, I, and Creativity: Self-Concepts of Eminent Creators," in *Creative Self,* ed. Karwowski and Kaufman, 137–52; and Carol A. Mullen, "Dynamic Creativity: Influential Theory, Public Discourse, and Generative Possibility," in *Dynamic Perspectives on Creativity: New Directions for Theory, Research, and Practice in Education,* ed. Ronald A. Beghetto and Giovanni Emanuele Corazza (Cham, Switzerland: Springer, 2019), 137–64.

50. Vlad Petre Glăveanu and Lene Tanggaard, "Creativity, Identity, and Representation: Towards a Socio-cultural Theory of Creative Identity," *New Ideas in Psychology* 34 (2014): 12; Vlad Petre Glăveanu, *Distributed Creativity: Thinking Outside the Box of the Creative Individual* (Cham, Switzerland: Springer, 2014), 9. See also Vlad Petre Glăveanu, "Creativity as a Sociocultural Act," *Journal of Creative Behavior* 49, no. 3 (2015): 165–80; and Vlad Petre Glăveanu and Iona Literat, "Distributed Creativity on the Internet: A Theoretical Foundation for Online Creative Participation," *International Journal of Communication* 16 (2018): 893–908.

51. Vlad Petre Glăveanu, "Paradigms in the Study of Creativity: Introducing the Perspective of Cultural Psychology," *New Ideas in Psychology* 28 (2010): 80–82, 84.

52. Glăveanu, *Distributed Creativity,* 9.

53. Campbell interview; Cecilia Aragon and Katie Davis, *Writers in the Secret Garden: Fanfiction, Youth, and New Forms of Mentoring* (Cambridge, MA: MIT Press, 2019), 10.

54. Bec Sampson, interview, November 3, 2017; Slatter interview.

55. Slatter interview; Hannett interview; David Burkus, *The Myths of Creativity* (San Francisco: Wiley, 2014), 17.

56. Hannett interview.

57. Slatter interview; Hannett interview.

58. Hannett interview; Sampson interview.

59. Dart-Thornton interview; London interview; Candice Fox, interview, October 7, 2016.

60. Campbell interview.

61. Enlund interview.

62. Cuthbert interview.

63. Hannett interview.

64. Slatter interview; Hannett interview; Slatter interview; Williams interview.

65. For more detail, see Cassandra Clare and Holly Black, "Why We Love Writing the Epic Magisterium Series Together," *Guardian*, September 11, 2014, www.theguardian.com.

66. Fox interview.

67. Fox interview.

68. See Ken Gelder, *Popular Fiction: The Logics and Practices of a Literary Field* (Abingdon: Routledge, 2004).

69. Barbara Dunlop, interview, July 29, 2017.

70. Dunlop interview.

71. Garry Disher, interview, February 27, 2018; Michael Robotham, interview, February 24, 2017.

72. Dart-Thornton interview.

73. Forsyth interview; Grace Lucas-Pennington, interview, February 14, 2019; Coleman interview.

74. Coleman interview; Robert Watkins, interview, February 19, 2019.

CHAPTER 5: Genre Sociality Online and in Person

1. See José van Dijck, *The Culture of Connectivity: A Critical History of Social Media* (Oxford: Oxford University Press, 2013); and Jean Burgess, Alice Marwick, and Thomas Poell, eds., *The SAGE Handbook of Social Media* (London and New York: SAGE, 2017), esp. chap. 13, "The Affordances of Social Media," by Taina Bucher and Anne Helmond.

2. Dijck, *Culture of Connectivity*, 24.

3. Alice E. Marwick and danah boyd, "I Tweet Honestly, I Tweet Passionately: Twitter Users, Context Collapse, and the Imagined Audience," *New Media & Society* 13, no. 1 (2011): 116.

4. See Sybil Nolan and Alexandra Dane, "A Sharper Conversation: Book Publishers' Use of Social Media Marketing in the Age of the Algorithm," *Media International Australia* 168, no. 1 (2018): 153–66; Anne Thoring, "Corporate Tweeting: Analysing the Use of Twitter as a Marketing Tool by UK Trade Publishers," *Publishing Research Quarterly* 27, no. 2 (2011): 141–58; Xuemei Tian and Bill Martin, "Digitization and Publishing in Australia: A Recent Snapshot," *Logos* 21, no. 1 (2010): 59–75; and Millicent Weber

and Beth Driscoll, "Playful Twitter Accounts and the Socialisation of Literary Institutions," *First Monday* 24, no. 3 (2019).

5. See Christina Shane-Simpson et al., "Why Do College Students Prefer Facebook, Twitter, or Instagram? Site Affordances, Tensions between Privacy and Self-Expression, and Implications for Social Capital," *Computers in Human Behavior* 86 (September 1, 2018): 276–88; and Sabine Trepte, Michael Scharkow, and Tobias Dienlin, "The Privacy Calculus Contextualized: The Influence of Affordances," *Computers in Human Behavior* 104 (March 1, 2020): 106–15.

6. Simone Murray and Millicent Weber, "'Live and Local'? The Significance of Digital Media for Writers' Festivals," *Convergence* 23, no. 1 (2017): 61–78.

7. Emma Viskic, interview, July 21, 2017.

8. Janette Currie, email, January 5, 2018.

9. Viskic interview; Angela Meyer, interview, July 28, 2017.

10. Iain Ryan, interview, August 4, 2017.

11. Lisa Hannett, interview, April 10, 2017.

12. Nick Couldry and José van Dijck, "Researching Social Media as If the Social Mattered," *Social Media + Society* 1, no. 2 (2015): 1.

13. See Marwick and boyd, "I Tweet Honestly, I Tweet Passionately," on the mix of personal and professional identities online; and, relatedly, Kathleen Kuehn and Thomas F. Corrigan, "Hope Labor: The Role of Employment Prospects in Online Social Production," *Political Economy of Communication* 1, no. 1 (2013): 9–25.

14. Nolan and Dane, "Sharper Conversation."

15. Kate Forsyth, interview, November 30, 2017.

16. Ryan interview.

17. Kelly Hunter, interview, September 4, 2017; Anna Campbell, interview, November 11, 2017.

18. Angela Savage, interview, December 1, 2017.

19. On parasociality, intimacy, and online communications, see Chris Rojek, *Presumed Intimacy: Para-social Relationships in Media, Society and Celebrity Culture* (Cambridge: Polity, 2016); and Beth Driscoll and DeNel Rehberg Sedo, "Faraway, So Close: Seeing the Intimacy in Goodreads Reviews," *Qualitative Inquiry* 25, no. 3 (2019): 248–59.

20. Alison Green, interview, December 14, 2017.

21. Amy Tannenbaum, interview, June 10, 2017; Beverley Cousins, interview, April 20, 2016.

22. Cousins interview.

23. Flo Nicoll, interview, July 29, 2017.

24. Kat Mayo, interview, October 27, 2016.

25. James Paul Gee, "Semiotic Social Spaces and Affinity Spaces," in *Beyond Communities of Practice: Language, Power and Social Context*, ed. David Barton and Karin Tusting (Cambridge: Cambridge University Press, 2005); Beth Driscoll, "Book Blogs as Tastemakers," *Participations Journal of Audience and Reception Studies* 16, no. 1 (2019): 280–305; Driscoll and Sedo, "Faraway, So Close"; Emmett Stinson and Beth Driscoll, "Difficult Literature on Goodreads: Reading Alexis Wright's *The Swan Book*," *Textual Practice* (2020).

26. Mayo interview.

27. See Kathleen Hale, "'Am I Being Catfished?' An Author Confronts Her Number One Online Critic," *Guardian,* October 18, 2014, www.theguardian.com, discussed in Beth Driscoll, "Readers of Popular Fiction and Emotion Online," in *New Directions in Popular Fiction: Genre, Distribution, Reproduction,* ed. Ken Gelder (London: Palgrave Macmillan, 2016), 425–49.

28. Savage interview.

29. Nicoll interview; Anna Valdinger, interview, February 18, 2019; Meyer interview.

30. Angela Slatter, interview, April 6, 2017; Sean Williams, interview, April 11, 2017; Mitchell Hogan, interview, October 23, 2017.

31. This group was set up by one of the authors of this book, Kim Wilkins, in her role as an author of fantasy fiction; interviewee Fox brought the group up unprompted.

32. Candice Fox, interview, October 7, 2016.

33. Mayo interview.

34. For more on private and public online book clubs, see DeNel Rehberg Sedo, ed., *Reading Communities from Salons to Cyberspace* (New York: Palgrave Macmillan, 2011).

35. Cecilia Dart-Thornton, interview, June 3, 2017.

36. Dart-Thornton interview.

37. Stephen Jones, interview, August 11, 2017.

38. People who attend cons are known as "members" because they buy a membership to attend.

39. Ryan interview.

40. Slatter interview.

41. Fox interview; Cousins interview; Slatter interview; Sarah Fairhall, interview, August 22, 2015.

42. Lindy Cameron, interview, September 18, 2017.

43. "Global Pitching Fest," https://sites.grenadine.co/sites/worldcon75/en/w75/items/10732 (no longer available).

44. George R. R. Martin, "The Hugo Losers Party," *Not a Blog* (blog), August 26, 2015, https://grrm.livejournal.com/439464.html.

45. Morgan Glass (@themorganglass), "This is awful and demeaning . . . ," Twitter, September 2, 2019, https://twitter.com/themorganglass/status/116817994966186 8033?s=20; George R. R. Martin, "GRRM on the Hugo Losers Party," *File 770* (blog), August 31, 2019, http://file770.com/grrm-on-the-hugo-losers-party/.

46. Hannett interview.

47. Ryan interview.

48. Jo Fletcher, interview, August 10, 2017.

49. Jones interview.

50. Hannett interview; Williams interview.

51. Hannett interview.

52. Hunter interview.

53. Juliet Marillier, "The Other Side of the World: Space, Place, and Australian Fantasy," Worldcon, August 11, 2017; Jonathan Strahan, interview, August 10, 2017.

54. At the time of writing, the global coronavirus pandemic had forced the 2020

Worldcon and ConZealand into online format. It remains to be seen whether the con spaces can be successfully transformed into wholly digital spaces.

CHAPTER 6: Genre Worlds on the Page

1. Garry Disher, *Bitter Wash Road* (Melbourne: Text, 2013).

2. Kelly Hunter, *Maggie's Run* (Tule, 2018).

3. Sara Douglass, *Battleaxe* (Sydney: Voyager Books, 1995).

4. Tim Lloyd, "When the Fantasy Finally Grows Up," *Adelaide Advertiser,* May 22, 1999.

5. Matt Hills, "Media Academics as Media Audiences: Aesthetic Judgments in Media and Cultural Studies," in *Fandom: Identities and Communities in a Mediated World,* ed. Jonathan Gray, C. Lee Harrington, and Cornel Sandvoss (New York: New York University Press, 2007), 39.

6. For example, see Anne Cranny-Francis, *Feminist Fiction: Feminist Uses of Generic Fiction* (New York: St. Martin's Press, 1990); Jessica Luther, "Beyond Bodice-Rippers: How Romance Novels Came to Embrace Feminism," *Atlantic,* March 18, 2013, www.theatlantic.com; Trisha Brown, "Romance Novels Are for Feminists," Book Riot, March 24, 2016, https://bookriot.com; Christina Lauren, "Writing Romance Novels Is a Feminist Act," *Time,* March 30, 2017, https://time.com; Anna Michelson, "The Politics of Happily-Ever-After: Romance Genre Fiction as Aesthetic Public Sphere," *American Journal of Cultural Sociology* (January 13, 2021).

7. China Miéville, "Tolkien—Middle Earth Meets Middle England," *Socialist Review* (January 2002), http://socialistreview.org.uk; Michael Moorcock, *Wizardry and Wild Romance: A Study of Epic Fantasy* (London: Victor Gollancz, 1987).

8. Rita Felski, *Uses of Literature* (Malden, MA: Blackwell, 2008), 14; Rita Felski, *The Limits of Critique* (Chicago: University of Chicago Press, 2015), 1.

9. Felski, *The Limits of Critique,* 29; Rita Felski, "After Suspicion," *Profession* 11 (2009): 31, 33.

10. Felski, *The Limits of Critique,* 108.

11. Daniel O'Malley, *The Rook* (New York: Hachette, 2012), 111; Michael Robotham, *Lost* (Sydney: Hachette Australia, 2005), 150, 195.

12. Megan Abbott, *Queenpin* (New York: Simon & Schuster, 2007); O'Malley, *The Rook,* 50.

13. Mitchell Hogan, *A Crucible of Souls* (New York: HarperCollins, 2015), 27–28.

14. Kylie Scott, *Play* (London: Pan Macmillan, 2015), 126.

15. Anna Valdinger, interview, February 18, 2019.

16. Rachael Johns, interview, February 24, 2017; Sue Brockhoff, interview, June 5, 2017.

17. Fiona McIntosh, *Bye Bye Baby* (Melbourne: Penguin Australia, 2019); Fiona McIntosh, *Beautiful Death* (Melbourne: Penguin Australia, 2019); Kate Forsyth, *Bitter Greens* (New York: St. Martin's Press, 2014), 88; Meredith Curnow, interview, October 24, 2017.

18. Lindy Cameron, interview, September 18, 2017.

19. Cameron interview.

20. Kim Wilkins, *Young Adult Fantasy Fiction: Conventions, Originality, Reproducibility* (Cambridge: Cambridge University Press, 2019), 2.

21. Keri Arthur, *Full Moon Rising* (New York: Bantam, 2006); Miriam Kriss, interview, March 22, 2018; review of *Full Moon Rising,* by Arthur, *Kirkus,* December 15, 2005, www.kirkusreviews.com; Arthur, *Full Moon Rising,* 222.

22. Jane Harper, *The Dry* (Sydney: Pan Macmillan, 2016), 313–15.

23. "Identity Amnesia," TV Tropes, https://tvtropes.org; Angela Slatter, *Vigil* (London: Jo Fletcher Books, 2016), loc. 1094 of 4457, Kindle.

24. Gerard Genette, *Paratexts: Thresholds of Interpretation,* trans. Jane E. Lewin (Cambridge: Cambridge University Press, 1997).

25. "*Mabo* Case," AIATSIS, https://aiatsis.gov.au/explore/articles/mabo-case.

26. Claire G. Coleman, interview, May 14, 2018. See also Veronica Sullivan, "'Speculative Fiction Is a Powerful Political Tool': From *War of the Worlds* to *Terra Nullius,*" *Guardian,* August 22, 2017, www.theguardian.com.

27. Darko Suvin, "On the Poetics of the Science Fiction Genre," *College English* 34, no. 3 (1972): 372–82; "About," *Full Stop,* www.full-stop.net/masthead/; Benjamin Murphy, "*Terra Nullius*—Claire G. Coleman," *Full Stop,* March 28, 2019, www.full-stop.net.

28. Kate Grenville, *The Secret River* (Melbourne: Text, 2005); Claire G. Coleman, *Terra Nullius* (Sydney: Hachette, 2017), loc. 925 of 4572, Kindle; Alison Whittaker, review of *Terra Nullius,* by Coleman, *Sydney Review of Books,* August 29, 2017, https://sydneyreviewofbooks.com.

29. Coleman, *Terra Nullius,* locs. 4028 and 4035 of 4572, Kindle.

30. Coleman, *Terra Nullius,* loc. 2466 of 4572, Kindle.

31. Coleman, *Terra Nullius,* locs. 3947 and 3898 of 4572, Kindle; Coleman interview.

32. Coleman interview; Coleman, *Terra Nullius,* loc. 229 of 4572, Kindle.

33. Coleman, *Terra Nullius,* locs. 1985 and 319 of 4572, Kindle.

34. Kim Wilkins, "From Middle Earth to Westeros: Medievalism, Proliferation and Paratextuality," in *New Directions in Popular Fiction: Genre, Distribution, Reproduction,* ed. Ken Gelder (London: Palgrave Macmillan, 2016), 212; Max Brooks, *World War Z: An Oral History of the Zombie War* (New York: Random House, 2006); Christopher Priest, *The Islanders* (London: Gollancz, 2011).

35. Robert Watkins, interview, February 19, 2019; Coleman, *Terra Nullius,* loc. 3076 of 4572, Kindle.

CHAPTER 7: Genre Worlds and Change

1. Angela Savage, interview, December 1, 2017; Miriam Kriss, interview, March 22, 2018; Angela Slatter, interview, April 6, 2017.

2. Iain Ryan, interview, August 4, 2017.

3. Grace Lucas-Pennington, interview, February 14, 2019.

4. Angela Savage, "Red Shoes," Sisters in Crime Australia, 2013, www.sistersincrime .org.au; "About," Staunch Book Prize, http://staunchbookprize.com/about-2/.

5. Kate Cuthbert, "Consenting Adults: Kate Cuthbert on the Romance Novel and Representations of Sexuality after #MeToo," *Books + Publishing* (September 12, 2018), www.booksandpublishing.com.

6. Lois Beckett, "A Romance Novelist Spoke Out about Racism. An Uproar Ensued," *Guardian,* January 1, 2020, www.theguardian.com.

7. Larry Correia, "An Explanation about the Hugo Awards Controversy," *Monster Hunter Nation,* April 24, 2014, http://monsterhunternation.com; Emily Todd Van-DerWerff, "How Conservatives Took Over Sci-Fi's Most Prestigious Award," *Vox,* April 26, 2015, www.vox.com.

8. Joel Cunningham, "Read N. K. Jemisin's Historic Hugo Speech," *The B&N Sci-Fi and Fantasy Blog* (blog), August 20, 2018, www.barnesandnoble.com/blog/sci-fi-fantasy /read-n-k-jemisins-historic-hugo-speech/.

9. Michael Patrick Hicks, "Controversy Erupts around ChiZine Publications, High Fever Books," November 17, 2019, www.highfeverbooks.com.

Index

Page references in *italics* refer to figures and tables.

Kim Wilkins was born in London and received her PhD from the University of Queensland, where she is currently a professor of writing and publishing. She is author of more than thirty novels of popular fiction and has been published in more than twenty languages. Her most recent scholarly book is *Young Adult Fantasy Fiction: Conventions, Originality, Reproducibility* (2019). She lives in Brisbane, Australia, with her husband and two children.

Beth Driscoll was born in Lismore, New South Wales, and holds a PhD from the University of Melbourne, where she is now associate professor of publishing and communications. She is author of *The New Literary Middlebrow: Tastemakers and Reading in the Twenty-First Century* (2014) and coauthor of *The Frankfurt Book Fair and Bestseller Business* (2020) with Claire Squires. She lives in Melbourne with her partner and two children.

Lisa Fletcher was born in Melbourne and received her PhD from the University of Melbourne. Her books include *Historical Romance Fiction: Heterosexuality and Performativity* (2008) and *Popular Fiction and Spatiality: Reading Genre Settings* (2016). She is professor of English and head of the School of Humanities at the University of Tasmania.

Lightning Source UK Ltd.
Milton Keynes UK
UKHW012132180822
407504UK00002B/582